As one of the world's longe[...]
and best-known [...]
Thomas Cook are the ex[...]

For [...] an 13[...]
guidebooks h[...]
of destin[...]
sharing with tr[...]
experience and a passion for travel.

**Rely on Thomas Cook as your
travelling companion on your next trip
and benefit from our unique heritage.**

2

Thomas Cook **driving** guides

# NEW ZEALAND

## Gareth Powell

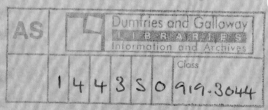
Thomas
Cook

Your travelling companion since 1873

**Written by Gareth Powell, updated by Darroch Donald**
Original photography by Larry Dunmire

**Published by Thomas Cook Publishing**
A division of Thomas Cook Tour Operations Limited
Company registration no. 3772199 England
The Thomas Cook Business Park, Unit 9, Coningsby Road,
Peterborough PE3 8SB, United Kingdom
Email: books@thomascook.com, Tel: + 44 (0) 1733 416477
www.thomascookpublishing.com

**Produced by Cambridge Publishing Management Limited**
Burr Elm Court, Main Street, Caldecote CB23 7NU

ISBN: 978-1-84848-209-8

© 2005, 2008 Thomas Cook Publishing
This third edition © 2009
Text © Thomas Cook Publishing
Maps © Thomas Cook Publishing/PCGraphics (UK) Limited

Series Editor: Adam Royal
Production/DTP: Steven Collins

Printed and bound in India by Ajanta Offset & Packaging Ltd

Cover photography: © Thomas Cook

# About the author

**Gareth Powell** first went to New Zealand in 1963 to interview and be interviewed by Barry Crump whose book, *A Good Keen Man*, has become a small New Zealand classic. Since then, the author has been in New Zealand some thirty times. He learned to ski at the Remarkables above Queenstown; he had dinner in Parnell with David Bowie (a small claim to fame). Although he has never bungee jumped, he has seen many hundreds of foolhardy adventurers hurl themselves into space and saved from an awful fate by 96 strands of knicker elastic tied to their ankles.

For this book he revisited every area of New Zealand, stayed in 72 hotels and motels, drove over 11,000km, carried away over 40kg of brochures (thus massively exceeding his airline allowance), interviewed dozens of tour operators, took uncounted sightseeing trips and learned to love Anzac biscuits (a non-slimming but delicious snack made from golden syrup and oatmeal).

# Contents

# About driving guides

Thomas Cook's driving guides are designed to provide you with a comprehensive but flexible reference source to guide you as you tour a country or region by car. This guide divides New Zealand into touring areas – one per chapter. Major cultural centres or cities form chapters in their own right. Each chapter contains enough attractions to provide at least a day's worth of activities – often more.

## Ratings

To make it easier for you to plan your time and decide what to see, every area is rated according to its attractions in categories such as Architecture, Entertainment and Children.

## Chapter contents

Every chapter has an introduction summing up the main attractions of the area, and a ratings box, which will highlight the area's strengths and weaknesses – some areas may be more attractive to families travelling with children, others to wine-lovers visiting vineyards, and others to people interested in finding castles, churches, nature reserves or good beaches.

Each chapter is then divided into an alphabetical gazetteer, and a suggested tour. You can select whether you just want to visit a particular sight or attraction, choosing from those described in the gazetteer, or whether you want to tour the area comprehensively. If the latter, you can construct your own itinerary, or follow the author's suggested tour, which comes at the end of every area chapter.

## Symbol Key

1 Tourist Information Centre

2 Advice on arriving or departing

P Parking locations

Q Advice on getting around

3 Directions

1 Sights and attractions

C Accommodation

1 Eating

O Shopping

9 Sport

O Entertainment

### The gazetteer

The gazetteer section describes all the major attractions in the area – the villages, towns, historic sites, nature reserves, parks or museums that you are most likely to want to see. Maps of the area highlight all the places mentioned in the text. Using this comprehensive overview of the area, you may choose just to visit one or two sights.

**Right**
Queenstown jet boat

**Practical information**

The practical information in the page margins, or sidebars, will help you locate the services you need as an independent traveller – including the tourist information centre, car parks and public transport facilities. You will also find the opening times of sights, museums, churches and other attractions, as well as useful tips on shopping, market days, cultural events, entertainment, festivals and sports facilities.

One way to use the guide is simply to find individual sights that interest you, using the index or overview map, and read what our author has to say about them. This will help you decide whether to visit the sight. If you do, you will find plenty of practical information, such as the street address, the telephone number for enquiries, and opening times.

Alternatively, you can choose a hotel, perhaps with the help of the accommodation recommendations contained in this guide. You can then turn to the overall map on pages 8–9 to help you work out which chapters in the book describe those cities and regions that lie closest to your chosen touring base.

**Driving tours**

The suggested tour is just that – a suggestion, with plenty of optional detours and one or two ideas for making your own discoveries, under the heading *Also worth exploring*. The routes are designed to link the attractions described in the gazetteer section, and to cover outstandingly scenic coastal, mountain and rural landscapes. The total distance is given for each tour, as is the time it will take you to drive the complete route, but bear in mind that this indication is just for the driving time: you will need to add on extra time for visiting attractions along the way.

Many of the routes are circular, so that you can join them at any point. Where the nature of the terrain dictates that the route has to be linear, the route can either be followed out and back, or you can use it as a link route, to get from one area in the book to another.

As you follow the route descriptions, you will find names picked out in bold capital letters – this means that the place is described fully in the gazetteer. Other names picked out in bold indicate additional villages or attractions worth a brief stop along the route.

**Accommodation and food**

In every chapter you will find lodging and eating recommendations for individual towns, or for the area as a whole. These are designed to cover a range of price brackets and concentrate on more characterful small or individualistic hotels and restaurants. In addition, you will find information in the *Travel facts* chapter on chain hotels, with an address to which you can write for a guide, map or directory. The price indications used in the guide have the following meanings:

$       budget level
$$      typical/average prices
$$$     de luxe.

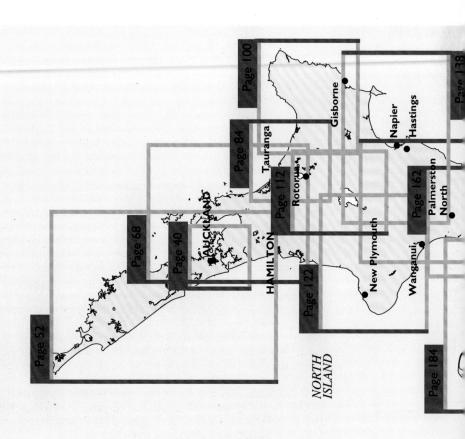

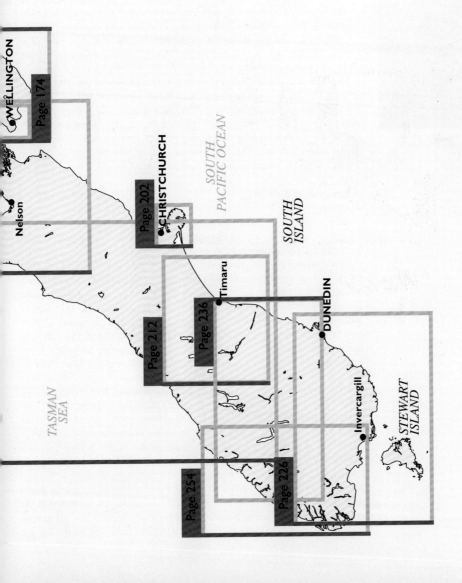

# Introduction

**Above**
New Zealand's verdant
countryside

New Zealand is one of the great tourist destinations of the world. Within its small compass it has an amazing range of scenery, a complete portfolio of every sport that you can think of, some sophisticated cities, superb skiing and surfing and some excellent wines. Finally, and perhaps most importantly, it is not very expensive.

Many potential visitors keep getting it wrong and therefore, for the record, New Zealand is in the southwest Pacific and has two large islands (North Island and the South Island), plus one smaller island, and numerous much smaller islands.

The Maori of New Zealand, who were there before the Europeans, refer to the country as Aotearoa, which can be translated as 'Land of the Long White Cloud'. More and more people favour using the name Aotearoa to replace New Zealand. Indeed, Maori place names generally are taking over from the European. Ones that have not changed are North Island (which in Maori is Te Ika a Maui, 'The Fish of Maui') and South Island (Te Waka a Maui, 'The Canoe of Maui').

### Geographical diversity

Altogether, New Zealand has an area of some 268,704sq km and a coastline of 15,134km in length. As a result of what is known as the 'Queens Chain' law, all coastline and river banks for up to 20m inland are available for public use and all coastline is public land.

New Zealand is a long narrow country, oriented very roughly north to south and with mountain ranges running for most of its length. It is a bit bigger than Great Britain, slightly smaller than Italy and the same size as Colorado. It contains, in its relatively small compass, as complete a range of scenic delights as you will find anywhere in the world.

It is sometimes thought that New Zealand is an island just offshore from Australia. It is not. New Zealand is the same distance from Australia as London is from Moscow. And New Zealand is as close to the equator as Buenos Aires in South America.

Apart from the two main islands, New Zealand has dependencies across the Pacific. These include the Chatham Islands, Campbell Island, Tokelau and Raoul Island in the Kermadecs, plus a 414,000sq km slab of Antarctica, which is administered as the Ross Dependency.

The distance between the very north of the North Island and the southern tip of the South Island is over 1,600km. Within that range there is a tremendous geographical and geological variety. In the North there are areas of thermal activity that create bubbling pools and mist-enshrouded forests and lakes. The North Island's main mountains – Ruapehu, Ngauruhoe and Tongariro – are all active volcanoes: only Taranaki to the west and Rangitoto in Auckland are considered dormant. On the South Island the scenery is even more spectacular, with 20 mountains rising to more than 3,000m high. Mount Cook, known by the Maori as Aoraki (the 'Cloud Piercer'), soars to 3,754m. Here, too, are fiords as scenic as any in Scandinavia.

These extremes of geographical type and formation give New Zealand some 15 separate climatic environments, though most of the country enjoys conditions that are ideal for farming – and for tourism – combining generous amounts of sunshine and rainfall.

## Population

As a generalisation, it could be said that South Island consists mainly of green national parks and agriculture, while North Island is more densely populated and has most of the industry. Indeed, that division has held true since the first humans arrived, for North Island was also the main focus of Maori settlement.

The Maori trace their descent from the chiefs of Hawaiki, who sailed to Aotearoa in voyaging canoes, starting some 1,200 years ago. No one knows exactly where Hawaiki is, except that it is certainly not near Hawaii. The theory that the Maori arrived in a single migration, derived from the Maori's own folk history, is not now thought to be accurate. New Zealand was probably colonised in a series of migration waves triggered by problems in the land of their origin – perhaps tidal waves, or inter-tribal warfare. The area around Auckland, the former capital, was not settled until some 700 years ago.

Most Maori strongly resisted European settlement, but they were disunited in their attempts to drive off the new invaders. The result was that, by 1840, the British had established control. They selected Auckland as their capital, naming it after the ruling viceroy of India.

## Hospitality

Tourism is one of New Zealand's biggest earners. In 2008, international visitors contributed NZ$5.9 billion to the economy, and around 1 per cent of the population was employed in the tourism sector. But perhaps as a result of its population, married with the inherently casual attitudes of most New Zealanders, any rapid growth is a relatively new phenomenon. Even more so than their Australian counterparts, 'Kiwis' are renowned for being visitor-friendly and are almost equally and blissfully laid-back about life. To an extent, the nation is far less commercially rapacious than other countries in which the 'get rich quick', 'most for least' mantra rules, and thankfully in tourism this ethic (so far, anyway) has only just begun to raise its ugly head.

So, in summary you will generally find that Kiwis, be it the public per se or the tourism operator, will genuinely want you to have a good time and will go out of their way to make sure they are the catalyst for that. However, beware – there are a growing number of exceptions, with large, corporate conglomerates buying up old and traditional tourism concerns en masse, and although they would fervently deny it, they have only two things on their mind – bums on seats and profit margins.

# Travel facts

## Go as you please

If you just turn up without a booking, you will rarely have problems getting accommodation, except at the main resorts like Queenstown during the peak season and public holidays. During these periods advance booking is almost essential. The rest of the time you can reserve rooms on a day-by-day basis using the visitor information centres to book ahead.

## Seasonal bargains

In tourist areas it is perfectly possible to get attractive reductions outside of the season. The way to do this is simply to go to the nearest visitor centre and ask what bargains are on offer.

## Homestays

Information on homestays and farmstays is available from all visitor centres. Alternatively, you can visit www.holidayhomes.co.nz for a comprehensive listing of private accommodation throughout New Zealand.

**Right**
Accommodation is easily found

## Accommodation

In New Zealand accommodation is relatively inexpensive and generally of a good to excellent quality, although there are few hotels, if any, that could be counted among the great hotels of the world. Also, to an increasing degree international hotel chains are represented here in the same way that they are, for example, in Australia.

Most motels are affiliated to such marketing organisations as Golden Chain, Budget, Flag and Best Western and the standard is, generally, very high. Except in the main tourist areas these motels do not depend on tourists for their main income – they cater for travelling business people, which keeps the standard of the accommodation and the fixtures and fittings extremely high. It also keeps the prices comparatively low, and it also means that they are relatively empty at the weekends, even if sometimes booked well ahead on weekdays (this especially applies to motels near to cities).

There are two excellent guides to accommodation in New Zealand. One is published by the New Zealand Automobile Association (www.aatravel.co.nz) and the other is Jason's (www.jasons.com/New-Zealand), published by a company that specialises in travel directories. Although you will see both on sale in bookshops, you can also pick up copies free at visitor information centres and in most motels.

New Zealand has its very own star qualification system which is Qualmark. You can read all about it at www.qualmark.co.nz/about_us.php. Think of it as New Zealand tourism's official quality agency which issues stars and the right to add the symbol Qualmark. This is pretty serious stuff for it is a government–private sector partnership between Tourism New Zealand and the New Zealand Automobile Association, which ran an earlier star system. It used to be by colours, but now it is, as in the rest of the world, by stars.

The assessments are specific to the type of accommodation experience offered – Backpackers, Guest & Hosted, Holiday Park, Hotel and Self Contained & Serviced – and result in a star grade that is used with the quality mark. So star ratings are only valid if accompanied by the Qualmark and that is the case throughout New Zealand.

The standard for one star is that it is acceptable, and that it meets customers' minimum requirements. Basic, clean and comfortable accommodation. Two stars is good. Defined as 'exceeds customers' minimum requirements with

## Airports

The two main ports of entry are Auckland and Christchurch. Note that Wellington, although it is the capital of the country, is not a major international airport because the runway is too short for the largest planes and wind sometimes closes the airport. Auckland and Christchurch are true international airports, and have all the essential facilities and the information centres are, in both cases, superb.

## Entry formalities

Tourists coming for less than six months do not require visas under normal circumstances. Your passport has to be valid for three months after your arrival date and you must have a valid return airline ticket. It is possible for students to obtain working and study visas. For full information on how this might apply in any particular case, apply to the New Zealand embassy or consulate in your country, and visit the website *www.immigration.govt.nz*

some additional facilities and services'. Three stars is very good. Provides a range of facilities and services and achieves good to very good quality standards. Four stars is excellent. Consistently achieves high quality levels with a wide range of facilities and services. Five stars is exceptional. Which means among the best available in New Zealand. Assessments are conducted by Qualmark's own assessment team – think of them as Michelin inspectors and you will not be far wrong. Qualmark works with most of the major agencies and seems to operate very well.

Although the star ratings follow a well-defined series of standards, they do, of course, vary as to the type of accommodation offered. You can go to the website – *www.qualmark.co.nz.index.jsp* – enter in what you want, where and get back selected places from the 800-plus accommodation properties (and there are some 80 backpacker places listed in there) right across the country.

To get the feel of this, let us look at a few examples. Aspiring Camper Van Park at Lake Wanaka is a five-star camper-van park. You might think this a contradiction in terms until you learn it has a family-size sauna, a seriously well-equipped kitchen, a lounge area with a log fire, a spa pool, a large barbecue pavilion and a van wash and cleaning area with an industrial vacuum cleaner provided. So though it is a camper-van park, plainly it is at the very high end of such accommodation and gets five stars.

Another example: there are six Heritage Inns and all of them are four star or more in the Qualmark 'Guest and Hosted' category. The 'Guest & Hosted' category includes bed and breakfasts, farm- and homestays, guesthouses, inns, country hotels, boutique lodges and similar accommodation that has a 'home-like' or particular NZ 'character'. The only problem with schemes like this is that no one wants to boast they are at the bottom end. The obvious question is, 'are there any places boasting about getting a one star rating?' Not that can be found with a cursory inspection. Indeed, there appear to be none boasting two or three stars. We then get into the slightly daft situation where establishments are advertising they have 4$\frac{1}{2}$ stars which makes judgement a bit iffy. Basic rule of thumb is that if any accommodation has a Qualmark rating it will be very good indeed within its class. It does, indeed, appear to be a mark of quality.

The easiest way to make bookings at any time is through one of the country's 85-plus I-site information centres, which are all part of the accredited Visitor Information Network – look for the white 'i' in a green circle sign. They will book you accommodation at any level you choose, and you can pre-pay at the centre using American Express – not always universally accepted at motels – VISA or MasterCard. These centres also have access to a database and can book ahead for your next stop.

Camper vans are a major part of the tourist scene in New Zealand. The minimum hiring age is 21. There are 2-, 4- or 6-berth camper vans, and most have a diesel engine, which is extremely economical to run in New Zealand. Most also have exhaust brakes and power steering,

and are relatively easy to drive. Most camper-van users spend the night at campsites – they are banned from parking overnight in national parks, except in specified areas, and camping by the roadside is frowned upon in most places.

Campsites, which provide power and toilet and shower facilities, are very inexpensive. There is thus a great saving on cost, even if the accommodation is not luxurious. Most users plan to stay at a motel one night out of seven for a taste of luxury, even though almost all camper vans offer hot water, an on-board toilet, cooking facilities, and so on. All in all, they are ideal for people who are not pushed for time, who want to see the whole country and who can put up with some small amount of discomfort.

## Children

New Zealand is a children's paradise and it is difficult to think of anything which is barred to them except bungee jumping. Serious efforts are made to cater for children. One good example is skiing, where every major resort has a children's programme, with clubs, training, minders, the lot. New Zealand also has a great and wonderful tradition of childcare, born of the sense that children represent the country's future.

## Climate

New Zealand is a very green country because it has a mild climate and a lot of rainfall. Sometimes you hear tourists complaining about the rain, but it is an essential part of the whole package. The average is usually between 640 and 1,500mm a year, with more than 2,400mm in some parts. Generally the rainfall is distributed evenly throughout the year, but there are some regional differences, mainly between the east and west coasts. The wettest areas in the South Island are the West Coast and Southern Alps. Otago, Canterbury, Marlborough and Nelson experience the lowest rainfall. In the North Island, the wettest areas are Northland, North Taranaki, Coromandel and the Bay of Plenty. There are no very dry or desert regions, although on the North Island there is a rain shadow to the east of the central mountains, through which the Desert Road (SH1) runs.

This abundance of water does not mean that there is a lack of sunshine. New Zealand rejoices in a very sunny climate regularly interspersed with rain showers, and enjoys a staggering 2,000 hours of sunshine a year – that's an average of four hours a day. The sunniest areas – such as Nelson, Blenheim, Tauranga and Napier – average over 2,350 hours of sunshine a year.

Winters are generally mild, although there is snow for skiing in the high mountains. Winds are mainly from the west throughout the year, although the mountains can cause variations.

**Left**
Christ Church in Russell, New Zealand's oldest surviving church

**Duty-free on arrival**

Bringing wine to New Zealand is a very silly idea. It is cheaper and better bought locally. Auckland, Christchurch and Wellington have duty-free shops in the arrivals area so that you do not have to carry the goods with you from the airport you departed from. Get them when you arrive in the time it takes to wait for your luggage to be got off the plane.

**Pure as snow**

Nowhere in the world will you drink purer water than in New Zealand. In Christchurch the water is often nominated as the purest city water in the world. That people still buy bottled water merely shows the power of advertising.

Visitors from the northern hemisphere should bear in mind that January and February are the warmest months of the year and July is the coldest – though it never gets seriously cold, except in the high mountains. You must also reverse your orientation: plants in New Zealand enjoy their sunniest conditions on north-facing walls, and the further south you go, the lower the temperature drops, although there is not as much difference in temperature between the North and South Islands as you might imagine. New Zealand's climate-change issues do not seem as ominous as those in Australia, but predictions are for warmer temperatures and wetter weather.

## Currency

New Zealand uses dollars and cents. Credit cards are pretty much universally accepted for payment, with one exception: a substantial percentage of motels will not accept payment by American Express card. You can use ATMs (cash machines) to draw funds, provided that you know your PIN. Traveller's cheques are accepted in any bank and can be replaced if lost.

## Customs regulations

Arriving passengers can bring in 200 cigarettes, 4.5 litres of wine and a bottle of spirits (up to 1.125 litres). You cannot bring in any animal or foodstuffs without declaring them, and the customs are very serious about this. They do not want you to bring fruit or plants into the country. Scanners can spot an apple in the bottom of your hand-luggage. There are bins just before customs where you should dump all fruit before entering. If in doubt, ask. Drugs are, of course, absolutely barred. Despite these warnings, you will find that going through customs in New Zealand is generally a relaxed experience. For further information refer to *www.customs.govt.nz*

## Drinking

New Zealand café latte is easing its way to becoming a national drink. This wondrous concoction comes in a bowl you could almost swim across and will perk you up for the day – especially when enjoyed with a monster Anzac biscuit, which is made from golden syrup and oatmeal. Sadly, it must be said that this is not a slimming mixture.

Beer is a standard New Zealand drink. The Lion Nathan brewery produces Steinlager, which is one of the world's most garlanded beers. Interesting, eclectic and esoteric beers are also being produced all over the country by the strong microbrewery movement.

New Zealand wine has gone from being dubious – it was once asserted that the vintners ate the grapes first – to being among the best in the world. White wines are generally held to be far better than

## Festivals

New Zealand doesn't have any big ethnic festivals. Given this, there is now talk of an annual 'New Zealand Day' celebrating all ethnicities, similar to 'Australia Day'. Waitangi Day, which commemorates the peace treaty signed between the Maori and the Europeans in 1840, is commemorated on 6 February, but even in Waitangi itself the celebrations can be muted, or even non-existent, following a series of serious demonstrations by Maori activists.

Anzac Day is 25 April, a very important date, for New Zealand sent, as a percentage of its population, more troops to both World War I and II than any other Allied country. On Anzac Day, if you have served in the forces, you pin your medals to your chest and you march to the memorial service. Then you go and sink a few cleansing ales, renew old friendships and frolic in the streets without fear of interference by the police.

## Health precautions

Although New Zealand has a generally mild climate, you can still get a nasty sunburn because the air is so clear. You need to use sun block, sunglasses and a hat. You will also need insect repellent if you are exploring the bush or any of the mangrove areas, or walking in Southland, the Fiords or the West Coast.

the reds, but this is changing as the red wines have recently improved beyond measure. The author of this book is ever willing to listen to argument for the other side, but, in his carefully considered opinion, he thinks that Cloudy Bay, which comes from the Marlborough Region, is the best white wine in the world. No risk. Many other wine authorities are in agreement. If you leave New Zealand without taking your duty-free allowance in wine, you are making a terrible mistake, because finding the better New Zealand wines outside the country is not at all easy.

## Eating out

At the basic level there is fish and chips or, as New Zealanders pronounce it, 'fush and chups'. These are quite magnificent as a takeaway meal, or eaten on the premises. They are cooked to order, so be prepared for a wait, particularly on Friday evenings. The fish is superb and the chips – an overabundant helping – are crisp and golden. The other standby at the low end is the pie. There is an old joke that says that a balanced New Zealand diet is a pie in each hand. In fact, the range of pies available is quite remarkable. Pizza Hut and many of the other international purveyors of fast food are also well represented throughout the country. If this isn't to your taste, every New Zealand town, no matter how small, will have a store selling freshly made sandwiches (and, probably, hot pies). Coffee shops abound selling excellent café latte and light snacks, and vegetarians are very well catered for. Generally speaking, the food is excellent, the quantity amazing and the service friendly, if not oversophisticated.

Ethnic restaurants exist, but are often a disappointment, because the original cooking tradition has been debased to suit New Zealand tastes. The vast majority are Chinese (which means Cantonese). There are also some Thai restaurants, and a few curry houses.

Then there are the medium-priced restaurants without pretensions. At the only seafood restaurant on the waterfront in Paihia, you can eat John Dory – a particularly succulent fish – so fresh that it was probably caught two hours previously. And the price is low to middling. New Zealand abounds in restaurants like this. Make your own discoveries. Motel owners are very good at giving an unbiased opinion on local options.

At the top there are restaurants with pretensions to culinary grandeur. In the main they are just that – pretensions. Except for a handful of restaurants in Parnell, Queenstown and Wellington, one or two in Christchurch and one in Nelson, it would be fair to say that New Zealand has no restaurants that would be considered worth one of Michelin's stars. Some of them can be seriously expensive, and you have to ask whether you are paying for special food or for napery, wine waiters, and that sort of pretension.

**Right**
Pick-me-up on South Island

## Electricity

The electricity supply is 230 volts and uses the Australian-style plug with three thin pins, angled not straight.

## Food

One of the great joys of driving around New Zealand is buying fruit from the roadside stalls. First of all, it is sold at a price that makes you almost embarrassed to pay so little. Secondly, it is available in a variety that you have probably never experienced before. Well over a hundred species and subspecies of fruit are grown in New Zealand, and many will be new to you.

New Zealand claims to have invented the pavlova. So does Australia. It is difficult to know why either wants to be renowned for this nauseously sweet meringue creation, which is impossible to eat tidily. Far, far better are Anzac biscuits, invented in World War I by servicemen in France and consisting, essentially, of rolled oats and syrup. They come in different sizes, with the biggest being about the size of a small dinner plate. (The editors have pointed out this is already the third reference to this culinary treat in 20 short pages. Indeed. And there will be more.)

It is a sadness that you will probably never taste one of the great delicacies of New Zealand – toheroa soup. This is made from a succulent shellfish once abundant on the beaches of North Island – Ninety Mile Beach was a favourite hunting ground. The dish became so popular that the shellfish reached a point where it was in danger of extinction, and has been declared a protected species. Large green-lipped mussels are another Kiwi favourite.

## Health

New Zealand's heath facilities are excellent, and visitors need take no special precautions. All the usual medications are available at chemists' shops, but if you are taking a very specific treatment it is best to bring a full supply of medicine to cover the whole of your trip. Though health facilities are excellent, they are not free. For that reason, travel insurance is absolutely essential.

## Information

The signage at information offices in New Zealand can be misleading. There is nothing to prevent anyone from erecting an 'i' sign, which is universally understood to indicate a tourist information centre. Frequently that is the case, but sometimes it is used to attract customers to a commercial enterprise pushing particular products.

If there is a green circle on the sign the office is part of the country's accredited I-site information network and has to keep to certain standards. Those standards are extremely high. The information offices are generally superior to those that you will find in, for example, the United States or the UK. Sometimes the offices are manned by volunteers, who are full of enthusiasm and local knowledge, and who enjoy a good gossip.

## The Internet

| | |
|---|---|
| AA New Zealand Travel Guide | www.aatravel.co.nz |
| Department of Conservation | www.doc.govt.nz |
| Discover New Zealand | www.discovernewzealand.com |
| Ecotours | www.ecotours.co.nz |
| Hiking New Zealand | www.hikingnewzealand.com |
| Mountain Biking in New Zealand | www.mountainbike.co.nz |
| New Zealand events | www.nzlive.com |
| New Zealand Tourism Board | www.purenz.com |
| New Zealand Travel & Tourism Information | www.travel-library.com/pacific/new_zealand |
| Regional news | www.nzcity.co.nz |
| Top 10 Holiday Parks | www.top10.co.nz |
| Virtual New Zealand | www.vnz.co.nz |

## Flora and fauna

Geomorphologists will tell you that New Zealand is a small sliver of Gondwanaland, the original landmass of the southern hemisphere. New Zealand became detached from the main mass something over 100 million years ago. One result is that much of the animal and plant life is unique to New Zealand. The forests of the islands contain some of the longest-lived plant species in the world. There are, for example, some specimens of the massive kauri tree that are known to be 2,000 years old. The country has the world's largest flightless parrot, delightfully called the kakapo, an alpine parrot called the kea and a lizard, called the tuatara, that dates back to the age of the dinosaurs. The symbol of the country is the flightless kiwi, now both rare and protected.

**Below**
Early printing press

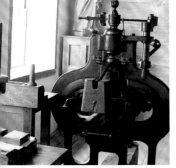

The New Zealand Tourism Board has an excellent internet site of which it is very proud, and which is continually being updated. It is a great starting point for planning your trip.

## Insurance

You will need standard travel insurance to cover health-care costs and other risks. Visitors are also covered by the New Zealand government's Accidents Compensation and Rehabilitation Insurance Scheme for personal injury caused by an accident. You can make a claim irrespective of fault (*www.acc.co.nz*).

## Maps

The maps used to research this book were produced by the New Zealand Automobile Association. Every bookseller – and New Zealand has more and better bookshops than most other countries on Earth – will stock a wide range. Highly spoken of are the series produced by International Travel Maps and those published by Bartholomew's.

## Museums

Throughout New Zealand there are two kinds of museum. First there are those in the cities which are of a very high standard and which, typically, are open Monday to Saturday from 0900–1700. Some of them are also open on Sundays. This especially applies to the glorious Te Papa in Wellington, the finest museum in New Zealand (*see page 180*).

Then there are the small museums run by the historical societies of the smaller towns. Often you find that these only open on something like the fourth Sunday of a month from 1000–1100. As they are run by volunteers you can hardly complain. Many of them are interesting, but you will find quite a few that consist of little but displays of early agricultural equipment. On the other hand, there are some small museums – Russell and Akaroa both spring to mind – which are fascinating, intelligent, amusing and well run.

## National parks

Entrance to every national park is free, and they are open right through the year. Every national park has an office – sometimes several – staffed by rangers who are enthusiastic, concerned and infinitely helpful. Where camping is allowed in national parks – this is not always the case – it is normally in designated areas. National parks are the responsibility of the Department of Conservation. This publishes some splendid small guides on

## Parks and reserves

New Zealand has more national parks, as a percentage of the country's land area, than any other country in the world. Official figures vary, because there is some debate about what to include, but if you work on the basis that 20 per cent of the country is park you will not go far wrong. The first national park was Tongariro on North Island, which opened on 23 September 1887. It was the fourth national park to be declared in the world, and it is now a World Heritage Site. Altogether, there are now 14 national parks, 19 forest parks and probably around 4,000 other regional and local parks and reserves.

## Sport

New Zealand is sport mad. Every sport that you can think of is played here, and played at a very high level. In Rugby Union – the game played in heaven – the country moves from interest to total obsession. The All Blacks, the New Zealand Rugby Union side, are revered as gods as long as they keep winning. Sometimes, very rarely, they have a losing streak and the country goes into deep mourning. At some time during your visit you will be asked your opinion of the All Blacks side. No matter what you actually think, you will say that this is the greatest rugby team the world has ever seen. Such diplomacy will make your visit to New Zealand much more enjoyable.

specific features, which are available at all good information offices for very low prices.

Dogs are not allowed in any national park. Some of these parks are serious wilderness areas and you would be well advised to take advice from the rangers on the prevailing conditions and any necessary precautions before embarking on an ambitious expedition.

## Opening times

The great New Zealand Sunday, when even petrol stations closed and the country was forced into somnolence, is now almost a thing of the past. In the main cities you will find shops that are open seven days a week, and this is true of petrol stations throughout the country. Most tourist offices are open on a seven-day basis, as are all of the fast-food outlets and many restaurants. Banks are open from 0900–1600; currency exchange bureaux are also to be found in main tourist centres, and these stay open much later.

## Postal services

Postal services in New Zealand are dependable and relatively speedy. There are two levels: standard post is said to deliver the next day in the same city and within two to three working days throughout New Zealand. Fast post covers international mail and also guarantees a next-day delivery between major towns and cities within the country.

## Public holidays

The public holidays are New Year (which includes 1 and 2 January) Waitangi Day (National Day) on 6 February, Good Friday and Easter Monday, Anzac Day on 25 April, the Queen's Birthday on 2 June, Labour Day on 27 October, Christmas Day and Boxing Day. January is very much the holiday season – the school holidays run from late December until late January – and during this time seaside resorts tend to be heavily booked up.

## Public transport

It is perfectly possible to see the whole of New Zealand using public transport. First there are the airlines, which cover the whole of the country, even down to the smaller towns. Then there is a sparse rail service, with a few 'Tranzscenic' routes. It also connects Auckland with Wellington and Christchurch. Reservation throughout the system is by a freephone number – 0800 872 467.

There are also scheduled passenger bus services throughout the country. The biggest operator is InterCity coach lines, which connects almost every city, town and tourist destination. It claims to service

## Packing

When packing for a trip to New Zealand, it is more of a question of what to leave out than what to take. New Zealand is a very informal country. Men are unlikely ever to need a tie, unless you are going to one of those restaurants where style is more important than the food – and probably not even then. A suit simply isn't needed. A blazer and slacks for men is the equivalent of formal dressing. Women also dress very informally and casually. Unless you are going to be invited to take tea with the Prime Minister – an unlikely event – you need to pack only casual clothes. You will, however, need a truly waterproof – and not just showerproof – coat of some kind, preferably one with a hood.

## Safety and security

New Zealand is a relatively safe destination, but petty theft is common and tourists are often targeted. All the usual precautions should be taken and travel insurance should be considered essential.

## Shopping

New Zealand is not a place you would visit for its shops. It has shops selling hand-knitted sweaters and other garments, and there is carved jade work and other jewellery, but on the whole people come to New Zealand for scenery, sport and food – not for shopping.

600 towns. There are several passes offering travel throughout specific regions, available for periods of up to three months. Another pass is available which allows travel on InterCity coaches, the rail service and the ferry services across the Cook Strait, separating the two main islands. It is available for various periods and can be bought from most accredited travel agencies, as well as any travel centre in New Zealand.

## Reading

The best-known New Zealand author is Katherine Mansfield, which was the pen name of Kathleen Mansfield Beauchamp. She was born in Wellington in 1888 and raised in New Zealand. In her short life – 35 years – she wrote a series of works that are reminiscent of Chekhov. She died in Paris in 1923. It is not generally known that the novelist Fay Weldon is also a New Zealander, having been born and raised on the Coromandel Peninsula. But that is an accident of birth: her New Zealand upbringing appears to have had no effect on her writings.

In most bookshops you will see a display of the works of the late Barry Crump. The best of these is *A Good Keen Man*. Barry Crump was, in truth, not a great writer, but his memory is revered in New Zealand and his books give a very accurate flavour of the country.

Finally, one must not forget that Ngaio Marsh, the detective writer and distinguished theatre director, was also a Kiwi.

## Taxes

New Zealand has its own form of purchase tax, similar to the iniquitous VAT in Europe and sales tax in parts of the US. It is called GST (Goods and Services Tax) and it is added, currently at 12.5 per cent, to pretty much everything. However, unlike, say, the United States, it is the practice here to quote prices inclusive of GST. Visitors can recover GST at the exit airport if the amount is sufficiently large – ask for details at the time that you make your purchase.

## Telephones, telecoms and internet

Pay phones come in two different colours. Yellow means you can use almost any credit card. Green means you have to use the telephone company's proprietary phonecard. Most of the public telephones in New Zealand are yellow. CardPhones and cards are widely available from newsagents, post offices and petrol stations. Mobile coverage is excellent in main centres and along highways, but patchy in remote

## Smoking

Smoking is banned in most indoor public areas, including bars and restaurants, and in all places of work. The display of tobacco products in shops is also restricted.

## Time warp

Many coffee shops appear to have been designed with a 60s look. You might think that this is the result of clever new-wave retro design. You would be wrong. New Zealanders, when it comes to coffee shop design, stay with what they find comfortable.

and rugged areas. Consult your service provider before you leave home to see whether your phone is enabled for use in New Zealand.

The important numbers to know are emergency services 111, international operator 0170 and international direct dialling 00 (followed by the country code, the area code (without the initial 0) and the local number). Freephone (0800) numbers apply to calls made within New Zealand only.

Most New Zealand telephones now have tone dialling. Computer users need to know that almost all newer switchboards do not use a pause when dialling out.

Email is a good way to keep in touch. New Zealand has dozens of internet cafés (main libraries also offer this service). A booklet listing every internet café is sold at most tourist offices. If you have a device that facilitates wireless mobile, then short-term connection services are becoming increasingly available in New Zealand (*www.vodafone.co.nz*).

## Time

New Zealand is where the new day begins, for the International Date Line runs some 300km to the east of New Zealand's Chatham Islands. The local time is 12 hours ahead of GMT and a couple of hours ahead of Australia. Depending on which part of the United States you are referring to, New Zealand is 17–22 hours ahead. New Zealand has daylight saving time during summer. The reverse of the northern hemisphere, this runs from the first Sunday in October to the third Sunday in March.

## Tipping

You simply do not need to leave tips while you are in New Zealand. Taxi drivers do not expect it; tour guides feel insulted at the idea. Only in the top restaurants (and especially in international hotels) has this practice begun to creep into the country – and 10 per cent of the bill is a good guideline to follow if you have received good and friendly service. There is rarely a service charge in restaurants – you can therefore apply the old standard of tipping only for superlative service.

## Travellers with disabilities

Serious moves are afoot to cater properly for travellers with disabilities. In truth, although a good start has been made it is still not entirely satisfactory. The best way to check what is available is to contact the Disability Resource Centre (*PO Box 24-042, Royal Oak, Auckland; tel: (09) 625 8069; fax: (09) 624 1633; www.disabilityresource.org.nz*). As an overseas tourist you can apply for an Operation Mobility Card for a nominal fee. This allows you use of specially designated car parking throughout the country. If your disability is not obvious, you will need a medical certificate.

# Driver's guide

## Automobile clubs

Many automobile clubs have reciprocal agreements with the Automobile Association in New Zealand. In Britain the AA, in Australia the NRMA, RVAC and others all have such arrangements, so check with your own organisation before you go. Where reciprocal arrangements exist, you can visit any New Zealand AA office and come away with a bundle of free maps and guides.

## Camper-van hire

All the following rental companies will accept bookings or enquiries via email:

**Maui/Britz Campervan Rentals**
*Private Bag 92133, Auckland, New Zealand; tel: freephone 0800 651 080 (within New Zealand); 00 800 200 80 801 (outside New Zealand); www.maui.co.nz, www.britz.co.nz*

**Britz Campervan Rentals**
*Tel: (09) 275 9090 or 0800 831 900; fax: (09) 275 1834; www.britz.co.nz*

**Spaceships**
*50 Fort St, Auckland; tel: 0800 772 237 or (+649) 526 2130; www.spaceshipsrentals.co.nz*

## Accidents

Your chances of being in an accident are not high. New Zealand is a low motoring accident zone compared with the rest of the world. Working on the basis of accidents as a ratio to population, then New Zealand's figures are better than Australia, Britain or the United States. The same comparison as a ratio to vehicles is even more reassuring, with New Zealand running typically at half the rate of Britain and well below most other developed countries.

So your chances of being in a collision are not high if you take reasonable care and precautions. That said, do note that city driving, especially in Auckland, can be a bit hairy and extra care is required. If you are in a collision of any sort you must stop. That is absolute and mandatory. Stop, get out and look to see if anyone is injured and assist any injured person. Remember to look inside any other vehicle for injured people. If a person is injured, you must report the accident to the police as soon as practicable and not more than 24 hours after the accident, if a person is seriously injured, of course, contact the emergency services immediately. If there is damage to another vehicle or property (such as fences, power poles, traffic signs, etc), you must either notify the owner of the vehicle or property, or report the accident to the police within 48 hours of the accident.

How you proceed from there depends on the extent of the damage. If it is minor damage you must report it immediately to your hire company. If anyone is even slightly hurt, or there is a potential of later injury, you must report it to the police. The police emergency number is 111. When you hire your car your car-hire company will give you clear details of what to do in the event of an accident. If you are not given them, ask for them.

## Breakdowns

First, make sure you and the vehicle are safe. Get it as far off the road as you safely can and, if need be, turn on the hazard lights. If you are leaving the vehicle to find help, leave a note on the windscreen.

Most hire companies will let you have anything fixed on a hire car up to a limit of about $100, but confirm this with the company upon hiring the car. After that you need permission.

You may have a reciprocal agreement with the New Zealand Automobile Association and you should check before you leave home. The AA, for example, runs such a scheme, but you need to make the

**Kea Campers**
*Tel: (09) 441 7833 or 0800 520 052; fax: (09) 444 2990; www. keacampers.com*

## Documents

New Zealand happily accepts most driving licences but it is never a bad thing to get an international licence from your motoring organisation. It does not cost much, it looks impressive, and you can never have too much documentation. It is possible to rent four-wheel-drive vehicles, but the restrictions are many and the insurance will not cover off-road driving, which rather defeats their purpose.

## Drinking and driving

Do not even think about drinking and driving in New Zealand. There is an official limit of 80mg of alcohol to 100ml of blood but there is a very active campaign to lower that limit and the police are absolute tigers. New Zealand simply doesn't tolerate drunk drivers. In that, the government should have your full support.

arrangements in Britain before going overseas. It does not work if you only try to do something after you have had a breakdown. Your car-hire company may also have such an arrangement and will provide details of what to do. Typically you call the NZAA toll free on *0800 500 216* and the vehicle is towed to the nearest AA Collision Management Centre or AA Collision Repairer. If the repair is going to take any length of time – multiply the estimated time by two – get a replacement vehicle from your hire company.

## Caravans and camper vans

This is one of the most popular hiring options in New Zealand. Note that in almost every case you are restricted to use on road. You cannot go charging off cross-country. The reason for this is very sound – these vehicles are not designed to handle rough terrain, and driving them in these conditions is extremely difficult.

Most of the hires are for totally self-contained vehicles rather than a towed caravan. These are not sprightly to drive, and you must adjust your driving style to the vehicle. Bear in mind that there are restrictions on where you may park them overnight – you will probably find that a camping site is the best bet. If you hire one, insist on a thorough briefing before you depart.

## Drivers with disabilities

New Zealand is perhaps unique in the Asia/Pacific area in having a company that specialises in renting motorhomes to drivers with a disability. Mobility Motorhomes – *www.mobilitymotorhomes.co.nz* – hires out custom coach-built vehicles based on the Mercedes Sprinter diesel. The camper van is fitted with hand controls and a detachable steering wheel knob. The fully adjustable hydraulic-suspension swivel seats allow easy transfer from a wheelchair. The motorhome is fitted with a self-operating electric wheelchair lift that retracts and folds away under the floor of the main entrance door. The wheel-in shower has an armless, height-adjustable, removable shower chair.

An optional extra is a PDQ PowerTrike for using on some of the many accessible walking tracks. This front wheel unit converts a normal wheelchair (folding or fixed-frame options available) into a motorised wheelchair. Some of the other hire companies offer modified vehicles, but on a more ad hoc basis. For the traveller with a disability in New Zealand, Mobility Motorhomes offers a solution which is world-class.

## Driving in New Zealand

Driving in New Zealand is an excellent way to see the country. Hire cars are relatively inexpensive and widely available. Driving is on the left-hand side of the road and in most respects is no different from

## Fines

Fines for driving over the speed limit range from $30 to $630. If you are in a hire car it will mostly, but not always, end up on your credit card. Drive more than 50kph over the limit and you are in serious trouble. This falls under the categories of careless, dangerous or reckless driving, depending on the circumstances, and there is a mandatory 28-day licence suspension.

As in most countries, seat belts must be worn by all occupants of the vehicle whenever the vehicle is moving. There is an instant fine of $150 for anyone not wearing a seat belt. Car seats are required for children under the age of 5.

driving anywhere else in the world, though this would not be New Zealand without one or two little idiosyncrasies.

Some road terms may not be familiar. Speed humps or traffic calmers are called judder bars in New Zealand. Signs painted on the surface of the road to warn you of coming hazards are painted in reverse order, presumably on the basis that you will read them one at a time as you come to them. In fact, you tend to take them in at a single glance and find yourself puzzling over 'Ahead road major'.

Many of the roads in New Zealand are graded tracks. This is especially true in the north of the North Island. Although these roads are very safe and drivable, some car-hire companies do not insure their cars for off-road driving. In other words, you cease to be insured the moment you go on to an unmetalled road. It is vital that you discover what the insurance on your hire car covers when collecting it. If necessary you should take out extra insurance (many of the country's roads are unmetalled, so this is advisable).

## Driving rules

If you are turning left at a crossroads (intersection), you must give way to any vehicle that is turning right from the other side of the intersection onto the road you intend to take. This can be most confusing if you are used to the left turn having priority, which is the case in almost every other country in the world. The car-hire companies will give you a diagram to explain what you must do.

Many roads are quite narrow, but heavy-goods vehicles and caravans are good at letting other motorists overtake. It is customary for them to signal that it is clear to overtake by switching on the right indicator. This signal normally means you can overtake in safety – but not always: it may just mean that the vehicle ahead is turning right. This can lead to moments of great excitement. When in doubt, hold back. You will also come across passing lanes: these are intended for overtaking slow vehicles, and are quite short. Don't hog them.

Many bridges in New Zealand are only one lane wide. If you have priority the sign is a blue square with a large white arrow on your side. A circular sign with a red border indicates that you must give way to oncoming traffic. In truth, you will find that the roads carry such a small amount of traffic that this is never a problem.

## Fuel

This is readily available but it is a good practice to fill up as soon as the needle gets to the halfway mark. There is nothing worse than driving along what appears to be an endless highway with the needle hovering around empty. All hire cars take unleaded petrol.

Most garages are self-service, but occasionally, when you stop for petrol, the attendant will come out, fill the car for you, clean the

## Lights

New Zealand drivers seem to switch to dipped lights as soon as there is any loss of visibility. This sensible idea means that dipped lights are used during heavy rain and in the late afternoon, just as the light is fading. Motorcycles drive permanently on dipped beams.

## Mobile phones

New Zealand has not yet changed the laws regarding mobile phones and driving, although there is a strong movement to make this happen. Talking on mobile phones (without hands free) while driving is unlawful in a large number of countries, but not in New Zealand. However, in the simple interests of personal safety this should be avoided.

windscreen and offer to check your oil. You may have forgotten that such courtesies existed. They still do in New Zealand.

## Parking

In keeping with the rest of the world, New Zealand suffers from parking problems in the larger towns and cities. In some places, like Hamilton and Auckland, the only way to deal with it is to leave your car in a long-stay car park and walk everywhere. Other places

**Right**
Coromandel Peninsula

are somewhat easier. In many places parking at a 45-degree angle to the kerb is standard. As almost everyone parks nose in, they reverse out, so driving past such parked cars requires extra care and attention.

In some towns there are parking meters and if you overstay your payment you will get a ticket. Do not think having a hire car will save you – you will get a supplementary charge on your credit card account at a later stage as a nasty reminder.

## Security

Car theft does happen, of course, but it is not something that should over-concern you. Just take sensible precautions: lock up when you leave the vehicle, and don't leave valuables visible.

## Speed limits

The Highway Patrol aims to make New Zealand roads safer by reducing driving speeds. The police are polite but firm, and also use speed cameras. You need to change mental gear and realise that you are driving in a country where the roads can be narrow and frequently winding and that the speed limits suggested are pretty sensible. Near the cities the police use unmarked cars.

Within built-up areas the limit is 50kph (roughly the same as 30mph). Once you get on the open road you can soar up to 100kph (almost exactly 60mph). In Low Speed Zones, marked by LSZ signs, you must temper your speed to the circumstances, but still with an absolute limit of 100kph. There are special speed limits at every school entrance, and these must be strictly observed. No leeway is given on any of these limits anywhere at any time. The police will stop and charge you if you are driving at 108kph in a 100kph zone. You need to adjust your driving attitudes to New Zealand conditions and abandon any press-on attitude. If you do, you will find that motoring has become a pleasant way to get around the country and to view the scenery.

## Road signs

Road signs follow standard international practice. One that you might not be familiar with is the LSZ (Low Speed Zone) sign which means that you can drive at 100kph (60mph) only if traffic conditions allow.

## NEW ZEALAND ROAD SIGNS

### Compulsory signs

Turn right

Keep left

You must not go
faster than 50km/h

You must not
drive into this road

You must
not turn left

You must not
make a u-turn

You must stop

You must slow
down and give way

### Hazard warning signs

Pedestrians crossing

Road narrows

Greasy surface

Road works

Left-hand lane closed

Slips

Metal surface

Stop on request

### Information signs

**TURN
LEFT**
**AT ANY TIME
WITH CARE**

You may turn left,
but first give way to
pedestrians and vehicles

Shows State Highway
number and distance in
kilometres to places shown

# Getting to New Zealand

If New Zealand has one disadvantage, it is that it is a very long way from pretty much anywhere else in the world. Therefore the only realistic way to visit is to fly. Opinion is divided as to whether to blast right through, in one journey, from Europe, or to take a break approximately halfway (at Hong Kong, Singapore, Bangkok or Kuala Lumpur on the Asian route, or Los Angeles if you are coming via the United States). Having made this journey over 100 times, the author would opt for breaking the journey if possible. Many packages to New Zealand include two nights' hotel accommodation at some stopover point. Make certain that, wherever you break your journey, you use the time for rest and adjustment, not for shopping and sightseeing.

If you fly straight through from Europe you are looking at a 25-hour journey on what will normally be a very full flight. This, especially in economy, is very fatiguing. Add to that the very real problems of jet lag and you will realise that, on a non-stop flight, you need to schedule a very low-key start to your visit to New Zealand, allowing time to recover and get back up to pace.

There are many suggested cures for jet lag, but the one that has worked for many people is spending time in the open air and letting the sun get to you. Avoiding alcohol on the flight also helps.

**Above**
Floatplane in Fiordland

**Opposite**
The road to Mount Cook

# Setting the scene

To experience your visit to New Zealand with optimum pleasure and enjoyment it is helpful if you first understand something of the history of the country and the forces that made it the way it is. This most desirable of destinations, widely accepted as being one of the major tourist attractions of the world, has been formed through a series of events that date back to prehistory.

The geographical layout of the country, and the way that it is formed on the volcanic Rim of Fire on the Pacific plate, has given it much of its stunning scenery and, of course, the thermal activity that is so great an attraction to this day.

The isolation of the country for so many centuries has given it some unique life forms and has kept it protected from many diseases and infections that have troubled other less fortunate places. (It is for this reason that you should not try to walk through customs with an apple illegally carried in your hand baggage – they have a fruit detector and you will be stopped and given a smart lecture before the offending fruit is sent off for incineration.)

**Below**
Prow of a Maori war canoe, or waka

The first people to arrive on the islands, the ancestors of the present-day Maori, helped change the country – not always with totally felicitous results. For example, when they arrived they found the moa, a large, flightless bird that was easy to hunt and gave a plentiful supply of food. Now the bird is extinct and only the bones of the moa remain to show us what once was. On the other hand, they explored the country from one end to the other. They settled mainly on the North Island but knew both islands well (which is more than can be said about many present-day New Zealanders). The Maori, for instance, used mountain passes for generations before they were 'discovered' and named after Europeans who were their supposed discoverers – the Haast Pass will do as just one example.

## European migration

Then came the Europeans. Unlike Australians, they all came to New Zealand voluntarily, arriving from the beginning of the 19th century. True, there were among them many people who were less than socially acceptable, especially among the sealers, whalers and gold miners – not the sort of people whom you would willingly invite around for tea. But, for the most part, they were serious immigrants who came to find a new life. The vast majority were from Britain, and many of them from Scotland, bringing the values of that non-conformist country with them (until late into the 19th century there were schools on the west coast of the South Island where the language of instruction was Gaelic).

The Europeans inevitably clashed with the Maori. They wanted to take over the country and farm it and there was serious trouble. The Maori, unlike the Australian Aboriginal people, were organised, war-like, and not easily fooled, even less cowed. And so came the famous Treaty of Waitangi, which, for generations, New Zealand children were taught was an example to all the world of how two races could be brought to live in harmony.

In reality, it was something far less than that. First it was not totally accepted by all the Maori. Next it was not clearly understood in all its implications by all the Maori. The translation was, at the very least, suspect. And the terms of the agreement were broken by the Europeans almost from the beginning. This led, inevitably, to warfare. The Maori, outgunned and out-equipped, nevertheless fought like demons to achieve what could, perhaps, be scored as a draw.

There is still friction between Maori and *pakeha* (the Maori name for New Zealanders of European extraction), and you will still hear racist jokes. But the truth is that the resolution of the relationships between the Maori and the *pakeha* is better in New Zealand than in any similar situation around the world, with the possible exception of Hawaii.

### Relations with the UK

Another great formative force has been the relationship between New Zealand and Britain. Britain was literally called 'home' until well into the 1950s, and the coming-of-age rite-of-passage for almost every New Zealander was 'The Trip' to Britain.

In each of the two world wars New Zealand joined in support of Britain within minutes of war being declared – and sent a large percentage of its people overseas to fight as part of the British army. They did this with great courage and substantial casualties. But they were fighting for Britain, and Britain was home. Thus, when Britain joined the European Community, New Zealand felt this like a most terrible kick in the teeth. It left New Zealand to find new markets for its agricultural produce that had traditionally been sold to Britain. Worse, it meant that New Zealanders visiting the Old Country had to fill in forms, queue at immigration and suffer restrictions, while visitors from the rest of Europe sailed through without a murmur.

It is difficult to this day to explain to anyone in Britain the sense of outrage that this created in New Zealand. In recent years the head of the British Tourist Authority told the press that if New Zealanders expected to be treated differently from the Chinese they could forget it. This was not a tactful message to send to a nation that had been Britain's staunchest ally for almost the whole of its existence.

## Made in New Zealand

Tourist guides do not hesitate to claim for their country that which is not strictly theirs. You will be told time and time again that the first bungee jumping occurred in New Zealand. It did not. It happened in Europe. The same applies to the gastronomic creation claimed by New Zealanders as their national dessert, the pavlova. This is a sort of meringue cake with a marshmallow centre, smothered with cream and fresh fruit. It was created in honour of the ballerina Anna Pavlova, who took both New Zealand and Australia by storm on her tour in 1926. New Zealand's claim to the pavlova's inception is strongly challenged by Australians.

The result is that New Zealand now has to redefine itself. And this it has done, becoming in the process a stronger, more mature, more individualistic nation. There are now no apron strings. Young New Zealanders still undergo their 'Big OE' (overseas experience), which may be a trip to Britain, or may be to a destination elsewhere in Europe, or in Southeast Asia.

### The New Zealand style

These changes have given New Zealand and New Zealanders a greater feeling of independence, of freedom, of their own style and destiny. New Zealand has always been a forward-looking nation. Arguably it was the first sovereign country in the world to give women the vote, and its education system has been the envy of many another nation. Its attitude towards health and welfare has, in some cases, led the world. It was able to do all of this because it was small, compact, relatively prosperous and inhabited by reasonable people. It is here that you get to the heart of what it is that defines New Zealand – the New Zealander. It does not actually matter from what ethnic background he or she comes – there is a style and an approach that sets the New Zealander apart – and that helps to define the country.

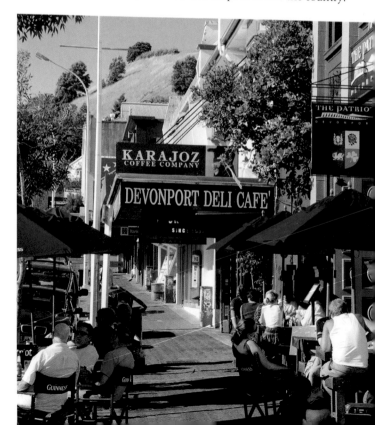

**Right**
Café life in Devonport

**Above**
Sporting options in
Queenstown

### The sporting life

All New Zealanders are sport mad. There is probably not a sport in the world that is not played somewhere in New Zealand. But the serious passion is reserved for yachting and rugby.

There are said to be more yachts per head of the population in New Zealand than in any other country in the world. In Auckland the figure is said to be one yacht for every 11 households, and there are those who would argue that the figure is greater than that, depending on the definition of the word 'yacht'. At the weekend Auckland harbour is a traffic jam of yachts. And most of them are desperately competing with other yachts.

New Zealanders are, indeed, yachting fanatics. But that fanaticism is as nothing compared to the New Zealand view of rugby. The All Blacks (the name of the team comes from the colour of the strip they play in) are venerated as gods (needless to say, New Zealanders, often without a trace of irony, refer to their country as 'God's own' – or 'Godzone'). When the All Blacks lose a match, especially against the arch enemy (Australia), the country goes into mourning. The All Blacks are expected not only to win, but to win consistently and in perpetuity. The team still holds the record for winning 15 international matches in a row – a fact that concerns New Zealanders not the slightest: what they want to know is what evil combination of circumstances led to the losing of the 16th match. When a prominent figure who has played for the All Blacks dies, it does not matter what else they achieved in their life. The obituary will always start with the fact that they played rugby for their country. All other achievements pale by comparison.

The New Zealander is a person of independent spirit who, if there is a flaw, albeit a venial one, suffers from being slightly unbalanced when it comes to the subject of sport.

### Good, keen men

A book that sells well in New Zealand, written by an author called Barry Crump, is called *A Good Keen Man*. And that, in truth, is how most male New Zealanders see themselves and each other. The feminist movement in New Zealand made all of its gains early on, and there is little or no feeling of a problem of equality between the sexes (one of the longest-serving prime ministers of New Zealand is a woman).

New Zealanders are independent, upright, pleasant, attractive and, generally, honest to a fault. If they have a problem – and this is not widely understood by the government departments of the country – it is that they are not over-keen on tourism. Note carefully that it is not tourists that they are against. You will never in your life meet such friendly courtesy as in New Zealand. No, it is the concept of tourism. Perhaps, more precisely, tourism in the American manner. By and large, New Zealanders do not want it. They would really much prefer to live in a green and pleasant country that is not distorted and disfigured for the sake of attracting more tourists. It is true that some places could be called tourist towns. Tourist development has been carried out very successfully in, for example, Queenstown, on the South Island, and with far less success at Franz Josef Glacier. But many places make no concessions at all to tourism. They say, in effect, this is the way we are. Take us as you find us.

This relaxed attitude towards tourism extends to all areas. On the one hand, you will almost never have to tip while you are in New Zealand. On the other hand, you will find that the quality of service is more on the matey level than following the international style. As most of the restaurants are of the middle range, rather than of international haute cuisine standard, this is rarely a problem. It becomes annoying only when you are in a restaurant with delusions of grandeur, charging as if it were a Michelin 3-star – but this does not happen often, except in a few restaurants in such cities as Auckland and Wellington. For the rest, tipping hardly ever arises. And you can cause some offence by pushing a tip where it is not welcome. Coach drivers, for example, do not want to be tipped.

**Below**
Kauri tree

### Cultural riches

Some New Zealanders are convinced that their country is some sort of a cultural desert. Nothing could be further from the truth. There is a thriving theatrical scene. The music played by local groups is rarely substandard, and is often world-class. Publishing thrives and there are more bookshops per head of the population in New Zealand than anywhere else in the world. All of the cities – and this is especially true of university cities – have a vibrant musical scene. Dunedin has a sound and style all of its own, which is recognised internationally.

Where New Zealand really shows its love of the arts is in its museums

## An agricultual economy

New Zealand has always been a successful agricultural nation. Its sheep and fruit have, of course, won world acclaim, but now there are other exports. The most notable of these is wine, where the country has made massive strides forward in the last 15 years. Certainly, New Zealand now produces white wines that are the equivalent of, or better than, those of any other wine nation in the world.

## The gift of the gab

Coach drivers view their charges with an attitude of amused tolerance and they tell stories to rival those of Baron Munchausen. In Rotorua, the author heard a coach driver describing some cooling towers as secret atomic power stations. He further explained that the dams on the river were there to create sufficient depth of water to enable South African submarines to come up the river and load a cargo of enriched uranium – at night, so that the locals would not be alarmed. You do not need to engage in extensive investigation to show that this and other stories like it are not based on anything resembling the truth.

and art galleries. The Te Papa museum in Wellington is world-class, and even the smallest town will have a museum. Sadly, many lean towards exhibitions of antique farm machinery – and you can quickly suffer sensory overload from exhibition after exhibition of antique ploughs. Overall, the museums and galleries are uniformly excellent, however, and the artistic life of New Zealand is alive and well. It is certainly far better than most New Zealanders appreciate.

## How green is my valley?

Another aspect of New Zealanders and their relationship with the country is that they are generally sensitive to conservation issues. The result is that a large percentage of the country is a national park – indeed, a larger percentage of the country than any other nation on Earth. And the New Zealanders love their national parks. They go tramping – the New Zealand term for hiking – along some of the finest walks in the world. The plan to have a continuous walking trail from one end of each island to the other is almost complete, and the whole foreshore throughout New Zealand is open to public access.

This greenness helps to make New Zealand forever and always one of the world's greatest tourist destinations. From the fiords and the majesty of Milford Sound in the deep south – if you go nowhere else in your lifetime you must visit Milford Sound, preferably when it is raining – to the wonders of Ninety Mile Beach in the north, New Zealand is one gloriously scenic spot after another. Luckily the country is so compact that exploring the main spots on a single visit is very feasible. You may get slightly overloaded with scenic splendour, but you will come away with images that will stay with you for the rest of your life.

**Right**
Local wildlife

# Highlights

Many visitors to New Zealand travel on a very limited time budget, allowing sometimes as little as seven days in which to see the country (although a schedule of fourteen days is more common).

If you want to see the highlights of New Zealand within such a limited time span, you have to be absolutely ruthless and concentrate on the highlights. On the plus side, you should not worry too much about what you will miss out this first time around. Visitors rarely come to New Zealand only once.

## Transport

If you are pushed for time you should use the excellent internal air services and hire cars at each destination within the two islands. You simply do not want the bother of driving along New Zealand's narrow (but adequate and safe) roads, to get from one point to another.

## Arrival

In almost every case you will arrive in Auckland, but this city need not detain you. It is the biggest city in New Zealand – although Wellington is the capital – but it is strangely untypical of the rest of the country, and you can safely leave it for another time.

Where you head first depends on whether you are most interested in scenery, culture, wine, hedonism or seeing the high alpine places of this mountainous country.

## Queenstown and Fiordland

The 'must-sees' on a short trip start with Milford Sound. If you go to New Zealand and miss Fiordland you have made a terrible mistake. This area is located in the southernmost part of the South Island. One way of setting up an itinerary would be to spend a night in Auckland to get over the stress and strain of a long flight and fly directly to Queenstown the next day.

You can easily use Queenstown as a base for exploring some of the more important scenic areas, including Fiordland. There are day trips from Queenstown to Milford Sound so that you can go by bus and let someone else do the driving. But if you want to enjoy the Sound at its best you need to book on one of the smaller boats and make the drive yourself.

From Queenstown you can also easily explore Lake Wanaka and Mount Cook. How much time you spend at these places depends on how long you have available. But if you were seriously rushed you could fly into Queenstown and do Milford Sound, Mount Cook and Lake Wanaka in three days. If it is within the constraints of your financial budget you can fly from Queenstown over Mount Cook to the Franz Josef and Fox glaciers and even land on them. This is, perhaps, the best way to approach the glaciers.

## Christchurch and the Marlborough Sounds

If you fly on from Queenstown to Christchurch, you can explore that quintessentially English city, the Banks Peninsula and Akaroa. If you have the time, take a day trip up and over Arthur's Pass to Greymouth. You can do this by train, which is very relaxing and definitely one of the better train journeys of the world. Next you need to see the Marlborough Sounds. When you get there you may well decide to revise your plans and go no further. Base yourself in Blenheim and drive very gently – there is no other way – along the road that winds around the Sounds, and see scenery that will bring peace to your soul.

While you are in Blenheim you are in the centre of the Marlborough wine country and you can go on a sampling tour. Let someone else do the driving. Do not, under any circumstances, miss out Cloudy Bay, the greatest white wine in the history of the world.

## North Island

Heading over to the North Island, it is best to fly directly to Rotorua for its hot springs, geysers and the volcanoes of the Central Plateau. The hot baths are wonderful and the lake can be magical. You can, if you wish, go to a Maori *hangi*, which is a type of feast. This will be strongly urged upon you by all the tourist authorities. If you decide not to, you have the perfect excuse – you can say that you are pressed for time and will include it on another visit.

Finally, returning from Rotorua to Auckland (which will almost certainly be your point of departure), you should try very hard to fit in a quick visit to Russell – a magical spot within easy striking distance. From there, take the day-long bus ride up to Ninety Mile Beach, which will take you to Cape Reinga at the very northern tip of the North Island. It brings this fast trip to an end with an enthralling drive along the beach and through the incoming waves.

This is a quick glimpse of the wonders of New Zealand. It is possible to pack all this into a week. The author did it on his first visit to New Zealand in 1965. He has been back since many, many times. Most visitors have the same experience.

**Below**
Bus trip along Ninety Mile Beach

# Auckland

## Ratings

| | |
|---|---|
| Dining | ●●●●● |
| Outdoor activities | ●●●●○ |
| Watersports | ●●●●○ |
| Children | ●●●●○ |
| Scenery | ●●●○○ |
| Historical sights | ●●●○○ |
| Museums | ●●●○○ |
| Heritage | ●●○○○ |

For most visitors, Auckland is the entry point to New Zealand. As the only true city in New Zealand, in the international sense, Auckland is quite unlike the rest of the country, and is unique to itself. Although it is full of tourist attractions, it is not a tourist city. Rather, it is a busy, cosmopolitan and thriving metropolis that accepts tourists with warm friendliness – but in a very businesslike manner.

Auckland is a beautiful city, built on a series of hills (extinct volcanoes, in fact) overlooking a harbour. As always, in this part of the world, the scenery transcends the architecture. The residents of Auckland are sailing mad. On a sunny Saturday you can barely see the water for the spinnakers and genoas. It is then that Auckland truly lives up to its nickname of the 'City of Sails'.

## History

**ⓘ Auckland Airport Visitor Centre**
*International airport terminal arrivals lounge, tel: (09) 275 6467; email: airport@aucklandnz.com. Open 0600 until the last flight. Very helpful in arranging accommodation and giving friendly and informed advice.*

The traditional name for the isthmus on which Auckland stands is Tamaki-makau-rau, the name that is now included on the signs welcoming air passengers at Auckland's Mangere airport. It means 'Tamaki of a hundred lovers' or 'Tamaki of the many rivers', a much sought-after and fought-over place, even in Maori times.

If Rome was built on seven hills, Auckland was built on seven extinct seaside volcanoes. The last eruption was on **Rangitoto Island** about 800 years ago. You can get there by ferry and, if you are relatively energetic, clamber to the top where you will have a spectacular view of Auckland. The extinct volcanic cones lent themselves to the building of *pas*, fortified Maori villages. The main ones were sited on Mount Eden, Mount Albert, Mount Wellington, One Tree Hill and Mount Hobson. Originally there were 36 volcanic cones, but they have been quarried away for road metal. Of those

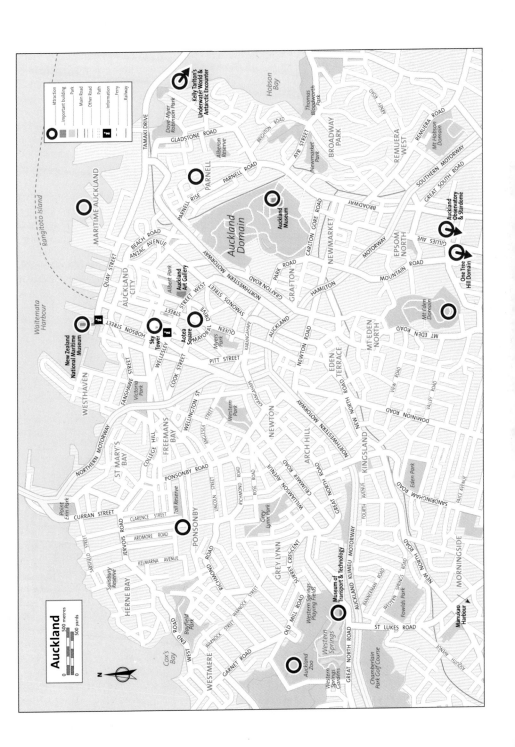

## Auckland

0 ————— 500 meters
0 ————— 500 yards

N

**Attraction**
Important building
Park
Main Road
Other Road
Path
Information
Ferry
Railway

Kelly Tarlton's
Underwater World &
Antarctic Encounter

Dove-Myer Robinson Park

TAMAKI DRIVE

GLADSTONE ROAD

Alberon Reserve

BRIGHTON ROAD

Hobson Bay

Thomas Bloodworth Park

AYR STREET

BROADWAY PARK

ARNEY ROAD

REMUERA ROAD

Mt Hobson Domain

REMUERA WEST

MARITIME AUCKLAND

PARNELL

PARNELL RISE

PARNELL ROAD

Newmarket Park

SOUTHERN MOTORWAY

GREAT SOUTH ROAD

Rangitoto Island

BEACH ROAD

ANZAC AVENUE

Auckland Museum

Auckland Domain

CARLTON GORE ROAD

BROADWAY

NEWMARKET

GILLIES AVE

Auckland Observatory & Stardome

QUAY STREET

Waitemata Harbour

Albert Park

Auckland Art Gallery

STREET WEST

NORTHWESTERN MOTORWAY

SYMONDS STREET

PARK ROAD

GRAFTON

HAMILTON

MOTORWAY

MOUNTAIN ROAD

EPSOM NORTH

One Tree Hill Domain

New Zealand
National Maritime
Museum

HOBSON STREET

WELLESLEY

Sky Tower

Aotea Square

MAYORAL DRIVE

QUEEN

KARANGAHAPE

GRAFTON ROAD

AUCKLAND

NEWTON ROAD

EDEN

Mt Eden North

MT EDEN ROAD

WESTHAVEN

FANSHAWE STREET

Victoria Park

COOK STREET

PITT STREET

NEWTON

NEW NORTH ROAD

Northern Motorway

WELLINGTON ST

Western Park

KARANGAHAPE

EDEN TERRACE

NEW ROAD

VALLEY ROAD

DOMINION ROAD

ST MARY'S BAY

COLLEGE HILL

FREEMANS BAY

LANCASEE STREET

RICHMOND ROAD

ROSE ROAD

ARCH HILL

GREAT NORTH ROAD

CRUMMER ROAD

WILLIAMSON AVENUE

NORTHWESTERN MOTORWAY

KINGSLAND

SANDRINGHAM ROAD

Eden Park

PACE AVENUE

Point Erin Park

CURRAN STREET

PONSONBY ROAD

LINCOLN STREET

Tole Reserve

Grey Lynn Park

FOURTH AVENUE

HERNE BAY

JERVOIS ROAD

CLARENCE STREET

ARDMORE ROAD

KELMARNA AVENUE

RICHMOND ROAD

GREY LYNN

SURREY CRESCENT

Museum of
Transport & Technology

AUCKLAND KUMEU MOTORWAY

BANNERMAN ROAD

Western Springs Playing Fields

WESTERN SPRINGS ROAD

Fowlds Park

NEW NORTH ROAD

MORNINGSIDE

SALSFIELD STREET

Salisbury Reserve

Bayfield Park

WEST END ROAD

Cox's Bay

WESTMERE

GARNET ROAD

WARNOCK STREET

Auckland Zoo

Western Springs

Western Springs Gardens

OLD MILL ROAD

GREAT NORTH ROAD

ST LUKES ROAD

Chamberlain Park Golf Course

Manukau Harbour

ASQUITH AVENUE

**ⓘ Tourism Auckland Head Office** *137 Quay St, Princes Wharf, Auckland; PO Box 5561, Wellesley St, Auckland 1001; tel: (09) 307 2614; fax: (09) 307 2614; email: nz@aucklandnz.com; www.aucklandnz.com. Open daily 0900–1700.*

**Auckland i-SITE Visitor Information Centre** *Cnr Skycity Atrium, Victoria St, Auckland; tel: 0800 AUCKLAND; fax: (09) 363 7181; email: skycity@aucklandnz.com; www.aucklandnz.com. Open daily 0800–2000.*

remaining, most carry the signs that a Maori *pa* was built there. Maori tradition attributes the volcanoes to a war between fairy people of Hunua and Waitakere. The Waitakere *tohunga*, or witch doctor, caused the isthmus to erupt as a Hunua war party crossed the intervening plain – hence the volcanoes.

When Governor William Hobson bought the city site from the Ngati Whatua tribe, it had been relatively depopulated because of inter-tribal conflict. But there is little doubt that this was always a settled area, and perhaps at one time as many as 50,000 Maori lived here.

The city was named after the first Earl of Auckland, George Eden, who was Governor-General of India when Governor Hobson founded Auckland in 1840 as a European settlement. Auckland briefly served as New Zealand's second capital. The first was Russell (*see pages 58–60*) – some 8km away from where the current Russell is situated – in the Bay of Islands. In 1865 Wellington was chosen as the new capital simply because it was more centrally placed in a long-stretched-out country of two islands, which still had great transport difficulties.

# Topography

**The city beat**

You can tell the difference between Auckland and the rest of New Zealand by the beat of the city. People in Auckland walk around at an average of about 5km an hour. Brisk. Energetic. Purposeful. Only two hours away, in Nelson, the speed is barely half of that.

**Coastal walk**

The waymarked walk between Waitemata Harbour and Manukau Harbour takes you from coast to coast across the Auckland isthmus. It takes about four hours and you can cop out and get on a bus if you get tired. The walk takes in Albert Park, Auckland University, Auckland Domain, Mount Eden and One Tree Hill.

**Harbour kayaks**

To experience Auckland's sparkling harbour first-hand, join a kayak expedition to Rangitoto and back. **Ferg's Kayaks**, *12 Tamaki Dr; tel: (09) 529 2230; email: ak@fergskayaks.co.nz*, runs guided tours and also hires out kayaks on an hourly basis.

Geographically, Auckland is one of the largest cities in the world – a massive urban sprawl of high-rise buildings and houses, straddled by two large harbours – Waitemata in the east and Manukau to the west. Though large, Auckland never feels dense or crowded because of its total integration with the sea. The stunning beauty of the harbour and the hills around help to compensate for the lack of fine architecture. Not that the architecture is truly dreadful. It is not. It is just something less than inspired. There is no great building in Auckland to compare with, say, the Opera House in Sydney. And the casino is, frankly, hideous. Not that this matters very much given that Auckland is dominated by the sea and by the hills.

The Pacific Ocean lies to one side of the city's isthmus, while the Tasman Sea is on the other. At its narrowest, this isthmus is only about 1km wide. The city, however, sprawls sideways along the shores of Waitemata and Manukau harbours and along the Hauraki Gulf. Rangitoto Island dominates Waitemata Harbour – the Sea of Sparkling Waters. You will be assured that the island's shape never changes, no matter from which angle you view it – needless to say, this simply isn't true.

Waitemata Harbour is spanned, to the east, by the Auckland Harbour Bridge, which links Freeman's Bay, on the southern side, and Northcote, on the northern. The bridge took four years to build and was opened in 1959. It was nowhere near big enough for the traffic it carried and so two more lanes in each direction were opened in 1969. These were hung on to the outside of the spans by Ishikawajima-Harima Heavy Industries and the bridge became known as the Nippon Clip-on. The bridge carries a daily average of 150,000 vehicles travelling in both directions.

The city's proximity to the water has two results. First, everyone in Auckland is bonkers mad on sailing. There is one boat to every dozen or so people. On some major regattas it appears as if all the 50,000 boats in Auckland have taken to the water at once. The other effect is that Auckland has a very temperate climate, for the sea moderates the excesses. Most of the rain falls in June, July and August, and the coldest month, July, averages about 13°C during the day.

Most of the inhabitants of New Zealand – 70 per cent of the total of around 4.3 million – live on North Island, and Auckland accounts for more than a million of them. It also claims to have the biggest Polynesian population of any city in the world.

**Left and right**
Maritime Auckland

# Sights

## Queen Street and the city centre

The *IMAX* **Entertainment Centre**, *Cnr Aotea Sq and Queen St*, is New Zealand's leading entertainment complex. In addition to the IMAX theatre, the architecturally stunning building houses a wide choice of bars, cafés and dance clubs, as well as a multiplex cinema.

**Opposite**
Auckland Harbour Bridge

The city's main thoroughfare, running north and south from the waterfront to the suburb of Newton, was built along the floor of a valley, so the side roads climb steeply away from the main road. **Queen Street** is home to many of the city's best retail outlets, and down its side streets and at its seaward end you will find many fine restaurants.

About halfway up Queen Street you'll find **Aotea Square**, which has the Council Buildings, the Old Town Hall and the Aotea Centre Cultural Complex. The square is very close to the **Auckland Art Gallery**, a beautiful old building dating from 1887 that houses the biggest collection of New Zealand paintings in the country. The gallery collection was founded on paintings donated by James Tannock Mackelvie, Sir George Grey and other citizens. In 1915 another Auckland citizen, Henry Edward Partridge, gave his collection of Gottfried Lindauer Maori portraits. The gallery also houses works by William Hodges painted during the voyages of Captain Cook, and an excellent modern New Zealand collection.

## The father and midwife of Auckland

Two great characters were responsible for the creation of Auckland. The first was Bill Webster, an American whaler who very probably jumped ship. He set up a trading station at the entrance to the Waiau River but later transferred to present-day Whanganui Island. The other was a medical doctor, John Logan Campbell, now called the Father of Auckland, who stayed with Billy Webster in 1840. Webster persuaded him what a great site Auckland was for a large city and offered to take him there for an on-the-spot assessment.

Billy Webster, John Campbell and three companions set out for Auckland in an open sailing boat, with eight Maori rowers, on 28 April 1840. Campbell was delighted with what he saw. He purchased land and eventually persuaded the authorities that Auckland was a superior site for New Zealand's capital city to Coromandel.

This took some considerable vision, as there were probably no more than 150 Europeans permanently resident in New Zealand at the time.

John Logan Campbell went on to found the Auckland Savings Bank and, in 1855, became Superintendent of the Province of Auckland. In 1901 he gave the city Campbell Park, the open land which contains One Tree Hill, and he was buried at the summit when he died in 1919 aged 95.

If John Campbell is the father of Auckland, then certainly Billy Webster was the midwife. He eventually had to leave New Zealand, penniless, stripped of his land and heavily in debt to Sydney merchants. A newspaper of the time reported that Billy Webster had 'overstepped the bounds of prudence in playing out his commercial transactions'. Perhaps, but he had also played a part in the birth of one of the greatest cities on Earth.

## Auckland Museum
*The Domain; tel: (09) 306 7067; www.aucklandmuseum.com; Open daily 1000–1700.*

## The Auckland Regatta
With Waitemata Harbour on the east and Manukau Harbour on the west, and the superb stretch of sheltered water outside Waitemata Harbour in the Hauraki Gulf, Auckland is the centre of yachting in New Zealand, and more than 80 per cent of the country's boats are owned and sailed there. On the Monday closest to 29 January, a regatta is held that dates back more than 160 years. More than 1,000 boats, ranging from dinghies to cruisers, enter the races.

The first regatta was held on 18 September 1840. A contemporary eyewitness, Sarah Felton Mathew, wrote: 'The gentlemen got up a boat race among themselves, another for the sailors, and a canoe race for the natives which all came off with great eclat. The amateurs pulled with the Surveyor-General's gig boat against that of the harbour master, for a purse of £5.'

## Explore NZ
Contact Explore NZ (Sail NZ) (*tel: 0800 397 567; www.explorenz.co.nz*) for sailing options in former America's Cup New Zealand yachts.

## Auckland Museum
Located on a hill in the southeast part of the Domain, **Auckland Museum** has the world's largest collection of Polynesian artefacts, as well as a great display of objects relating to New Zealand's natural history. There is a 30m-long Maori war canoe, carved from a single totara tree some 150 years ago. The three-level collection of Maori art is said to be one of the most significant in the world. Prominent is Hotunui, the large carved meeting house built in 1878, and Te Toki a Tapiri, the only surviving complete war canoe. On the front wall of the museum's central gallery are storehouse carvings found in a cave at Te Kaha. These are considered to be the finest Maori carvings in existence. Treasures from Polynesia, Melanesia and Micronesia include carved statues of goddesses from Tonga and Nukuoro. The most recent addition to the building is 'The Dome', a 4-storey suspended bowl, clad in Fijian Kaur, which hangs over the auditorium, and it certainly forms a striking first impression from the museum's south entrance.

## Maritime Auckland
To get the feel of this aspect of Auckland, take a 15-minute **ferry** ride across the harbour – much better than taking the bus – to Devonport, which has a small beach and thriving café culture. In fact, ferries can take you almost anywhere on the harbour and provide some of the least expensive and most enjoyable sightseeing trips available (*timetables and destinations from Fullers at the Ferry Building on Quay St; tel: (09) 367 9111, or call Maxx Regional Transport, tel: (09) 366 6400; www.maxx.co.nz, for all bus, train and ferry information*).

The **New Zealand National Maritime Museum** (*open daily, 0900–1800 summer; 0900–1700 winter; tel: (09) 373 0800 or 0800 725 897; www.nzmaritime.org*) fills in the detail, starting with the Polynesian migration from the legendary land of Hawaiki and ending with the America's Cup. It features the 1995 America's Cup-winning boat NZL32, and a tribute to the life and work of Kiwi yachting legend Sir Peter Blake.

## Sky Tower
For any visitor to Auckland, the view from the top of Auckland's iconic and much loved hypodermic landmark should be a must, provided of course the weather is favourable. Completed in 1997 and piercing 328m into the urban milieu, many Aucklanders initially criticised the tower, saying it was too futuristic and a blot on the landscape. But they have grown to love it – perhaps because it really is like a beacon and can be seen from as far away as the Coromandel Peninsula.

The observation deck offers stunning 360-degree views and there is a café and the obligatory revolving restaurant. You can even jump off it on a 'controlled' bungee descent.

**Sky Tower** *Corner of Victoria and Federal Sts. Enquiries and restaurant bookings, tel: (09) 363 6000; for more information, tel: 0800 7592 489; www.skycityauckland.co.nz.* For bungee madness contact **Sky Jump** (*tel: 0800 759 586, www.skyjump.co.nz*).

**Right**
Auckland's Sky Tower

## Miscellaneous sights

**Kelly Tarlton's Underwater World and Antarctic Encounter** (*Orakei Wharf, on Tamaki Drive; tel: (09) 528 0603 or 0800 805 050; www.kellytarltons.co.nz; open daily 0900–1700*) is a seawater aquarium built in old stormwater holding tanks. The Antarctic Encounter is a re-creation of an Antarctic environment and is better done than most. Also, given such emphasis it would be rude not to have a few penguins and there is a quality live exhibit.

**The Museum of Transport and Technology** (*Western Springs on Great North Road; www.motat.org.nz*) has an amazing range of machinery. Linked to it by an electric tramway is the aviation museum at Keith Park Memorial Airfield (*both open daily 1000–1700; tel: 0800 668 286*).

**Auckland Observatory and Stardome** near the Manukau Road entrance to the One Tree Hill Domain is regularly open to the public with a talk and, on clear nights, a viewing of the heavens. You can even adopt a star! (*For details, call 24hr helpline, tel: (09) 624 1246; www.stardome.org.nz.*)

⊘ **Waiheke Island**
Waiheke, the second-largest island in the Hauraki Gulf, has become famous for two things: its first-class red wines and its jazz festival (held on Easter weekend) which attracts many top international artists. The island is a 30-minute ferry ride from Queen St Wharf (*Fullers, tel: (09) 367 9111*) and boasts white-sand beaches and the picturesque village of Oneroa, 10 minutes' walk from the ferry. It also has public transport, taxis and an official wine tour service.

**Right**
Ring-tailed lemurs at Auckland Zoo

**Auckland Zoo** (*Motions Rd, Western Springs; tel: (09) 360 3805; www.aucklandzoo.co.nz; open daily 0930–1730*) is five minutes from downtown Auckland and features a nocturnal house with kiwis, though these are very shy birds and there is no guarantee that you will see them. The park has over 900 of the usual suspects in an impressive array of themed exhibits, but places a heavy emphasis on native wildlife and conservation issues.

## Accommodation and food

Note that parking is either not available at most city-centre hotels or it is prohibitively expensive. Most, however, have an arrangement with a nearby car park for a discounted rate.

**Café Cezanne $–$$** *296 Ponsonby Rd; tel: (09) 376 3338*. One of the oldest in the city, with a reputation for delicious cakes.

**Aspen House $$** *62 Emily Pl; tel: (09) 379 6633; www.aspenhouse.co.nz*. A no-nonsense, cheaper hotel option, well placed, clean and comfortable. Standard or connecting rooms with TV. Some rooms are small, which is reflected in the price. Wireless internet, free breakfast and undercover parking.

**Esplanade Hotel $$** *1 Victoria Rd, Devonport; tel: (09) 445 1291; www.esplanadehotel.co.nz*. One of Auckland's oldest hotels in Devonport's 'village within a city'.

**Great Ponsonby B&B $$** *30 Ponsonby Terr, Ponsonby; tel: (09) 376 5989; www.greatpons.co.nz*. One of the best in the city, with friendly, knowledgeable hosts.

**Iguacu Restaurant and Bar $$** *269 Parnell Rd, Parnell; tel: (09) 358 4804; www.iguacu.co.nz*. Thought by many to be, in this price range, the best restaurant in Auckland.

**Oaklands Lodge Backpackers $$** *5a Oaklands Rd, Mt Eden; tel: (09) 638 6545; email: info@oaklands.co.nz.* Tidy budget Victorian villa on the fringe of the CBD (Central Business District), and only a short walk to the summit of Mount Eden.

**Sawadee $$** *42A Ponsonby Road, Ponsonby; tel: (09) 376 0320; www.sawadee.co.nz.* Possibly the best Thai restaurant in New Zealand. Thai chefs – who are both Thai and chefs – turn out authentic Thai food. And the place has a great atmosphere.

**Soul $$** *Viaduct Harbour; tel: (09) 356 7249.* Open-air decks overlooking the harbour – the 'in' place to see and be seen.

**Hilton Hotel $$$** *Princes Wharf, 147 Quay St; tel: (09) 978 2000; www.hilton.com.* Built in a prime waterfront location and designed to look like a cruise liner; if you want to treat yourself, this is a fine luxury option.

**Kermadec Ocean Fresh Restaurant $$$** *1st Floor, Viaduct Quay, Viaduct Basin; tel: (09) 304 0454; www.kermadec.co.nz.* One of the best seafood restaurants, perhaps the very best, in Auckland.

**Orbit Restaurant $$$** *Sky Tower, corner Victoria St and Federal St; tel: (09) 363 6000.* Over two-thirds of the way up the Sky Tower, so they have the best views of any restaurants in the city.

**Below**
Rangitoto Island

# Northland

## Ratings

| | |
|---|---|
| Beaches | ●●●●● |
| Heritage | ●●●●● |
| Scenery | ●●●● |
| Children | ●●●○○ |
| Outdoor activities | ●●●○○ |
| Watersports | ●●○○○ |
| Dining | ●●○○○ |
| Museums | ●●○○○ |

Northland, forming the far northern peninsula of New Zealand, is packed with features worth visiting. It is an easy hour's drive from Auckland, reached by the road along the Hibiscus Coast which, though singularly free of hibiscus, is worth the drive in itself. Then there are two major attractions opposite each other: Russell, the first capital of New Zealand, positively reeks charm and history, while at Paihia are the house and grounds where the Treaty of Waitangi was signed. At the northernmost tip of Northland, Cape Reinga is sacred to the Maori as the stepping-off point to the hereafter. To the south lies Ninety Mile Beach, which is classified as a highway and is one of the most exciting drives in New Zealand.

## DARGAVILLE

 **Kauri Coast Information Centre** *Normanby St; tel: (09) 439 8360; www.kauricoast.co.nz*

Dargaville is at the centre of what is left of the New Zealand kauri forest. The kauri provided valuable gum, and its timber was precisely what the world's shipbuilders needed for making the spars and masts of their sailing ships in the late 19th century. As a result, little now remains of the once dense kauri forest that centres around Dargaville.

The country's two remaining large stands of kauri are at the **Trounson Kauri Park**, 39km north of Dargaville, and at the **Waipoua Forest Sanctuary**, 51km northwest of the township. The former was established in 1919 by James Trounson. The latter is a protected forest covering some 15,000ha. It survived only because of public protest. When the last of the mighty kauris were being harvested in 1952, a petition signed by more than 70,000 people convinced Parliament to set aside a large slab of the forest as a sanctuary. Since then it has been extended to its present size. The caretaker's cottage, built at the beginning of the 20th century, has been preserved as a museum.

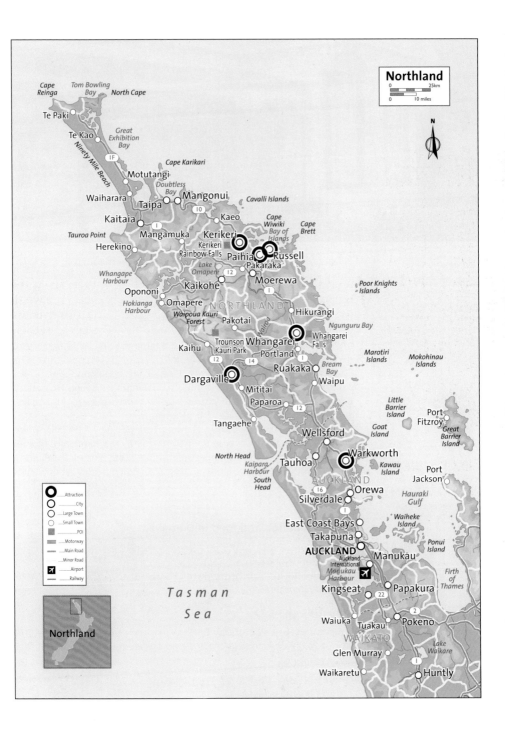

**Sweet potatoes**

Dargaville is also the centre of a major kumara-growing region. *Kumara* is the Maori name for the sweet potato, which is an important part of the Maori diet.

Dargaville was founded in 1872 and became a borough in 1908. The name comes from Joseph McMullen Dargaville, who emigrated from Ireland to Australia. He moved to New Zealand as a bank inspector and manager, but resigned to enter the kauri timber trade and bought the land where the town now stands, on the Northern Wairoa River, which was navigable to the sea.

The **Kauri Museum**, Church Rd, Matakohe (*tel: (09) 431 7417; www.kauri-museum.com; open daily 0900–1700*) is 44km southwest of Dargaville and well worth a look. One of the better museums in the country, it houses a number of highly imaginative displays that offer a detailed insight into the natural history of the kauri and man's exploitation and love affair with the great tree.

The **Dargaville Museum**, in Harding Park (*tel: (09) 439 7555; email: darg.museum@xtra.co.nz; open daily 0900–1600*), is a nautically themed museum with some intriguing displays, including part of the *Rainbow Warrior*, the Greenpeace ship sunk by the French Secret Service when they decided to play at being James Bond. In doing so they killed one innocent person.

## Accommodation and food in Dargaville

**Blah Blah Blah Cafe** $–$$ *101 Victoria St; tel: (09) 439 6300.*

**Awakino Point Boutique Motel** $$ *SH14; tel/fax: (09) 439 7870; www.awakinopoint.co.nz*

**Dargaville Motel** $$ *217 Victoria St; tel: (09) 439 7734.*

**Kauri Coast Top 10 Holiday Park** $$ *Trounson Park Rd, Kaihu; tel: (09) 439 0621; www.kauricoasttop10.co.nz.* Located 30km north. Guided night nature walks.

**Above**
Lodge House in the Waipoua
Forest Sanctuary

**Motel Hobson's Choice** $$ *212 Victoria St; tel: (09) 439 8551; fax: (09) 439 8553; www.motelhobsonschoice.co.nz*

# KERIKERI

**New Zealand on foot**

The first stage of a continuous long-distance walk, from one end of New Zealand to the other, was opened in February 1995. It runs between Kerikeri and Waitangi. This is the work of the Te Araroa – meaning the 'long pathway' – Trust, which was set up to create an uninterrupted trail from North Cape to the Bluff.

Kerikeri is 22km to the northwest of Paihia and contains two of the oldest buildings in New Zealand. Nowadays, Kerikeri is a small town of fewer than 3,000 people. The major industries are growing kiwi fruit and citrus fruit – a very wide variety – and a range of arts and crafts including jewellery, woodcarvings and ceramics. Its importance lies not in the town itself but in the Kerikeri Basin, 2km away (just down the hill from the Kerikeri Shopping Centre), which is where Christianity started in New Zealand. **The Stone Store** (*tel: (09) 407 9236; open daily during the summer 1000–1700; May–Oct 1000–1600*) was built by missionaries between 1832 and 1835 and it replaced an older wooden structure that had probably been there since 1819. For a time Bishop Selwyn used the top floor as a library. On display in the store is the first plough used in New Zealand, which was pulled by a team of six oxen in 1820.

Next door is the **Kerikeri Mission House** (*tel: (09) 407 9236; open daily Nov–Apr 1000–1700; May–Oct 1000–1600*), built in 1822 and the oldest stone building in the country. For the first ten years of its life it was used for the staff of the Church Missionary Society. It is now known as Kemp House after the family that lived in it from 1832 until 1974, when it was given to the Historic Places Trust. Even in the 20th century, one of the members of the family, Miss Gertrude Kemp, kept a light in the window to guide boats up the river basin. This tradition probably dated from the time when the house was built.

Don't miss the **chocolate factory** in Kerikeri Road (*tel: (09) 407 6800; https/secure.makana.co.nz*), where you can watch the chocolate being made and have a free tasting before you buy (it also runs a mail order service).

At 1 Landing Road there is an authentic replica of a **Maori fishing village**, reputed to have been the home of Rewa, the great Maori chief. The replica was built in 1969 (*access by way of the visitor centre; open daily 1000–1600*). Across the inlet from there is the fortified Maori *pa* which belonged to Hongi Hika, who once ruled over most of the North Island.

The striking **Kerikeri Rainbow Falls** are 4km out of town, off the Waipapa Road on Rainbow Falls Road and a ten-minute stroll from the car park.

## Accommodation and food in Kerikeri

**Café Jerusalem** $ *Cobblestone Mall; tel: (09) 407 1001.*

**Abilene Motel** $$ *136 Kerikeri Rd; tel: (09) 407 9203; www. abilenemotel.co.nz*

**Black Olive Pizzeria and Restaurant** $$ *308 Kerikeri Rd; tel: (09) 407 9693.*

**Kerikeri Park Motel** $$ *494 Kerikeri Rd; tel: (09) 407 7464;*
*www.kerikeriparkmotel.co.nz*

**The Landing Restaurant and Bar** $$ *Stone Store Basin; tel: (09) 407*
*8479.*

# The Treaty of Waitangi

In order to comprehend the nature of New Zealand it is important to have a basic understanding of the Treaty of Waitangi. This was signed in 1840 between what were then two sovereign states. One was the United Kingdom and the other was the United Tribes of New Zealand.

It has become plain since that the United Kingdom did not approach the Treaty as if it were an agreement between two equals. The British were motivated by two conflicting desires. The first was to stop the French who, they thought, were planning to settle in New Zealand – specifically on the Banks Peninsula. That was a very real threat. The second was to provide a buffer between the Maori and the settlers. The settlers, almost all British, were grabbing land as if it were undeveloped and therefore legally available, on the basis that the first to turn a sod owns it. Such imported legalistic concepts were totally alien to the Maori. Other settlers 'purchased' the land in unequal deals that were misunderstood by the Maori, who thought they were leasing their land for agriculture, not selling it for perpetuity.

In true Victorian British style William Hobson, a navy captain, was instructed to negotiate the transfer of sovereignty with 'the free and intelligent consent of the natives'. First an English document was drawn up and then a Maori translation made. It is possible to quibble about the accuracy of the translation.

The original treaty in Maori was signed by some 400 representatives of five Northern tribes in Waitangi. The Treaty was then taken around the country and many, but by no means all, Maori tribes signed it.

The terms of the agreement were broken almost from the beginning. The settlers wanted land and did not care how they got it. This especially applied once gold was found. The government was operating under severe financial restraint, and was unable (or unwilling) to reimburse the Maori people for the full worth of their land. The result was annoyance, leading to aggravation and eventually to conflict, which led to the Maori Wars.

Although the Treaty has been represented as an ideal pact between equals, and for decades was presented as such to New Zealand schoolchildren, it was plainly something less than that. The original Treaty in Maori is still treasured by some of the Maori tribes, but there has been a continuous stream of complaints.

In recent years these complaints, and the problems created by the Treaty, have resulted in the Waitangi Tribunal, which was set up under the Treaty of Waitangi Act 1975. It adjudicates on claims made by the Maori under the Treaty of Waitangi. Four of the sixteen members of the tribunal must be Maori. Initially the idea was that it would deal only with claims going back to 1975 but now it deals with claims going all the way back to the signing of the Treaty in 1840.

There are well over 400 claims registered and they concern not only disputed land but also other issues that are deemed to come under the terms of the Treaty. It is possible that now, with the appointment of the tribunal, the original intent of the Treaty of Waitangi might be met.

# PAIHIA

ℹ️ **Bay of Islands Information Centre** *Paihia Wharf, Marsden Rd; tel: (09) 402 7345; www.visitnorthland.co.nz*

**First press**

One of the first printing presses in the country was installed at Paihia by William Colenso, in 1835, and was used to print copies of the Treaty of Waitangi.

The glory of Paihia is the **Treaty House** where the Treaty of Waitangi was signed. This should serve as a splendid example for tourism organisations around the world on how to handle these matters with style and grace. The house was bought by the then Governor General, Lord Bledisloe, who presented it to the nation. It is historically important in that, for many years, the Treaty of Waitangi defined the attitudes of New Zealanders of European descent – the *pakeha* – towards the Maori. It was presented to New Zealand schoolchildren and to the world as an example of fair and equitable treatment. The fact that it was flawed in its execution does not detract from its historical importance, and this splendidly run site, with 400ha of surrounding gardens, does it justice.

A recent addition to the Waitangi experience is the **Culture North Treaty of Waitangi Night Show**, a Maori performance that is staged most evenings and is highly recommended (*1 Tau Henare Dr, Paihia; tel: (09) 402 7437; www.waitangi.net.nz*).

## Accommodation and food in Paihia

Paihia is almost wall-to-wall motels along the front and on the road entering the town. Except in the height of the season, around Christmas, you will be spoiled for choice. Out of season it is relatively easy to get a discount.

**Bay Adventurer and Bay View Apartments $** *28 Kings Rd; tel: 0800 112 127; www.bayadventurer.co.nz*

**Waikokopu Café $–$$** *Treaty Grounds, Waitangi; tel: (09) 402 6275.*

**Darryl's Dinner Cruise $$** *Tel: 0800 334 6637; www.dinnercruise.co.nz.* Popular cruise/dinner option.

**Allegra House $$$** *39 Bayview Rd; tel: (09) 402 7932; www.allegra.co.nz*

**Below**
The Treaty House in Paihia, where the Waitangi Treaty was signed

# RUSSELL

**① Bay of Islands Information Centre** *Paihia Wharf, Marsden Rd; tel: (09) 402 7345; www.visitnorthland.co.nz*

Russell, in the Bay of Islands, is a short car-ferry ride from Paihia, and is one of the most interesting and elegant towns in the country. It has so much going for it that it makes nearby Paihia seem, at times, like a deprived country cousin, and there is a distinct feeling of jealousy in the air. It is difficult to believe that Russell was once called the hell-hole of the Pacific, and it was where the ramping, stamping, tearing, swearing sailors and whalers came ashore to get very drunk and fornicate.

With sin came the missionaries. One Maori described them as having 'faces so solemn they looked like a relation had just been eaten'. Strong efforts are now being made to sanitise the history of Russell; to suggest that it was never that bad and that the missionaries were guilty of gilding the lily. But this is nonsense – it was a wicked, wicked place.

Take, for example, the Girls' War. This started in February 1830 when two Maori ladies fell out over the favours of a whaling captain.

**Below**
Russell harbour

**Dolphin Encounters**
*Maritime Building, Paihia;*
*tel: (09) 402 7421; www.*
*dolphincruises.co.nz.* Sail in a
catamaran and go swimming
with dolphins. You can visit
Urupukapuka Island and take
a further ride in an
underwater viewing vessel to
observe the seabed.

**Fullers** *(tel: (09) 402 7421)*
has several other cruises in
the Bay of Islands and coach
trips to Cape Reinga.

**Coastal Kayakers** *Paihia;*
*tel: (09) 402 8105;*
*www.coastalkayakers.co.nz.*
Guided tours explore the
mangrove forest and Haruru
Falls (4 hours); Motumaire
Island and the Waitangi
coast (full day); or
Urupukapuka Island (2 days
with an overnight camp).

The cat-fight gradually escalated into a full-scale war between two
tribes. Over 100 warriors were killed on the beach on the first day, and
40 on the next. Missionaries, led by Samuel 'The Flogging Parson'
Marsden, finally brought the situation under control. That is not an
incident that lends itself to whitewash.

Whaling ships, sealers and traders had been using the sheltered
anchorage from the 1820s. Living there were escaped convicts,
deserters, sailors who had jumped ship, released convicts from
Australia (New Zealand was never a penal colony) and other equally
upright members of the community.

Edward Markham, artist and writer, recorded the atmosphere in *New
Zealand, or Recollections of It*. He wrote: 'The Missionaries hate the
Ships to come into the Bay; the Reason is this. Thirty to five and
Thirty sail of Whalers come in for three weeks to the Bay and 400 to
500 sailors require as many Women, and they have been out one year.
I saw some that had been out Thirty two Months and of course their
Ladies were in great request, and even the Relations of those who are
living as Servants with the Missionaries go to Pihere and bring them
away in spite of all their prayer lessons. These young ladies go off to
the Ships, and three weeks on board are spent much to their
satisfaction as they get from the Sailors a Fowling piece for the Father
or Brother, Blankets, Gowns & as much as they would from the
Missionary in a year.'

At the time, Russell was called Kororareka. It acquired its new name
in honour of Lord John Russell, then the British Secretary of State for
the Colonies. Not far from Kororareka was Okiato, also known as Old
Russell, where Lieutenant Governor William Hobson originally set up
shop, making it the *de facto* capital of New Zealand (the capital moved
to Auckland in 1841). Russell's fate thereafter was to be destroyed by
fire, and then, four years later, to be attacked and pretty much
destroyed again by Hona Heke, the Maori leader. For years Russell was
a deserted town. Its recovery has been gradual – most of it occurring in
the last 30 years.

In a sense, Russell is now a living museum. It has the country's
oldest surviving church in **Christ Church**, which was built in 1836
(there are those who would argue that it is also the country's most
beautiful church). Then there is **Pompalier House** on the waterfront,
which was built from rammed earth in 1839 for use as a Roman
Catholic mission, and later as a printing press. For a further taste of
times gone by, try the **Duke of Marlborough Hotel** on the waterfront,
which has the oldest liquor licence in the country – dating from 1840
(and there was an unlicensed hotel there before that, starting in 1827).
The present building is the fourth pub that has stood on this spot.

**Russell Museum** is supremely well done, on a miniature scale, and
is full of local and maritime artefacts, including a very large-scale
model of the *Endeavour* (*tel: (09) 403 7701; www.russellmuseum.org.nz;
open daily 1000–1700*).

## Accommodation and food in Russell

**Birdie Num Nums** $ *2 Cass St; tel: (09) 403 7754.* Excellent fish and chips.

**Russell Top 10 Holiday Park** $–$$ *Long Beach Rd; tel: 0800 148 671; www.russelltop10.co.nz*

**Commodore's Lodge** $$$ *The Waterfront; tel: (09) 403 7899; email: commodoreslodge@xtra.co.nz; www.commodoreslodgemotel.co.nz*

**Duke of Marlborough Hotel** $$$ *The Waterfront; tel: (09) 403 7829; email: info@theduke.co.nz; www.theduke.co.nz.* Stay at the oldest licensed pub in New Zealand.

**Kamakura** $$$ *The Strand; tel: (09) 403 7771.* Top of the range with open deck and fine bay views.

# WARKWORTH

**🛈 Warkworth Visitor Information Centre** *I Baxter St; tel: (09) 425 9081; fax: (09) 425 7584; www.warkworthnz.com.* This is among the best of its kind, with a more positive approach to tourism than almost any other visitor centre in New Zealand.

Warkworth lies on the banks of the Mahurangi River, with wharves right in the centre of the town packed with leisure boats. The founder of the town, John Anderson Brown, was born in Warkworth in Northumberland, England. When he arrived here in 1843, he said the sweep of the Mahurangi River reminded him of the Coquet River near his home town. This helps to explain why so many of the streets are named after members of the noble families of Northumberland and the villages in that county.

In the beginning the only communication between Warkworth and Auckland was by ship. From this came about a deadly rivalry between the two shipping companies running services on the route. On the one side there were the Settlers, who supported the local company; on the other side were the MacGregors, supporters of the MacGregor Steam Ship Company. There were at least two major collisions between ships owned by the competing companies. The second was in 1905, when the *Claymore* of the MacGregors ran into, and sank, the *Kapanui*, a ship belonging to the Settlers, in Waitemata Harbour.

From the wharf and from nearby Sandspit there are cruises to **Kawau Island**, which is 40 minutes away. One such trip is run by Reubens Cruises, leaving at 1030 daily *(tel: (09) 425 8006)*. The great attraction of the island is the homestead at Mansion House Bay, once owned by New Zealand's first premier, Sir George Grey. He bought the island as a retreat in 1862 when he was Governor of New Zealand. The house has magnificent gardens and wildlife including wallabies, kookaburras, peacocks and the rare weka (a flightless bird).

Just outside **Warkworth Museum** are two kauri trees. The larger of the two is 800 years old and stands 120m high. The Parry Kauri Park was bought by residents because someone was, of course, going to cut

**Opposite**
Warkworth Museum

**SWAMP KAURI**

THIS LOG WAS DUG OUT OF A SWAMP ON RAY BRYANT'S
FARM AT PARORE, 6 KM NORTH OF DARGAVILLE.
IT WAS ONCE A KAURI TREE 3.7m (12 FEET) IN DIAMETER.
APPROXIMATELY 2800 YEARS AGO AN EARTH MOVEMENT OR
VOLCANIC ERUPTION DESTROYED THE FOREST,
NOW THE AREA IS A SWAMPY VALLEY CONTAINING MANY
KAURI LOGS.
THE FLAT SIDE OF THIS LOG WAS LEVEL WITH THE
GROUND. IT HAS BEEN EXPOSED FOR MANY YEARS
AND HAS GRADUALLY WEATHERED AWAY.
NOW LESS THAN HALF THE ORIGINAL LOG IS LEFT.
NOTE THE SEAM OF KAURI GUM IN WHAT WAS THE CENTRE
OF THE TREE.

**Above**
Historic kauri tree

the trees down. Within the museum there is a splendid display of kauri gum (*about 2km out of town on Tudor Collins Drive; tel: (09) 425 7093; open daily 0900–1600*).

**Sheepworld**, 4km outside town, runs shows demonstrating sheep-shearing and the use of sheepdogs. There is also a petting farm and a café (*tel: (09) 425 7444; www.sheepworldfarm.co.nz*).

Some 6km out of town is the **Moira Hill Walkway** which runs for 6km through native bush and takes a leisurely three hours to complete. There are two return routes – one through the Pohuehue Scenic Reserve.

The Warkworth region is also renowned for its quality vineyards, particularly around Matakana, a short drive east. The Visitor Information Centre has full listings of vineyards, vineyard restaurants and accommodation.

Offshore is the **Goat Island Marine Reserve**, set up in 1978. Because there is a total ban on fishing and collecting specimens in the waters around the island, the area has a thriving aquatic life. It is ideal for snorkelling, although skin diving is also available. Full-day and half-day trips are available, departing from Warkworth, and are moderately priced. The University of Auckland's Marine Laboratory is based on the island.

A neat detour out of town is the 8km Falls Road run, which takes you to a ford and a picturesque waterfall. Drive out of town along the Woodcocks Road, coming back by way of Falls Road.

### Accommodation and food in Warkworth

**Sawmill Café $** *142 Pakiri Rd, Leigh; tel: (09) 422 6019. Open summer daily 1000–late; winter Fri–Sun late.* The place to go in Leigh for fresh light meals, good coffee and occasional live music.

**Sandspit Holiday Park $–$$** *1334 Sandspit Rd; tel: (09) 425 8610; www.sandspitholidaypark.co.nz.* Beachside motorpark handy for cruises to Kawau Island.

**Ascension Wine Estate and Oak Grill Bistro $$** *480 Matakana Rd; tel: (09) 422 9601; www.ascensionwine.co.nz. Open daily for lunch from 1100 and for dinner at weekends.* Award-winning winery restaurant and cellar door.

**Matakana House Motel $$** *975 Matakana Rd, Matakana; tel: (09) 422 7497; www.matakanahouse.co.nz.* Mid-range and very tidy.

# WHANGAREI

**ⓘ Whangarei Visitors Bureau**
*Tarewa Park, 92 Otaika Rd; tel: (09) 438 1079; fax: (09) 438 2943; email: whangarei@i-site.org; www.whangareinz.org.nz.* Note that this office is 2km outside the town.

Whangarei, with a population of 44,000, is the main city of Northland. It is basically a commercial centre and port rather than a major tourist destination, though within the area are some of the finest beaches in the region. The town was settled in 1842, but because of the Maori Wars, most of the population moved to Auckland for protection, starting in 1845. The town remained sleepy until the 1960s when it established itself as a commercial centre.

The area has 2,000 hours of sunshine a year with an average rainfall of 1,555mm, which means that it effectively has a subtropical climate. The soil is volcanic and the result is the abundant growth to be seen in a series of beautiful parks and gardens.

Of these, **Cafler Park and Rose Gardens,** in the centre of town, and **Mair Park,** in Rurumoki Street, are worthy of note. From Mair Park there are well-marked trails to Parahaki, which was a fortified Maori *pa* and has views that go on for ever. It will take you an hour to make the easy climb to the top but the panorama is worth the effort.

Also well worth the effort is the **Mangrove Boardwalk,** starting at Ewing Road, just off the Ted Elliot Memorial Pool car park. This takes you through the mangroves of the Hatea River (as always when exploring mangroves, you need to wear insect repellent).

In the centre of the town is an attractive waterfront development called Quayside which houses the **Clapham's Clocks Collection,** the largest of its kind in the southern hemisphere (*open daily 1000–1700*). The Quayside also has a museum of fishes, a museum of dolls and a range of speciality shops and restaurants. Like most harbour developments around the world, much of the interest lies in the yachts moored along the promenade.

Called (by an optimistic tourist agency) the 'most photogenic waterfall' in New Zealand, the **Whangarei Falls** are 5km northeast of the town, at Tikipunga. There are two viewing platforms at the 25m-high falls, which are created by an old basalt lava flow.

**Cheviot Park Motor Lodge** $$ *Cnr Western Hills Dr and Cheviot St; tel: (09) 438 2341; email: cheviot-park@xtra.co.nz; www.cheviot-park.co.nz*

**Flames International** $$ *Waverley St; tel: (09) 436 2107; www.flameshotel.co.nz*

**Cherry Court** $$ *35 Otaika Rd; tel: (09) 438 3128; www.cherrycourt.co.nz*

**Killer Prawn** $$ *28 Bank St; tel: (09) 430 3333; www.killerprawn.co.nz.* Well-established restaurant/ bar offering a wide selection of traditional and specialist seafood. Try the namesake dish 'Killer Prawn'.

**Reva's on the Waterfront** $$ *31 Quayside, Town Basin; tel: (09) 438 8969.*

**Whangarei Museum** is at the Clarke Homestead and Kiwi House at Maunu, 6km out of town (*tel: (09) 438 9630; www.whangareimuseum.org.nz; open daily 1000–1600*). Its guided tour is more professionally run than most. There is also a nocturnal kiwi house so you can see New Zealand's national emblem. The surrounding 25ha of farmland and bushwalks are as attractive as the museum itself.

Brauhaus Frings Northland Breweries (*104 Lower Dent St; tel: (09) 438 4664; www.frings.co.nz; open Mon–Sat 0900–2200 with tours and free tastings*) is a microbrewery producing three traditional beer varieties, without the use of chemicals. The Northland Draught is especially well spoken of. Food is served – burgers, hot dogs, cheese platters.

## Suggested tour

**Total distance:** 555km (excluding the bus tour).

**Time:** 10 hours' driving (excluding sightseeing and the bus tour). Allow at least two days for the tour, and preferably three (the bus tour is a whole day's journey in its own right).

To enter the Northland take SH1 out of **Auckland** ❶ going through the suburb of Albany and then through Silverdale, Orewa and

**Hundertwasser's Loo**

Austrian-born artist Frederick Hundertwasser designed the public lavatory in Kawakawa – the most original in New Zealand. It is an *objet d'art*, with coloured tiles, windows made from wine bottles, bulbous pillars, a grass roof – and not a straight line in sight. The artist died in 2000, but is said to have completed other designs for various businesses in Kawakawa.

Waiwera to **WARKWORTH ②**. This is the first town of Northland, a major holiday area in its own right, and yet is only 66km from Auckland. From there the road goes north through Wellsford, Kaiwaka, Brynderwyn (one of the few Welsh place names in New Zealand) to the major town of **WHANGAREI ③** which is 170km from Auckland.

From there, go to Hikurangi, Whakapara, Kawakawa and then Pakaraka. All along this road there are turns to the right that will take you to the sea and the small seaside resorts of Ngunguru Bay, Sandy Bay and Whangaruru Harbour. At **PAKARAKA ④**, 237km from Auckland, you take the SH10 for 23km to **PAIHIA ⑤** and the site of the Waitangi Treaty. From there it is a vehicular ferry ride to **RUSSELL ⑥**, the first capital of New Zealand and a major destination in its own right. In theory you could drive from here to explore the rest of the Northland. A far better option is to see the rest on a bus tour (*see below*). The main reason is Ninety Mile Beach, an absolutely essential part of anyone's itinerary, for which private cars are totally unsuited, even if they are four-wheel drive. There are several places from which you can take the bus – indeed, pretty much every town in the Northland has a connection of one sort or another. The best bet is Paihia, which has two major bus lines operating from the centre. The day-long tour covers some 550km, costs the same as a moderate night's lodging and is one of the great delights of New Zealand.

After the tour, you can resume driving from Paihia, crossing the peninsula on the SH12 to **KAIKOHE ⑦**, and then to Omapere which is right on the major inlet known as Hokianga Harbour. From there the road turns south along the western side of the peninsula, through **DARGAVILLE ⑧** and back to Warkworth.

**Bus tour to Ninety Mile Beach**

Starting from **Paihia ⑤** the bus normally takes the following route, although there are variations on this theme, normally caused by the state of the tide. The route goes first through **WAIMATE NORTH ⑨**, the site of the first inland mission station in New Zealand, established by Samuel Marsden in 1830. Once an active volcanic area, this is now some of the most fertile farmland in the north. From here the journey continues through the **PUKETI KAURI FOREST ⑩**, which has a walkway around some kauri trees that are over 1,000 years old.

Next comes **KAITAIA ⑪**, the principal town of the Far North. It has a strong connection with the original Croatian settlers who came there in search of kauri gum. It is said that this is where the term 'gum boots' originated, but that is doubtful. Next stop is at the **ANCIENT KAURI KINGDOM ⑫**, a commercial enterprise that recovers huge kauri logs from swamps and converts them into furniture. The logs have been underground for up to 30,000 years. Kauri tends to be a featureless wood, with little figuring.

**Opposite**
Buses on the Ninety Mile Beach tour stop to allow passengers to surf down the Te Paki Quicksand Stream

**No ordinary bus**

The bus that takes you along Ninety Mile Beach is specially constructed for the job. The engine is located inside the body of the bus. The chassis is tipped up at the tail to give extra clearance. The whole chassis is also galvanised. At the end of every trip, while the passengers have a cup of coffee, the bus is carefully hosed down to remove all salt water from the chassis and body. Then, when the bus is returned to the depot each night, it is given another hosing. Each week it has a total grease job. This way the devastating effects of driving on the beach are kept at bay, and the buses have a long and useful life. No car can stand up to this treatment. For example, on a rough day, with the tide coming in and the wind behind the waves, the bus can actually be picked up and moved sideways up the beach – an exhilarating and awe-inspiring experience.

Next you encounter **NINETY MILE BEACH** ⓭, which is treated as a road by the authorities. It is, in fact, only 60 miles (90km) long but is full of interest – one of the world's most unusual bus drives!

At the northern end you will come to the **TE PAKI QUICKSAND STREAM** ⓮ which is the only access point. Again, crossing it is not something you could easily do in a normal car. Typically the bus stops near a sand dune to allow the passengers to go surfing down the face of the dune. Normally, this would be considered a piece of environmental vandalism but as the dunes are continuously shifting and being replaced by sand blowing across from other parts of the peninsula, it is not ecologically disturbing.

From the beach you head to **CAPE REINGA** ⓯, a special place as it is believed to be the departure point of Maori spirits. Representations by the Maori have stopped the sale of food at the post office and, as a common courtesy, visitors are asked to eat their lunch before they get to the Cape itself. The small Post Office is open most days to sell postcards that you can send stamped with a Cape Reinga postmark. The small lighthouse, erected in 1941, flashes every 26 seconds and can be seen from some 50km away. Although you may not be able to see it from the lighthouse, it is interesting to know that, about 500m offshore, the Tasman Sea meets the South Pacific Ocean in a stormy turmoil that, even on a calm day, is dangerous to shipping.

On the return journey, the bus goes through Mangonui Harbour, which was originally a port for both the kauri timber trade and for whalers. Finally the journey takes you through the deep and near-landlocked Whangaroa Harbour and from there back to Paihia.

## Also worth exploring

There is an unsealed road starting some 12km from Kaikohe, which is 32km from the Kawakawa turn-off, south of Russell. Although there is no tarmac it is normally well maintained and drivable. Take local advice before you set off from the Kaikohe tourist information office. The road runs for about 50km through forested countryside, passing the Trounson Kauri Park and ending up at **Parakao**. There is a turn to **Avoca** and then sealed road to Dargaville. The journey is about 80km.

The main road south from Dargaville runs on the east side of Kaipara Harbour, with a long narrow peninsula separating it from the sea. There is a sealed road running down the western side facing the Tasman Sea. At **Te Kopuru**, the road has a junction running down to the shore and Clinks Gully. Just before **Rototuna**, 30km down the road, the tarmac ends and you are on an unsealed but drivable road until you get to **Pouto**, which is on Kaipara Harbour and forms one of the heads in the outlet to the sea. This is remote country and, although not deserted, gives a strong feeling of isolation. The return journey covers a little over 100km.

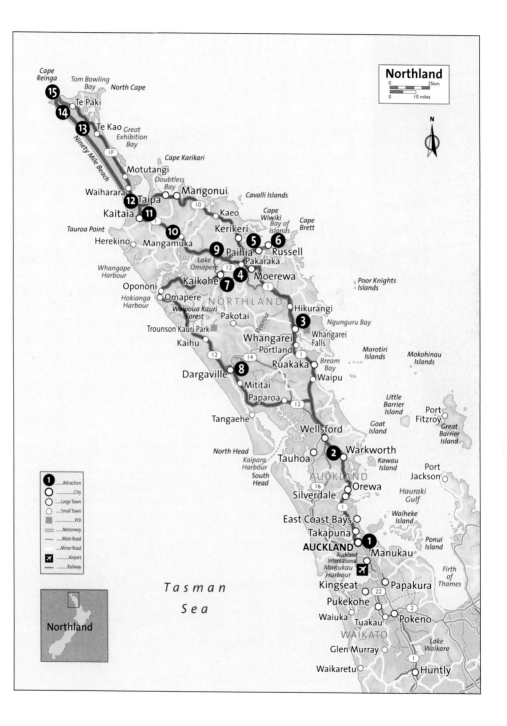

# The Coromandel Peninsula

## Ratings

| | |
|---|---|
| Beaches | ●●●●● |
| Scenery | ●●●●○ |
| Watersports | ●●●●○ |
| Children | ●●●● |
| Outdoor activities | ●●●●○ |
| Heritage | ●●○○○ |
| Dining | ●●○○○ |
| Museums | ●●○○○ |

Only 90 minutes' drive from Auckland lies the Coromandel Peninsula. In a sense it is a relief valve for Auckland, for it is clean, green and relatively undeveloped. It is populated by people who live by art and craft, a hippy haven with a very relaxed and laid-back alternative lifestyle.

The interior of the peninsula consists of a ridge crisscrossed with roads, some of them unpaved. The peninsula has no major town. Its centres are Thames, Coromandel and Whitianga, but these are small towns which cater for the surrounding area rather than for visitors.

Coromandel is near enough to Auckland to make it a day's drive, although it deserves much more. From just before Christmas to early February, the peninsula is packed with holidaymakers escaping from the capital. For the rest of the year, it is pleasant, quiet and remarkably interesting.

## COROMANDEL

**Coromandel Information Centre** 355 Kapanga Rd; tel: (07) 866 8598; fax: (07) 866 7285; email: coromandel@i-site.org; www.coromandeltown.co.nz

The most important attraction of Coromandel is its atmosphere. There is something in the air – perhaps as a result of its style and history – that makes this one of the loveliest of New Zealand towns to visit. You feel embraced, even cuddled, by its friendly atmosphere. It is not a big town – just one main drag and a population of under 1,500. Many of them are involved in the arts and crafts, and their wares are on display and on sale in well over 100 studios and retailers. Although the town has specific attractions, it is more a place for idle strolling and long lunches in one of the excellent pavement cafés, offering great food – much of it vegetarian – at very reasonable prices.

To understand what Coromandel was like in its glory days you must see it as a series of small towns linked together. Visitors disembarked at high tide at Fureys Creek stone jetty, which was the 'Lower Town' of Coromandel. What is now Moehau Takeaways and Tearooms was the bottom floor of the Moehau Hotel, an impressive two-storey

The Coromandel Peninsula

0 — 25km
0 — 10 miles

○ Attraction
○ City
○ Large Town
○ Small Town
■ POI
▬ Motorway
— Main Road
— Minor Road
✈ Airport
— Railway

building. The Golconda Hotel is much as it was originally. Today's Alpha Motel stands on the site of the original Star and Garter Hotel, which had floor shows and dancing girls and a fair line in naughtiness.

Away from that, Lower Town, on the road to Long Bay, was a tented city known as the town of Belleview. The main settlement of Coromandel was in the area of the Coromandel Hotel, which was originally a two-storey building.

The hospital is at the junction of Main Street and Kapanga Road. Opposite the hospital lived Doctor Berkinshaw, the surgeon, whose daughter is Fay Weldon, one of New Zealand's better-known novelists. The family home, a colonial mansion, still exists.

The town still has a feeling of prosperity, perhaps because it lies on a small fertile plain – the only one on the west side of the peninsula – and because it retains many buildings left over from the gold-rush era and from the prosperity that kauri logging brought to the area.

A reminder of the past is the **School of Mines Museum** (*841 Rings Rd; tel: (07) 866 8987; open daily 1000–1600 in summer, seasonal hours in winter*), housed in its original late-Victorian building. Also of historical interest is the **Gold Stamper Battery** (*410 Buffalo Rd; tel: (07) 866 7933*), a century-old water-powered plant used to extract the gold from solid rock. It is also home to the nation's biggest working waterwheel.

**Driving Creek Railway** (*tel: (07) 866 8703; www. drivingcreekrailway.co.nz; departures at 1015 and 1400, with extra 1245 and 1515 services in summer*) is 2.5km north of the town, and has been reconstructed by Barry Brickell, who originally started the railway to transport logs and clay to his pottery. It still does that when it is not

carrying visitors. It is the only narrow-gauge – as opposed to miniature and standard-gauge – service still running in New Zealand. The train runs for 3km through replanted kauri forest, with a final stop that takes in an excellent view of Coromandel from the 'Eyefull Tower'. You can also visit the brickworks and the pottery.

Some 3km out of town there is a beach with a camping and picnic site at Long Bay reserve. It has a series of signposted tracks so that you can explore the area.

Located 4km before the township on Highway 309 is **The Waiau Waterworks** *(tel: (07) 866 7191; www.waiauwaterworks.co.nz; open daily 0900–1700; closed in winter)*, a garden full of fascinating whimsical water sculptures and gadgets. Like the Driving Creek Railway, it is Kiwi ingenuity and imagination at its wonderfully eccentric best, and particularly popular with kids.

### Accommodation and food in Coromandel

**Colville Store and Café** $ *Colville; open daily 0930–1600, Fri–Sun also 1800–2000.* Don't miss this icon if venturing north to Colville.

**Success Café** $ *104 Kapanga Rd; tel: (07) 866 7100.* Good all-round café with seafood a speciality (try the mussels).

**Coromandel Motel and Holiday Park** $–$$ *636 Rings Rd; tel: (07) 866 8830; www.coromandelholidaypark.co.nz*

**Anchor Lodge Resort** $$ *448 Wharf Rd; tel: (07) 866 7992; www.anchorlodgecoromandel.co.nz*

**Coromandel Court Motel** $$ *365 Kapanga Rd, tel: (07) 866 8402 or 0800 267 626; www.coromandelcourtmotel.co.nz.* Right in the centre of the town just behind the Coromandel Information Centre.

**Pepper Tree Restaurant and Bar** $$ *31 Kapanga Road; tel: (07) 866 8211.* Great local seafood. Licensed.

**Pottery Lane Cottage** $$ *15 Pottery Lane; tel: (07) 866 7171; email: r&bmartin@xtra.co.nz.* Two good-value, self-contained cottages in a peaceful garden setting.

# PAEROA

**ⓘ Paeroa Information Centre** / *Belmont Rd; tel: (07) 862 8636; fax: (07) 862 8636; email: I-site@hauraki-dc.govt.nz*

Paeroa has a population of around 4,000 and the town is 30km to the southeast of Thames. The name of the town can be translated as 'Long Mountain Range' and refers to the Coromandel Range. The town is 'world-famous in New Zealand' for a fizzy drink called L&P, which stands for Lemon and Paeroa. It was the town's spring that originally produced the mineral water that added to the flavour. In commemoration of this there is a massive, and extremely ugly, bottle in the main street at the junction of the SH2 and SH26. Basically this is a country town servicing an agricultural area, specialising in dairy farming, on the edge of the Hauraki Plain. Originally it was a river port, and steamships used to come up the Waihou River bringing goods to and from Auckland. Paeroa was also strategically placed on the edge of a gold-mining area. Gold was discovered only a few kilometres from the town, on the Komata Reef, where there was a highly productive, if short-lived, mine.

### Accommodation and food in Paeroa

**L and P Café and Bar** $ *Cnr Taylors Ave and Seymour St; tel: (07) 862 7773.*

**Lazy Fish Cafe** $ *56 Belmont Rd; tel: (07) 862 8822.*

**Paeroa Motel** $ *2 Puke Rd; tel: (07) 862 8475; email: paeroamotel@ kol.co.nz*

**Casa Mexicana Motel** $$ *71 Puke Rd; tel: (07) 862 8216; email: casa.mexicana@slingshot.co.nz*

**Four Seasons Chinese Restaurant** $$ *Belmont Rd; tel: (07) 862 7616.*

# THAMES

 **Thames Information Centre** *206 Pollen St; tel: (07) 868 7284; fax: (07) 868 7584; email: thames@ i-site.org; www.thamesinfo. co.nz*

Thames is a town of something fewer than 7,000 people. In the glory days of the gold rush, in the 19th century, it had nearly three times that many. You can still get a feel of its past from its old wooden buildings in the main street.

The town is on the Firth of Thames and the site was originally spotted by Captain Cook. He sailed to the mouth of the Waihou River, then explored the river by longboat. He named what is now called the Waihou the River Thames, seeing a resemblance between the two rivers that has eluded later travellers. The Maori name for the river – Waihou, which possibly means 'New River' – has prevailed. Later, the name Cook had given the river became the name of the settlement on its bank, which was originally known as Shortland.

Like so many other towns in Australia and New Zealand, Thames grew to prominence because of its gold and timber. The timber was the kauri, which still exists, though in much diminished quantities. Gold was discovered in the early 1850s, but an arrangement had to be reached with the local Maori before serious prospecting could start. This did not happen until a dozen years later, and the first major strike was on 10 August 1867.

Immediately there was a gold stampede, and the town quadrupled in size almost overnight. By 1870 the population had increased to

**Opposite**
Nesting terns on the Coromandel Peninsula

around 20,000 – more than half as much again as the population of Auckland. The new residents, who were probably not the quietest and most decorous of people, were serviced by nearly 100 pubs. Now there are only a handful.

In 1870, Shortland was amalgamated with a nearby settlement known as Grahamstown, later renamed Thames. The new town became a borough in 1873. Shortland and Grahamstown were originally connected by a railway line.

Most of the attractions of this pleasant town help to give you an accurate historical perspective of the gold rush. Worth seeing is the **Thames Gold Mine and Stamper Battery** (*Pollen St; tel: (07) 868 8514; www.goldmine-experience.co.nz; open daily 1000–1600*), which offers regular 45-minute tours of the impressive ore-crushing stamper, various horizontal tunnels and a narrow-gauge railway, all with an informative commentary about the process and history of gold mining along the way. You can also try your hand (and your luck) gold panning.

Elsewhere, the **Thames School of Mines and Mineralogical Museum** (*corner of Brown and Cochrane Sts; tel: (07) 868 6227; open Wed–Sun 1100–1600*) stopped training mine managers in 1954, but it has a definitive collection of historical photographs and mineralogical samples. You might not think this could be interesting, but you would be wrong. The **Thames Historical Museum** is run by the local historical society and is better than most (*Pollen St, open daily 1300–1600*).

Around the town you will see many reminders of the golden days. Just behind the Power House, on the corner of Bell and Campbell Streets, is the **Queen of Beauty Pump**, which used to pump out floodwater from the local mines.

**Below**
The Coromandel Peninsula, near Thames

**Bird reserves**
Thames is a great
centre for birdwatchers,
who come for the avian
life that flocks to the
mudflats of the Firth of
Thames. There is a bird
hide off Brown Street,
near the town centre,
which overlooks the
mangrove swamps. The
best place for serious
birdwatchers is the
**Miranda Wildlife
Reserve** on the
Kaiaua–Miranda Road
(*tel: (09) 232 2781*).

## Accommodation and food in Thames

**Sola Café $–$$** *720 Pollen St; tel: (07) 868 8781.* Good lunch option
with an emphasis on vegetarian cuisine.

**Coastal Motel Lodge and Cottages $$** *608 Tarura Rd; tel: (07) 868
6843; www.stayatcoastal.co.nz.* This was one of the first motels in New
Zealand, and it has been superbly updated in recent years. The massive
rooms have fully equipped kitchens. Located opposite the yacht club.

**Cotswold Cottage B&B $$** *Maramarah Rd, Totara; tel: (07) 868 6306; www.
cotswoldcottage.co.nz.* Restored 1920s villa beside the Kauaeranga River.

**Old Thames Restaurant $$** *705 Pollen St; tel: (07) 868 7207.* Good
value with a loyal local following, all day and evening meal menus.
Licensed.

**Rolleston Motel $$** *105 Rolleston St; tel: (07) 868 8091 or 0800 776
644; www.rollestonmotel.co.nz*

# WAIHI

ℹ **Waihi Information
Centre** *Seddon St,
Waihi; tel: (07) 863 6715.
Open daily 0900–1700.*

Waihi was created by gold. For years the **Martha Mine** was one of the
richest gold producers in the world. In its first 66 years, it produced
8 million ounces of gold. It closed in 1952 but was reopened again in
1988 and still manages to produce some 70,000 ounces of gold a year.
The mine is almost in the centre of town and there are tours during
the week which take in the mine and the stamping machinery (*tel:
(07) 863 3030 for times and bookings; www.waihi.org.nz*).

The town also has the **Waihi Arts Centre and Museum** at 54 Kenny
St (*tel: (07) 863 8386; www.waihimuseum.co.nz; open Thu–Sun
1000–1500*) which explains the mining of gold with models and
displays. It also tells of the famous Waihi strike, which brought the
whole operation to a standstill in 1911. Another great reminder of
those times is the **Goldfields Railway** (*tel: (07) 863 9020;
www.waihirail.co.nz*), running between Waihi and Waikino – a 7km
journey. The ride lasts an hour (*daily departures from Waihi at 1000,
1145 & 1345*).

Nearby **Waihi Beach** is both a beach and a small hamlet. The beach
runs for 10km and the hamlet was originally planned as a retirement
town for miners. Now it is packed during the summer holidays but pretty
empty for the rest of the year. At the end is a bird sanctuary.

Between Waihi and Paeroa is the **Karangahake Gorge**, with a
footpath up the middle that follows part of a disused railway line.
Buses pick up and put down walkers at each end of the route. The
gorge was a major gold-mining area and is full of abandoned
machinery and mines.

## Accommodation and food in Waihi

Waitete Orchard Café $ *31 Orchard Rd (off SH2); tel: (07) 863 8980.* Organic flair, fruit wines and ice cream.

Chambers Wine Bar and Restaurant $$ *22 Haszard St; tel: (07) 863 7474.*

Sea Air Motel and Motor Park $$ *Emerton Rd, Waihi Beach; tel: (07) 863 5655; www.seaair.co.nz.* A good option in Waihi Beach.

Waihi Motel $$ *Tauranga Rd; tel: (07) 863 8095; www.waihimotel.co.nz.* Fair-sized units and spa pool.

# WHANGAMATA

**ⓘ Whangamata Information Centre** *616 Port Rd; tel: (07) 865 8340; fax: (07) 865 8341; email: whangamata@i-site.org; www.whangamatainfo.co.nz*

**Ecotours** Whangamata is the base for one of New Zealand's best-known tourist ventures: **Kiwi Dundee Adventures** (*PO Box 198, Whangamata; tel: (07) 865 8809; email: kiwi.dundee@xtra.co.nz; www.kiwidundee.co.nz*) provides most of the serious ecotours here.

**ⓕ Fishing and canoeing** Whangamata means 'Obsidian Harbour', so-called because pieces of this glass-like mineral, used for axes and arrowheads, were often washed here from Mayor Island. The harbour offers chartered boats for game fishing off the nearby islands. It is also ideal for canoeing: canoes can be hired from the Estuary Mini Market, *Marie Crescent; tel: (07) 865 8788.*

**Opposite** Whangamata Beach

This pleasant town's claim to fame is that it has one of the best surfing beaches in the country. **Ocean Beach** runs for 3.8km from the harbour entrance to the mouth of the Otahu River. The shore is protected by offshore islands: at low tide you can walk to the largest of these, **Hauturu.** The beach is patrolled during the holiday season. The surfing attracts thousands during the summer holidays when the population increases tenfold. The rest of the year it is very quiet.

The harbour stands at the opening of an estuary fed by the waters of the Whareki22uponga and Waiharakeke rivers. From the 1870s until the early 1900s, these rivers were used (with dams and booms) to transport massive kauri logs to the port. There the logs were assembled into rafts and floated to Auckland.

Just to the north of Whangamata is **Opoutere Beach** with its 5km of white sand dunes, without a single house or sign of civilisation. To get there, park at the beginning of Ohui Road and walk through the forest – a ten-minute stroll – and then over a wooden footbridge to the beach. Inshore from the beach is **Wharekawa Harbour,** a collection of estuarine mudflats and mangroves. This is a major birdwatching area, home to the **Wharekawa Wildlife Refuge.**

For a great walk, follow the SH25 south until you see the signposted turn-off to the Wentworth Valley Road. Follow that for 4km to the car park and campsite that marks the start of the track to **Wentworth Falls.** From here it is 5km to the falls, an easy hour's walking.

## Accommodation and food in Whangamata

Caffe Rossini $–$$ *646 Port Rd; tel: (07) 865 6117.* Good lunch option.

Oceanas $$ *328 Ocean Rd; tel: (07) 865 7157.* Good seafood and Pacific Rim cuisine.

Palm Pacific Resort $$ *413 Port Street; tel: (07) 865 9211; www.palmpacificresort.com.* Convenient location.

**Pipinui Motel $$** *805 Martyn Rd; tel: (07) 865 6796; www.pipinuimotel.co.nz.* Set away from the main road.

**Bushland Park Lodge and Nickel Strausse $$$** *444 Wentworth Valley Rd; tel: (07) 865 7468; www.bushlandparklodge.co.nz; closed Mon.* Luxury accommodation and a winery restaurant serving food with a Bavarian emphasis.

# WHITIANGA

**❶ Whitianga Information Centre** *66 Albert St, Whitianga; tel: (07) 866 5555; fax: (07) 866 2205; email: whitianga@i-site.org; www.whitianga.co.nz.* Open seven days a week.

Whitianga faces Mercury Bay, so-called because it was from here that Captain James Cook observed the transit of the planet Mercury, which was one of the many purposes of his expedition. It was also at Whitianga that, as his orders instructed, Cook took possession of New Zealand 'in the name of the King of Great Britain'. The Union Jack was hoisted on the shore on 15 November 1769. By coincidence, it was also here that Kupe, the leader of the Polynesian expedition, came ashore in about AD 950.

Today Whitianga is a pretty seaside town, small and easy to explore on foot, overlooking an estuary which makes a safe anchorage. In the

height of the summer season (part of December, all of January and the first week of February), it is jam-packed with holidaymakers who come for the six nearby beaches, all within easy strolling distance. One of the most attractive is **Buffalo Beach**, which extends for 4km and is safe for children (though it can get rough in winter – the beach is named after HMS *Buffalo*, which was wrecked here in a gale in 1840).

Opposite lies **Ferry Landing**, site of the original town. The passenger-only ferry *(daily from 0730 to 1830 and in the evening for half an hour at 1930 and 2130 with extra crossings at the height of the season)* saves a road trip of over 30km. The wharf at Ferry Landing is thought to be one of the oldest in the country, although the old stone blocks have been concreted over. It is

🐟 **Fishing** Whitianga's local fishing fleet specialises in crayfish. There is also much big-game fishing, with charters available, and skin diving.

well worth taking the trip just to climb to **Shakespeare's Lookout** above Ferry Landing, where you can enjoy staggering views over the whole of Mercury Bay. Also at the lookout is a memorial to Captain Cook.

Whitianga is home to the Mercury Bay Boating Club, one of the contenders in the 1988 America's Cup – the one that ended farcically in court with the cup being retained by the United States. New Zealand got its revenge when it won in 1995. The event is commemorated in the small museum run by the local historic society *(tel: (07) 866 5995 for opening times)*.

## Accommodation and food in Whitianga

**Seafari Motel $** *7 Mill Rd; tel: (07) 866 5263; www.seafarimotel.co.nz*

**Snapper Jacks $** *Albert St; tel: (07) 866 5482*. Reputedly the best fish and chips in town.

**Fireplace Restaurant and Bar $$** *Esplanade; tel: (07) 866 4828*. Aesthetically one of the best, with a lovely fireplace. Pizza and lamb a speciality.

**Above**
The view over the estuary

**Mercury Bay Beach Front Resort $$** *113 Buffalo Beach Rd; tel: (07) 866 5637; www.beachfrontresort.co.nz*. All the units are opposite the beach.

**Left**
Cathedral Cove

**The Waterfront $$** *2 Buffalo Beach Rd; tel: (07) 869 5994; www. waterfrontmotel.co.nz*. Modern beachfront accommodation.

**Walks in the Coromandel Forest Park**

From Thames, a road (unpaved for part of the way) runs inland along the rugged Kauaeranga Valley. The name means 'No crossing here'. After about 13km, there is an office run by the Department of Conservation (*tel: (07) 867 9080*). The office provides a complete series of guides to walks in the area, including the fairly tough Kauaeranga Kauri Trail, which takes you to the Pinnacles Hut where you can stay overnight. The very fit could do the walk in a day. There are several shorter walks, including Billygoat Landing, which is a 20-minute stroll over 1.5km and allows a view of the Billygoat Falls.

From Tapu the road continues along the coast through Waikawau and Kereta, and around the Manaia inlet to **COROMANDEL** ❹. Just before you reach Coromandel, you can detour on a sealed road across the peninsula that will take you to Matarangi Beach – as does the main road beyond Coromandel. Beyond Matarangi Beach the road runs down the east side of the peninsula to the resort of **WHITIANGA** ❺.

From there it curves inland to get around Whitianga Harbour until it reaches **COROGLEN** ❻. Here you can detour to Hahei, a small seaside town reached by driving to **WHENUAKITE** ❼ and turning left. **HAHEI** ❽ has perhaps the best beach on the Coromandel Peninsula, protected by a series of offshore islands. It is part of a marine reserve and has superb scuba diving. You can also visit the caves at Cathedral Cove at low tide. A little way to the south is **HOT WATER BEACH** ❾. To reach it, drive back inland 4km from Hahei and then swing back to the coast for another 4km. You need to get there two hours after or two hours before low tide. Dig a hole in the sand, which will soon fill up with hot thermal water to create your very own spa pool. This is the only place in New Zealand where you can do this.

Back at Coroglen, the main road heads through Whenuakite to the west coast at **TAIRUA** ❿, whose sister town, **PAUANUI** ⓫, faces it across the inlet. The road then drops down through the Tairua Forest until it reaches **WHANGAMATA** ⓬. From there it runs inland to **WAIHI** ⓭, with **WAIHI BEACH** ⓮ as a detour, and then back inland to **PAEROA** ⓯, before turning north again to return to Thames.

## Also worth exploring

From Coromandel the road north runs slightly inland and ends up at Colville. This is the last place you can get petrol and provisions if you are exploring further. It is also the end of the sealed road, but the road ahead (which has gates across it at intervals) is in excellent condition most of the year and is easily drivable in a standard saloon.

The road continues right to the end of the peninsula, swinging around Fantail Bay, passing the very tip, at Cape Colville, and then continuing for a kilometre or so to Port Jackson. From here the only way back is the way you came: though there is a footpath that extends from here right around the peninsula to the road at Stony Bay and then down through Port Charles to Little Bay. This is not a drivable route, so you will have to retrace your route to Colville.

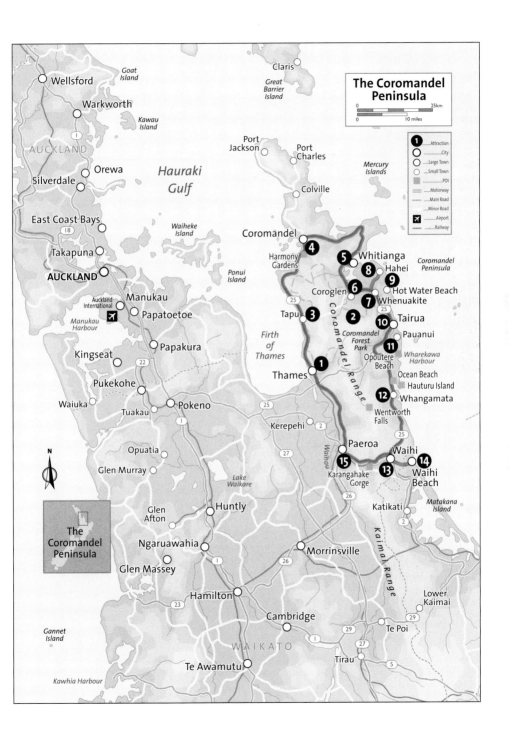

# Tauranga and Rotorua

## Ratings

| | |
|---|---|
| Scenery | ●●●● |
| Children | ●●●● |
| Outdoor activities | ●●●● |
| Heritage | ●●●● |
| Historic sights | ●●●● |
| Museums | ●●● |
| Dining | ●●● |
| Watersports | ●● |

The city of Rotorua is the main centre for tourism on the North Island. Rotorua itself is a smallish town – though New Zealanders like to call it a city – with almost everything a traveller needs, including excellent bookshops, a wide range of accommodation, many good restaurants and the Polynesian Spa – which is worth the journey on its own.

The triangle formed by Rotorua, Whakatane and Tauranga encloses one of the world's most active areas of geothermal activity, as well as large tracts of forest, including the Kaimai-Mamaku Forest Park and the largest tree plantation in the world at the Kaingaroa Forest. If that were not enough, the nearby Bay of Plenty coast has an amazing range of beaches, and dolphins that will come and swim with you. What other area in the world can offer all this?

## ROTORUA

**ⓘ Rotorua Visitor Centre** *1167 Fenton St; tel: (07) 348 5179 or 0800 768 678; fax: (07) 348 6044; email: rotorua@i-site.org; www. rotoruanz.com.* Located in the centre of town, this early 20th-century building with its large tower looks like a misplaced Austrian ski lodge crossed with Tudor architecture. It was built as the Rotorua Post Office and incorporates a memorial town clock erected in honour of

Rotorua lies at the southwestern end of Lake Rotorua. It was founded in the early 1870s and became a city in the early 1960s. The main industry is tourism, with timber, sheep, beef and dairy farming tagging along behind. There are extensive tree plantations, begun in the 1920s, which supply large sawmills and pulp and paper plants. The Forest Research Institute, founded at Rotorua in 1947, coordinates all research of the New Zealand Forest Service.

The key to the city's attraction is that it is set on a volcanic plateau right in the heart of the North Island's thermal belt. The result is that all round Rotorua there is an extraordinary range of geysers and hot springs, boiling and bubbling pools, and general thermal activity. In some areas the building of houses can be precarious because digging the foundations can release unexpected thermal activity. Some people have woken up to find that their front garden has been turned, overnight, into a hot bath. Much of this activity is harnessed to

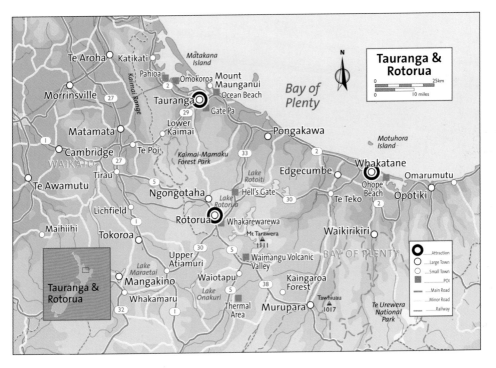

Premier Richard Seddon who died in 1906. The visitor centre is the place to book tours. The staff are well informed and try hard to save you money, but they all seem to believe that going to a Maori feast – a *hangi* – followed or preceded by a concert is an essential part of the Rotorua experience. It is not – it is expensive and the food, to some tastes, is inedible. If you find such staged cultural events mawkish, give this a miss, no matter what the visitor centre says.

**ⓘ Rotorua 5-star Attractions**
*tel: (07) 349 0388; email: info@rotorua5star.co.nz; www.rotorua5star.co.nz*

provide heating for the city – and entertainment, if not health, for the visitors. Almost every hotel and motel offers thermally fed hot baths. As you walk around Rotorua you will literally see evidence of all this thermal activity – plumes of steam if nothing else – almost everywhere you walk.

The city is built on the shores of **Lake Rotorua**, which is the largest of the group of 20 so-called Hot Lakes. Lake Rotorua is actually part of the city, helping to shape and define it. The best time to view the lake is at dusk when large flocks of ducks and black swans come to the lakeside. The lake itself is pear-shaped and is 12km by 9.5km. Its name comes from the Maori, meaning 'crater lake', and it was created by an immense volcanic explosion that left a crater extending over 80sq km. The lake drains a 526sq km basin and the waters are discharged through the Ohau River to Rotoiti.

One of the great delights of a visit to Rotorua is a **cruise** on the lake. Most of the cruises leave from a jetty opposite Tutenakai Street. There are several options including a high-speed catamaran and jet boats. Then there is always the option of a scenic flight by seaplane (*tel: 0800 800848; www.volcanicair.co.nz*).

In the last century people used to drink the local waters as well as soak in them on the basis that anything that tasted so disgusting must do you good. Nowadays, most visitors just luxuriate in the water. The

## Smelly or not?

Everyone says that a strong smell permeates Rotorua – the rotten egg smell of hydrogen sulphide. There seems to be a certain amount of hyperbole involved here. The author has visited Rotorua more than a dozen times and has yet to notice the strong smell for which it is notorious. When asked, guides always say that 'at some times of the year, when the wind is in a certain direction, there is a strong whiff in the air'. This may be the case. But many visitors go to Rotorua and never notice it. Plainly, it is not something that should deter you from visiting this splendid city.

best place in Rotorua to experience the waters is, beyond doubt, the **Polynesian Spa** (*Hinemoa St; tel: (07) 348 1328; www.polynesianspa.co.nz; open 0630–2300*), considered the best spa complex on the North Island. The spa offers a choice of pools, but the best experience comes from the Lake Spa, a series of five outdoor pools overlooking Lake Rotorua that are graded by temperature. The hottest of these pools is so warm that most visitors can only stand it for a few minutes. This does not appear to apply to Japanese tourists, who are plainly used to warmer waters. The changing rooms here are elegantly designed, in a very spacious Scandinavian manner, and even the toilets have won awards for their style and cleanliness. It is possible to have a massage after taking the waters, and the licensed Hot Springs Café serves post-bathing refreshments, as well as a full à la carte menu. Note, it can get busy and the best times to visit are at lunch and dinner-time when the tour buses are elsewhere.

An older spa is located in the glorious **Government Gardens** down by the lakeside, where the central feature is a Tudor-style – that term being used in its widest and loosest sense – bathhouse, built in 1906 in an attempt to capture the flavour of a European spa. Now it contains **The Rotorua Museum of Art and History** (*tel: (07) 350 1814; www.rotoruamuseum.co.nz; open daily in summer 0900–2000; in winter 0900–1700*), with a large section devoted to the local people of Te Arawa. Bear in mind that this is the most Maori of New Zealand cities and you will understand the importance of this display. The museum also describes very clearly the experience of the Tarawera eruption (*see feature, page 88*). The formal gardens surrounding the gallery are unusual and possibly unique in the world in that they, too, have thermal activity so that, as you walk around, you see parts of the garden as through a cloud of mist. In the centre of the town, near the visitor centre, is the main **Rotorua Library**, a treasure cave of information on the area – especially on all aspects of Maori life. The librarians have signs on their desks reading 'Please interrupt'.

Further out of the city, it is possible to climb **Mount Tarawera** and to descend right into the crater. The crater lies on Maori Reserve land: this is not a public park and therefore there is no automatic right of access. The best way to see it is on a guided four-wheel-drive tour, which can be arranged through the Tourism Rotorua Visitor Centre. You will be driven up to the top car park over very rough roads and your guide will encourage you to glissade to the bottom of the crater, and then struggle back to the top. Many visitors achieve this with considerable difficulty. Your guide, who skips ahead like a young lamb, may well be into his 70s. Such energy is ascribed by the locals to the health-giving properties of the air.

To get an overall perspective of the area, you can also ride the 900m **Skyline Gondola** (*open daily 0900 until after sunset; tel: (07) 347 0027; www.skylineskyrides.co.nz*). The complex has several attractions including the infamous luge – considered a Rotorua 'must do'.

**Left**
Mineral colours at Rotorua

There are 11 official angling lakes in the area and several streams that provide excellent fishing for rainbow trout. Only Lake Rotorua is open for fishing all the year round – the rest have a season lasting from 1 Oct–30 June. An excellent guide book, called *Trout Fishing Maps and Information*, is published by the Rotorua Anglers' Association and is available for a nominal sum at the visitor centre.

The most famous thermal area in New Zealand is based around **Whakarewarewa**, which is a suburb of Rotorua, located on the banks of the Puarenga River, about 3km from the centre of Rotorua. Its full name is Te Whakarewarewatanga-o-te-ope-a-Wahiao, meaning 'the uprising of the war party at Wahiao'. Locally it is known simply as Whaka and commercially as Te Puia. Also on site is the **New Zealand Maori Arts & Craft Institute** (*Hemo Rd; tel: (07) 348 9047*). The Institute has continuous demonstrations of carving and weaving. Nearby is the **Whakarewarewa Forest**, which covers 4,052ha. It has an amazing variety of trees, and offers mountain biking and horse riding as well as running and walking. Contact the Fletcher Challenge Forest Visitor Centre (*tel: (07) 350 0110*).

Further out, about 30km along the SH5, is a splendid thermal reserve called **Waiotapu** (*tel: (07) 366 6333; www.geyserland.co.nz*) with excellent walkways and informative signs taking you to bubbling mud pools, boiling springs and silica terraces. This reserve boasts the **Lady Knox Geyser**, which is one of the more predictable of the geysers. A ranger sets it off every day at 1015 by dropping soap into a cairn. The dubious story you are told is that the geyser went off in the first place when prisoners were taken there to wash, and the soap caused the pool to erupt. It is true that the soap breaks down some of the surface tension of the water but the story sounds much too romantic to be true. The cairn was built to restrict the geyser and force it to shoot upwards. It was named in 1904 after the daughter of Governor-General Lord Ranfurly.

## Pink and White Terraces

Once upon a time, the Pink and White Terraces were one of Rotorua's major tourist attractions. Created from the deposition of silica, they formed steps or terraces that swept down to the shores of Lake Tarawera. The White Terrace, also known as Te Tarata, fell 240m in steps from a giant hot spring 30m above the lake. It provided a perfect series of natural temperature-graded swimming pools. The Pink Terrace, Otukapuarangi, was on the other side of the lake and was of a similar, if smoother, configuration. They can be seen in paintings and some early photographs, as well as in contemporary advertisements (Thomas Cook ran tours to New Zealand with the Pink and White Terraces as a featured attraction).

This all came to an end on the night of 10 June 1886, when the volcano Tarawera erupted and volcanic ash, dust and mud was distributed over 4,800sq km of the surrounding countryside. It is thought that the biggest of the eruptions lasted four hours. The explosions were heard as far away as Auckland, Napier, Hokianga, Nelson and Marlborough but – as far as is known – no one locally who actually saw the eruption lived to tell the tale. The whole settlement of Moura slipped into Lake Tarawera, while people in the village of Ariki were buried alive. The village of Wairoa was buried under 2m of ash and 153 people were killed. Alongside all this human tragedy, the eruption totally wiped out the Pink and White Terraces at Lake Tarawera.

The ruins of Wairoa have since been excavated and can now be visited as the Buried Village. There are hopes that a new set of similar terraces will eventually grow but it will be many decades before they will even remotely rival the original Pink and White Terraces of Rotorua.

**Above**
Steaming mud pools at
Whakarewarewa Thermal Park

The **Waimangu Volcanic Valley** (*tel: (07) 366 6137; www.waimangu.com; open daily 0830–1545; Jan 1645*) is some 26km southeast of Rotorua on the SH5. This is the southern end of the Taiwera eruption and is still a very active thermal area containing the world's largest boiling lake. There are also huge steaming cliffs, numerous boiling springs and terraces that are a small version of the famous Pink and White Terraces (*see feature opposite*).

**Hell's Gate** (*tel: (07) 345 3151; www.hellsgate.co.nz; open daily 0830–2030*) is 15km north out of town on SH30. It contains a wealth of violently boiling springs, mud holes and some eerie sulphur vents as well as a mud bath and spa complex. There is also a hot waterfall. When George Bernard Shaw visited Hell's Gate he said, 'It reminds me too vividly of the fate theologians have promised me.'

# Hinemoa

The small island of Mokoia, in Lake Rotorua, is the setting for a well-known Maori legend. The story concerns a maiden of the local Arawa tribe called Hinemoa. She fell in love with a young man called Tutanekai who lived on the island. In order to see him, she planned to paddle over in a canoe at night guided by Tutanekai playing his flute. Her family, suspecting that she was going to see her lover, hid all the canoes. Hinemoa decided to swim across, taking dry gourds with her for buoyancy.

Reaching Mokoia, she headed straight for the Waikimihia hot pool to warm herself after the cold swim. While she was bathing naked Tutanekai's servant came to the spring to fill a drinking gourd. For reasons unexplained in the legend Hinemoa pretended to be a man and broke the servant's gourds every time he came to fill them (there may be some symbolism here). Eventually Tutanekai came to check out the problem. According to the legend he cried, 'Who dares annoy me?'

Hinemoa, still without the benefit of raiment, stepped forward and said, 'It is I, Hinemoa, who has come to you.' Fade out to sound of soft violins.

The next morning a servant was sent to check on Tutanekai who, understandably, was having a bit of a lie-in. The servant came running back, shouting, 'It is Hinemoa. It is Hinemoa who lies with Tutanekai.' His people then noticed canoes heading towards the island. It was Hinemoa's family and it was feared that a battle would take place. In fact, everyone got on like a house on fire and swore eternal peace and friendship.

The hot spring on Mokoia is now called Hinemoa's Pool – and Hinemoa Point, on the shore of the lake, is where she is said to have started her swim to the island. So fascinated were early film-makers by this great romantic story, that no less than three directors made it into a feature film.

## Accommodation and food in Rotorua

Fenton Street claims to be the longest street in New Zealand, and it certainly is the longest street of motels – there are hundreds to choose from. Confused by the choice, your best bet is to go to the Rotorua Information Centre, tell them your budget, explain what you want and have it arranged for you.

**Fat Dog Café $** *1161 Arawa St; tel: (07) 347 7586.* A Rotorua institution and consistently rated as the best café in town.

**Heywood's Motor Lodge $$** *249 Fenton St; tel: (07) 348 5586; email: reservations@ heywoodsmotel.co.nz; www.heywoodsmotel.co.nz.* Big rooms, lots of parking space. Rooms at the back are quieter.

**Pig and Whistle $$** *Cnr Haupapa and Tutanekai Sts; tel: (07) 347 3025.* This was a police station until 1969. Good food. Locally brewed beers.

**Regal Palms $$** *350 Fenton St; tel: (07) 350 3232 or 0800 743 000; www.regalpalms.co.nz.* One of the most modern motor lodges.

**Maclaren Falls Park**
in the Kaimai Ranges,
11km east of Tauranga, has
well-marked walks through
the native bush, natural pools
for swimming and canoeing,
and an animal park.

**Matakana Island**, accessible
on a day-trip from Tauranga,
has 24km of beach, good
surfing, a shop and pub.
Make the 15-minute journey
on the *Forest Lady*.

**Mills Reef Winery**
*143 Moffat Rd,
Bethlehem, 6km east of
Tauranga on the SH2; tel: (07)
576 8800; www.millsreef.co.nz.*
The winery offers daily
tastings of its world-class
wines, 1000–1700, and a 45-
minute tour. The restaurant
is open 1100–1500 and 1800
until late, with live jazz Sun
lunchtime.

Range to the Mamakus in the south. Running through it is the 9km
Kaimai railway tunnel – the longest tunnel in New Zealand. It was
begun in 1969 and was put into operation seven years later. The
**Kaimai-Mamaku Forest Park** was established in 1975 and covers
37,141ha. It runs from the Ohinemuri River near Paeroa to the
Mamaku Plateau.

During the winter, a terrible wind roars over the Kaimai Ranges,
between Tauranga and the Hauraki Plains. With typical New Zealand
understatement, it is called the Kaimai Breeze. It can topple haystacks
and even buildings, and was credited with bringing down an airliner
in 1963.

The twin town of Tauranga is Mt Maunganui, located on a long
peninsula on the other side of Tauranga Harbour. The two are
connected by a harbour bridge. Mt Maunganui – known locally as
'The Mount' – lies at the foot of the **Maunganui mountain**. This is a
slab of solid rock, 232m high. It takes an hour to walk up – some
climbing is involved – but the view makes the effort well worthwhile.

The major attraction of Tauranga is the beach life. The beaches here
are consistently superb and on the inland side are totally protected.
The Mount has two major beaches almost abutting each other. **Ocean
Beach** is 15km long and is one of the finest surfing beaches in the
country. **Mount Maunganui Beach**, on the other side of the
peninsula, has several kilometres of golden sand.

Within Tauranga Harbour – using that name in the sense of the
geographical feature rather than the port – there are numerous
sheltered beaches, for the harbour is almost landlocked. Two of the
best are **Omokoroa**, which is 21km northwest of Tauranga, and
**Pahioa**, 22km in the same direction.

Tauranga is an excellent resort for walking. Within the area there
are over 20 waymarked walks and the information centre has a
pamphlet listing them. One of the great walks of the area consists of
two paths that join together to follow the shores of the **Waikareao
Estuary**, taking around two hours and starting at the end of Maxwells
Road. It connects to McCardles Bush Boardwalk, which takes you
through mangroves (don't forget the insect repellent).

## Accommodation and food in Tauranga

**Collar and Thai** $ *21 Devonport Rd; tel: (07) 577 6655.* The author of
this guide collects titles of Thai restaurants. Current top favourite is
'Thai Me Kangaroo Down' in Perth, but this one is certainly worth a
special mention.

**Crown and Badger** $$ *Cnr Strand and Wharf Sts; tel: (07) 571 3038.*
Waterfront pub lunches.

**Harbour City Motor Inn** $$ *50 Wharf St; tel: (07) 571 1435 or 0800
253 525; www.taurangaharbourcity.co.nz*

**Above**
Matakana Island viewed from
Mount Maunganui

**Harbourside Restaurant $$** *The Strand; tel: (07) 571 0520;*
*www.harboursidetauranga.co.nz.* Tauranga's best restaurant on the
waterfront offering an excellent and imaginative all-day blackboard
and à la carte menu, with an emphasis on local seafood.

**Harbour View Motel $$** *7 Fifth Ave E; tel: (07) 578 8621;*
*www.harbourviewmotel.co.nz*

**Hotel on Devonport $$** *Devonport Towers, 72 Devonport Rd; tel: (07)*
*578 2668; www.hotelondevonport.net.nz.* Quality boutique hotel,
centrally located.

**Somerset Cottage $$** *30 Bethlehem Rd; tel: (07) 576 6889.* Well-
regarded rural restaurant.

# WHAKATANE

**Whakatane Information Centre** Cnr Quay St and Kakahoroa Drive; tel: (07) 308 6058; fax: (07) 308 6020; email: whakatane@ i-site.org; www.whakatane.com

This town, at the mouth of the Whakatane River, is the main service centre for the eastern part of the Bay of Plenty. Behind the town are the forests that supply the local paper mills and timber processing plants.

The story behind the name of the town is very romantic. Literally it means 'to play the part of a man'. When one of the first Maori canoes arrived in the 14th century, Wairaka, the daughter of the chief Toroa, grabbed a paddle and helped guide the canoe to the shore, even though it was forbidden for women to handle the paddles. As she did so she said, 'Me whakatane au i au', meaning, 'I will act as a man.' A statue of **Wairaka** now stands at the Whakatane Heads, at the mouth of the river.

The occupants of the canoe, the *Mataatua*, were probably not the first Maori explorers to arrive. Toi te Huatahi, the famous Maori adventurer and navigator, is said to have landed at Whakatane during his visit to New Zealand in the 12th century, which is probably two centuries before the arrival of the great fleet. It has been suggested that Toi built a *pa*, or fort, on Whakatane Heads and, indeed, there are the remains of two *pas* to be found there. However, no conclusive date has yet been determined for their construction. There is a splendid circular footpath called **Nga Tapuwae O Toi** that starts by going up to the original *pa* earthworks, then around Kohi Point to Ohope Beach. The whole walk would take an easy seven hours but you can join or leave at any place on the route. Maps can be had from the visitor centre.

The first permanent European resident was Philip Tapsell, who established a store there in 1830. In 1865 the Hau Hau rebellion caused the government to declare martial law in the whole area. Four years later, Te Kooti, the Maori insurgent, came out of Urewara Country, which was effectively impregnable, and launched an attack on the town. He was held up by a small redoubt manned by a French flour miller, Jean Guerren, and six men. They held up the 200-strong band of Te Kooti supporters for two days and nights until they were

**Wet 'n' Wild Rafting** (tel: (07) 348 3191; www.wetnwildrafting.co.nz) offer white-water rafting on the Motu River. You can travel by helicopter or four-wheel-drive to the Motu and other rivers in the area.

**Kiwi Jet Boat Tours** (tel: (07) 307 0663 or 0800 800 538; www. kiwijetboattours.com) run tours on the Rangitaiki River.

overrun. Te Kooti and his men then sacked Whakatane and burned many buildings. There is a memorial to **Guerren** 5.5km south on the main road to Opotiki. Appropriately, it consists of a stone from his mill.

Running through the centre of Whakatane is The Strand, while the crossroad is Boon Street, where you will find the small **Whakatane Museum and Gallery** (*open Mon–Fri 1000–1630*). In the centre of the town is a model of the *Mataatua* canoe in which Wairaka and her fellow Maori explorers arrived. It stands by the Pohaturoa Rock, once a Maori sacred place and now the centre of a small park and a memorial to the dead of World War I. At its base are karaka trees, said to have been grown from seeds which arrived on the *Mataatua*. Next to the rock stands a statue of Te Hurinui Apanui, a local chief.

Further afield, the **Te Urewera National Park** offers a wealth of walking opportunities. Ask the Visitor Centre for details.

The Whakatane area boasts some amazing beaches. To the west of the town is the 18km **Ohope Beach**, a great favourite with surfers. It is backed by the beautiful pohutukawa – the New Zealand Christmas Tree – so-called because it comes into bloom during the weeks leading up to Christmas.

Perhaps the great attraction of Whakatane is the opportunity to swim with dolphins. **Dolphins Down Under** (*Green Wharf; tel: 0800 354 7737; www.dolphinswim.co.nz*) specialises in providing everything needed, including hot showers after the trip.

Offshore is the volcanic **White Island** – Whakaari – which has a tendency to erupt regularly. The last time it did so was in 1992. You can go there by boat from Whakatane with Pee Jay Charters (*tel: (07) 308 9588; www.whiteisland.co.nz*). Alternatively, Vulcan Helicopters run helicopter expeditions to White Island (*tel: 0800 804 354*). Also offshore is Whale Island, a wildlife reserve controlled by the Department of Conservation.

## Accommodation and food in Whakatane

**Ground Zero $** *163 The Strand; tel: (07) 308 8548.* Café.

**Tuscany Villas $$** *57 The Strand; tel: (07) 308 2244; fax: (07) 308 2255; email: reservations@tuscanyvillas.co.nz*

**Wharf Shed $$** *Strand East; tel: (07) 308 5698.* Seafood a speciality – try the chowder.

**White Island Rendezvous $$** *15 Strand East; tel: (07) 308 9500; www.whiteisland.co.nz.* Modern motel and B&B accommodation operated by Pee Jay White Island tour/cruise company.

# Suggested tour

**Total distance:** 275km.

**Time:** 5 hours' driving (excluding sightseeing).

**Links:** East Cape (*see page 100*) lies immediately to the east.

The road from **WHAKATANE ❶** goes straight inland, through **TE TEKO ❷** to **MURUPARA ❸**, right on the edge of the **TE UREWERA NATIONAL PARK ❹** and the Ikawhenua Range of mountains from which many of the rivers which feed into Lake Rotorua originate. From there the road becomes the SH38 and skirts the **KAINGAROA FOREST ❺**. It joins the SH5 almost opposite the **WAIKITE THERMAL BATHS ❻**. It runs alongside the start of the **WAIMANGU THERMAL VALLEY ❼** and then passes the

WHAKAREWAREWA FOREST ❽ , before running into ROTORUA ❾ itself.

From there, the SH5 continues to NGONGOTAHA ❿ and then across to TIRAU ⓫. Some 12km out of Tirau on the SH27, a right turn on the SH29 goes to TE POI ⓬ and then over the Kaimai Range, with

KAIMAI-MAMAKU FOREST PARK ⓭ to the right, down through LOWER KAIMAI ⓮ to TAURANGA ⓯. From there the coast road, the SH2, leads back, mainly along the shore of the Bay of Plenty, to Whakatane.

## Also worth exploring

The coastal road from Whakatane to **Katikati**, along the SH2, runs parallel to Matakana Island, in the Bay of Plenty, through a series of small towns. Katikati is a small town with an amazing collection of murals right along its main street. It is almost as if the town had become an open-air art gallery. Why did it happen? Some time around 1990 the suggestion was that the SH2 should be diverted around the town. In other towns, in other countries, such a diversion might be a cause for rejoicing. But for Katikati it apparently meant commercial death. So the decision was taken to make the town irresistible so that no one would ever want to by-pass it.

What attraction could be created? The answer was a series of murals. By 1991 there were three, and now there are 44 – with more planned. At the information centre you can buy brochures explaining each mural. It is worth a special trip just to see how the town succeeded in stopping a by-pass by the use of art.

**Left**
Waimangu Thermal Park

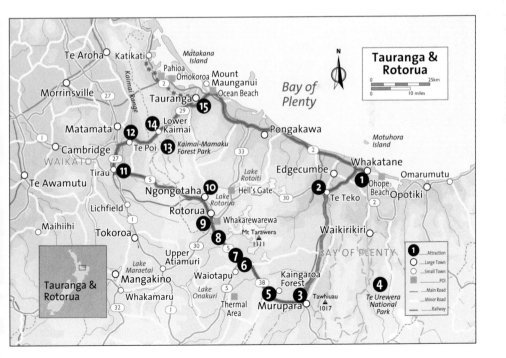

# East Cape

## Ratings

| | |
|---|---|
| Scenery | ●●●●○ |
| Watersports | ●●●●○ |
| Children | ●●●●○ |
| Outdoor activities | ●●●○○ |
| Historic sights | ●●●○○ |
| Museums | ●●●○○ |
| Dining | ●●○○○ |
| Heritage | ●○○○○ |

East Cape is almost a separate slice of New Zealand. Although it is no longer isolated from the rest of the country, it has a special style of its own. It is friendly, sophisticated despite its isolation, and has a feeling of community that is, perhaps, missing in other areas.

It also has some of the most dramatic scenery in New Zealand. Travelling from Auckland you will probably enter East Cape at Opotiki, a former whaling and fishing district. The SH35, skirting the coast from Opotiki to Gisborne, is one of the country's great scenic drives. You are never out of sight of the sea for a minute. On the other hand, the inland route, which takes you on the SH2 from Opotiki over the mountains to Gisborne, is dramatic in its own right and can sometimes be a challenging drive.

## GISBORNE

 **Gisborne Visitor Information Centre** *209 Grey St; tel: (06) 868 6139; fax: (06) 868 6138; email: gisborne@i-site.org; www.gisbornenz.com.* Very active and willing to give intelligent and apposite advice. One of the best of its kind.

Gisborne is the city closest in the world to the International Date Line. Inevitably it markets itself as the town that is the 'First To See The Light', and there is much truth to this claim, perhaps in more senses than one.

Gisborne is sited on Poverty Bay, which is a total misnomer and utterly misleading. That was the name given by Captain Cook when he failed to find provisions here. No one has had that problem since. Captain Cook arrived here on 9 October 1769 and a party was sent ashore two days later, landing on Kaiti Beach. Sadly, this first contact ended in bloodshed when the landing crew thought that a Maori was trying to steal a sword. Thus it was, in this isolated area of New Zealand, that Europeans landed in the country for the first time.

There are several monuments to commemorate the remarkable Captain Cook. One is a somewhat inappropriate **totem pole**, donated

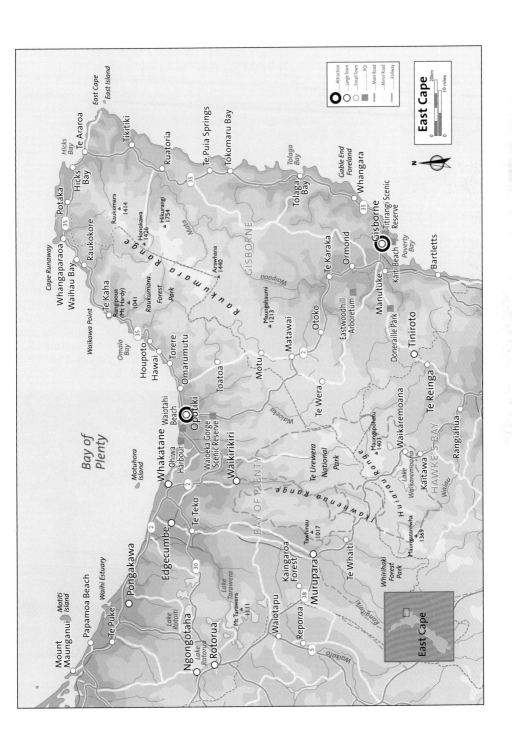

East Cape

East Island
East Cape

Te Araroa
Tikitiki
Ruatoria
Te Puia Springs
Tokomaru Bay
Tolaga Bay
Gable End Foreland
Whangara
Tolaga Bay

Hicks Bay
Hicks Bay
Potaka
Raukokore
Raukumara 1414
Hikurangi 1754
Honokawa 1426

Cape Runaway
Whangaparaoa
Waihau Bay
Te Kaha

Raukumara Range

Arawhana 1440

GISBORNE

Te Karaka
Ormond

Gisborne
Titirangi Scenic Reserve
Kaiti Beach
Poverty Bay
Bartletts

Waikawa Point

Rangipoua (Mt Hardy) 1041

Raukumara Forest Park

Maungahaumi 1213

Eastwoodhill Arboretum
Manutuke

Omalo Bay
Houpoto
Hawai
Torere
Omarumutu
Toatoa

Matawai
Otoko

Doneraille Park
Tiniroto

Motu

Te Wera

Waikaremoana
Te Reinga
Rangiahua

Waiotahi Beach
Opotiki
Waioeka Gorge Scenic Reserve
Waikirikiri

Te Urewera National Park

Maungapohatu 1403

Kaitawa

HAWKE'S BAY

Waioeka

Whakatane
Ohiwa Harbour

Te Waihenua Range

Huiarau Range

Waikaremoana
Lake Waikaremoana

Bay of Plenty

Motuhora Island

Te Teko

BAY OF PLENTY

Tawhinau 1017

Maungataniwha 1369

Motiti Island

Edgecumbe

Waiotapu

Kaingaroa Forest

Te Whaiti

Whirihaki Forest Park

Mount Maunganui
Papamoa Beach
Waihi Estuary

Pongakawa

Te Puke

Lake Rotoiti

Lake Rotorua

Lake Rotoma

Lake Tarawera
Mt Tarawera 1111

Ngongotaha
Rotorua

Waiotapu
Reporoa
Murupara

East Cape

Mata
Waipaoa
Waioeka
Hangaroa
Ruakituri
Waikato

by the Canadian government. It stands next to the Information Centre and is where the out-of-town buses pull up. Another is an obelisk on **Kaiti Beach** which was raised by national subscription, with each schoolchild contributing a penny towards its construction. It marks the place where Captain Cook landed on 9 October 1769 (note: the date engraved on the obelisk is incorrect by one day).

On Kaiti Hill there is also the **Cook Observatory**, with public viewings on Tuesdays (at 1930 in the winter and 2030 in the summer) run by the local amateur astronomy society.

At **Waikanae Beach**, where the Taruheru River comes out to the sea, there is a statue – a sculpture not, perhaps, to everyone's taste – of Nicholas Young, who was the first of Cook's crew to sight New Zealand. He was a surgeon's boy on the *Endeavour* and was 12 years of age at the time. His prize for the sighting was a gallon of rum. The beach is actually within the city, and can be crowded during the holidays and at weekends in the summer. The rest of the time it enjoys splendid isolation.

Gisborne is at the confluence of the Waimata and Taruheru rivers, which join to form the Turanganui – reputedly the shortest river in New Zealand at just 1,390m. There are **footpaths** along all three of the rivers, which make exploring the compact yet charming town very pleasant. **Gisborne Harbour** was built in the 1920s by constructing a diversion wall in the Turanganui River. This provided an inner harbour, which is now a marina and a centre for restaurants and cafés.

**Below**
Statue of Captain Cook, Gisborne

One of the best views of the city is from the **Titirangi Scenic Reserve**, which encompasses Kaiti Hill. This was originally a Maori *pa* – a fortified village – and on a clear day you can see right across Poverty Bay to Young Nick's Head at the southern end of the bay. Incidentally, this cliff was not, despite its name, the first piece of land spotted from the *Endeavour*. The mountains further inland would have been spotted first. There are pathways leading down to the Captain Cook landing site.

One of the largest Maori meeting houses in New Zealand is at the bottom of the hill. **Te Poho-o-rawiri meeting house** opened in 1930 and is one of the most decorated Maori buildings in New Zealand, but you need permission (*obtainable from the information centre, tel: (06) 868 5364*) before you enter.

The history of the area, and especially the Maori culture, is excellently shown in the **Tairawhiti Museum and Arts Centre** (*tel: (06) 867 3832; www.tairawhitimuseum.org.nz; open Mon–Sat 1000–1600, Sun 1330–1600*). In its grounds is the six-room Wyllie Cottage, built in 1872 and the oldest building in Gisborne, furnished in 19th-century style. Nearby, and included in the same complex, is a small but interesting **Maritime Museum** containing some of the superstructure of the *Star of Canada*, which was wrecked on Kaiti Beach. For some years the wreckage was used as a house.

Gisborne is bounded by rich river flats, giving generally excellent agricultural land, mainly used as market gardens and vineyards. This agricultural fecundity extends to the city, which has an excellent **Botanical Garden** in Aberdeen Road, on the banks of the Taruheru River and covering 4ha, with a major display of native plants. **Gisborne Rose Garden** is across the road from Kelvin Park.

The **East Coast Museum of Technology** (*tel: (06) 868 8254; open 0930–1600*), in Makaraka, near the showground, consists mainly of agricultural machinery and is just like many similar museums around New Zealand – once you have seen one knackered, broken-down chaff cutter, you have seen them all.

More interesting is the **Te Kuri** footpath. The true significance of this will only be apparent to fans of Murray Ball, the cartoonist, whose great creation – *Footrot Flats* – is one of New Zealand's greatest exports. *Footrot Flats* followers will know that the cartoon's central character is a farmer called Wal, the archetypal New Zealander, but that his dog, called Dog, is the true hero of the series. (The cat was called Horse, but let us not confuse you.) Te Kuri is Maori for 'The Dog', hence the name of this walk, which starts 4km to the north of the town at the end of Shelley Road. It then circles around the farm of Murray Ball, where Wal lives his imaginary bachelor life. The walk takes about three hours and wends through farmland and forest and has one amazing viewpoint.

Worth visiting further out is **Eastwoodhill Arboretum**, located just beyond Ngatapa, 35km west of Gisborne. Founded in 1918, it is home

**Gisborne's famous**

The city is named after the then colonial secretary because the original Maori name – Turanganui-a-Kiwa – was often confused with Tauranga in the Bay of Plenty. Despite its *pakeha* name, Gisborne is very proud of its Maori past and the fact that many Maori from the area – not all of them good and decent characters – made a mark on New Zealand history. Among them are Te Kooti, the infamous trader, prophet, general stirrer and church founder, Aspirina Ngata, who was the first Maori graduate, and Dame Kiri Te Kanawa, the celebrated diva.

Gisborne is a good
surfing area and
surfing reports are given
each day after the news on
Radio 89.3FM.

to a massive collection of northern-hemisphere plants and trees. There
is a gentle 45-minute stroll along marked paths that take in the whole
of the garden (*open daily 0900–1600*).

## Accommodation and food in Gisborne

**Café Ruba $** *14 Childers Rd; tel: (06) 868 6516.* Award winner, good coffee.

**Fettuccine Bros $** *12 Peel St; tel: (06) 868 5700.* Good and authentic
Italian food. Licensed and BYO.

**Irish Rover $–$$** *69 Peel St; tel: (06) 867 1112.* Good atmosphere and
pub food.

**Colonial Motor Lodge $$** *715 Gladstone Rd; tel: (06) 867 9165;
www.gisbornecolonial.co.nz*

**Portside Hotel $$** *2 Reads Quay; tel: 0800 767 874; www.portside
gisborne.co.nz.* Modern hotel set in centrally located waterfront position.

**Repongaere Estate $$** *Lavenham Rd, Patutahi; tel: (06) 862 7515;
www.repongaere.co.nz.* Luxury vineyard accommodation.

**Senator Motor Inn $$** *2 Childers Rd; tel: (06) 868 8877; www.
senatormotorinn.co.nz.* New and harbourside.

**Wainui Beach Motel $$** *37 Wairere Rd, Wainui Beach; tel: (06) 868 5882;
www.wainuibeachmotel.co.nz*

**The Wharf Café $$** *60 The Esplanade; tel: (06) 868 4876.*

**Whispering Sands Beachfront Motel $$** *18 Salisbury Rd; tel: (06) 867
1319; www.whisperingsands.co.nz*

# OPOTIKI

**❶ Opotiki
Information
Centre** *Cnr St John and
Elliot Sts; tel: (07) 315
3031; fax: (07) 315
3032; www.opotikinz.com*

**The name Opotiki**

This comes from O-
Potiki-Mai-Tawhit, a
spring on the eastern bluff
above Waiotahi Beach.
The name literally means
'place of the children
from Tawhiti'.

Opotiki has much to offer, including four-wheel drives to the scenic
Motu River, jet boating and white-water rafting. Your first stop should
be the Information Centre, where you will be positively brainwashed
on the delights of the area. Two rivers join at the harbour – the Otara
and Waioeka – and both offer excellent boating and yachting, which
extends out into the Bay of Plenty. There are numerous safe swim-
ming beaches and bays in the area. A popular beach is **Waiotahi**,
which is only 6km out of town and is patrolled by the surf club during
the season.

   **Jet boat rides** are offered along the spectacular and turbulent
lengths of the Motu River, to the east of the town. These trips are not
inexpensive but are certainly thrilling. Try Motu River Jet Boat Tours
(*tel: (07) 325 2735; www.motujet.com*); you need to book at least a day
ahead. For multi-day rafting trips contact **Wet-n-Wild** (*tel: (07) 348
3191; www.wetnwildrafting.co.nz*) – they offer a truly superb wilderness
river adventure.

Well worth visiting is **St Stephen's Anglican Church,** on Church Street, which was built by the Reverend Carl Sylvus Volkner in 1864. He was reputedly murdered by the Hau Hau (*see feature, page 107*). That is the official *pakeha* (European) version. The Maori version is that, like many missionaries, Volkner supported land-grabbing by settlers and it was for this that he was executed. The truth probably falls somewhere between the two versions.

At the northern end of Church Street is the **Heritage and Agricultural Society Museum** (*open Mon–Sat 1000–1530, Sun 1330–1600*), another New Zealand town museum packed full of ill-assorted

**Below**
Eastwoodhill Arboretum, Gisborne

**Ancient tree**

In the Hukutaia Domain, within the town, is a puriri tree that is thought to be between 1,000 and 2,000 years old. These subtropical trees, whose timber is as durable as teak, grow only in the northern half of the North Island.

mementoes and only interesting if you are fascinated by odd implements and gadgets of a certain age. More interesting is the fact that Opotiki is the centre of a major Maori area, and it is much easier to get a feeling for the authentic Maori way here than it is with cultural shows in the big cities.

Some 16km away from Opotiki is **Ohiwa Harbour**, which is not only very beautiful, it is also the most northerly site for New Zealand black beech trees and the most southerly site for mangroves – a curious mixture. The beach is lined with the New Zealand Christmas tree – the pohutukawa – which flowers in December and January.

## Accommodation and food in Opotiki

**Flying Pig Café $** *95 Church St; tel: (07) 315 7618.* BYO. Despite the name, it has a good selection of vegetarian dishes.

**Hot Bread Shop Café $–$$** *43 St John St; tel: (07) 315 6795.*

**Right**
Logging near Opotiki

**Left**
Sunrise at Wainui Beach near Gisborne

**Magnolia Court Motel $$** *Cnr Bridge and Nelson Sts; tel: (07) 315 8490; www.magnoliaopotiki.co.nz*

**Capeview Cottages $$$** *Tablelands Rd; tel: (07) 315 7877.* Luxurious cottage with its own web page – *www.capeview.co.nz*

# Hau Hau

The bloodthirsty wars fought between the Maori and the British settlers showed time and time again that the Maori were natural warriors. One particular group, the Hau Hau, wanted all *pakeha* – Europeans – out of New Zealand. Its followers believed that they could not be wounded or killed by bullets. The way to achieve this invincibility was to hold a hand above the head with the palm facing forward while making a barking sound, Hau Hau. The Hau Hau also had a habit of carrying the heads of their victims in front of them on long stakes as totems.

Although this unique method of bullet-proofing had fatal conceptual flaws, the Hau Hau inflicted some dreadful blows on the *pakeha*. One was the famous killing of the missionary, the Reverend Carl Volkner, who was murdered in March 1865 at Opotiki. The propaganda of the time alleged that the Hau Hau, led by the prophet, Kereopa Te Rau, drank his blood.

Elements of the Hau Hau religion were handed down to the Ringatu religion, which was founded by Te Kooti Rikiraugi. He was arrested in 1865 during the battle at Waerenga-a-hika, tried as a Hau Hau spy and deported with others to Chatham. Three years later, in 1868, Te Kooti and 200 followers escaped and carried out the Poverty Bay Massacre in which between 60 and 70 – the exact number is unclear – Maori and Europeans were murdered and houses and farm buildings burned to the ground. A reminder of this is the tiny church at Matawhero, which stands at the crossroads on the SH2. The church, then a school house, was the only building in the immediate vicinity to survive the destruction.

## Chardonnay capital

Gisborne is known as the Chardonnay capital of New Zealand, being at the centre of one of the largest grape-growing regions in the country. Some 1,500ha are under vines, producing about 35 per cent of the national crop of the Chardonnay grape, which is used to make a lush and strongly flavoured wine. The first grapes in the area were planted by Marist missionaries in the 1850s, but they moved on to establish the Hawke's Bay wine industry. The first serious move came from Friedrich Wohnsiedler. He emigrated to Gisborne around the turn of the century and established a small factory producing German-style sausages. This was wrecked during World War I when anything German was suspect. Wohnsiedler then moved to Ormond, just out of town, and planted vines. His first crop was harvested in 1921 and by the time of his death, in the mid-1950s, his Waihirere vineyard was a major property, later to be acquired by the massive Montana wine-making company.

## Suggested tour

**Total distance:** 425km.

**Time:** 7 hours' driving (excluding sightseeing).

**Links:** Tauranga and Rotorua (*see page 84*) lie immediately to the west.

Start at **OPOTIKI** ❶ where you must make the difficult decision on how to travel the circuit that traverses East Cape. You can choose to go around the Pacific Coast Highway – the SH35 – which runs through some of the most beautiful scenery in New Zealand for 334km until it reaches Gisborne. Alternatively, you can follow the SH2 for 147km through the magnificent Waioeka Gorge and over the mountains to Gisborne. Best of all, you can decide whether to take the coastal route one way and come back overland, or vice versa.

Going the long way around, the SH35 goes around the coast through a series of very small villages – Omarumutu, Opape, Torere, Hawai, Houpoto and Whitianga – not to be confused with the town of the same name in Coromandel – where the Motu River comes to the sea. From there it follows the coast through Omaio, Whanarua Bay, **RAUKOKORE** ❷ – which has a tourist information centre – Waihau Bay and then Whangaparaoa. From there it goes a very short way inland to Potaka and then comes down to the coast at Hicks Bay on the way to **TE ARAROA** ❸ which is, compared to the other towns listed, of a reasonable size and also has a tourist information centre.

The road cuts across the East Cape to Tikitiki on the Waiapu River and then runs along its northern bank until it crosses the river near Ruatoria, with Mount Hikurangi in the background. From there it continues along the coast to Te Puia Springs and then Tolaga Bay followed by a string of minute seaside communities until it reaches **GISBORNE** ❹.

For an interesting diversion from Gisborne, leave on the Tiniroto Road to Wairoa. After 53km you will come to **DONERAILLE PARK** ❺, a native bush reserve on the Hangaroa River, with safe swimming and picnic sites. Carry on along the road to **TINIROTO** ❻ to visit **HACKFALLS ARBORETUM** ❼ *(tel: (06) 863 7091)*. This is privately owned and has an important collection of trees planted round the lakes on a sheep and cattle station. Nearby, the **TINIROTO LAKES** ❽ are scenic and provide first-rate trout fishing. Just beyond are the **REINGA FALLS** ❾ and then you can, if you wish, turn inland to the **TE UREWERA NATIONAL PARK** ❿ in the Urewera Ranges. The park gains its name from a tradition that a Nga Potiki chief, old and feeble, lay down beside a fire and was fatally burnt in the genitals. A literal translation of Urewera is 'burnt penis'. You now possibly know more about Urewera than you wanted to. The park has scenic waterfalls, bush walks and caves, and Lake Waikaremoana offers trout fishing and pleasure boating.

The **SH2** inland road ⓫ that takes you back from Gisborne to Opotiki starts its journey by following the banks of the Waipaoa River to Te Karaka and then climbing through Puha to Matawai. From there the SH2 runs down the Wairata and then through the magnificence of the **WAIOEKA GORGE SCENIC RESERVE** ⓬ to Opotiki.

Instead of following the road from Matawai to the coast you can also get down to Opotiki along an older route. This is a much rougher and unsealed route, with two fords to cross. If you are driving a hired car

**Right**
Tolaga Bay wharf, north of Gisborne

you must make sure in advance that your insurance covers this segment. It takes you first to **MOTU ⓫**, with Motu Falls just beyond. You then follow the Old Motu Coach Road down to **OMARUMUTU ⓮** , on the coast and from there back to Opotiki.

## Also worth exploring

It is possible to make a tour of some of the winemakers in the Gisborne area, but you should understand that these are individual vineyards and you would be wise to make a booking before you turn up. Many of them have cellar sales and some have restaurants attached showcasing the products of the vineyard. The Visitor Information Centre has full listings.

**Matawhero Wines** *The Vineyard, Riverpoint Rd, Gisborne; tel: (06) 867 6140.* Former owner Denis Irwin began making wine in the mid-1970s and achieved almost instant success. The vineyard was bought by the Searle family in 2008 and is being redeveloped.

**Millton Vineyard** *119 Papatu Rd, Gisborne (15 mins from centre); tel: (06) 862 8680 or 0800 464 588 for appointments; www.millton.co.nz.* This is a green, clean vineyard which uses no insecticide or soluble fertiliser, being New Zealand's first commercial fully certified organic vineyard. Its 1992 Chardonnay was selected as the best organic wine in the world at a competition in the UK. Millton wines also came second and third.

**Montana** *Solander St, Gisborne; tel: (06) 868 2757; www.pernod-ricard-nz.com/pages/wineries/gisborne; open daily 1030–1400.* Not surprisingly, the country's largest and best-known winemaker has a high profile in the region and winery tours and tastings are available at the Lindauer Cellars. A popular feature of the tour is the Lindauer Cellars Museum housed in the former cuvé room, and there is also a fine à la carte restaurant *(open daily from 1130)*.

**Pouparae Park Wines** *385 Bushmere Rd; tel: (06) 867 7931; open daily 1000–1800.* Although no grapes are actually grown on this elegant property, it is surrounded by vineyards and produces a good line in Chardonnay, sold at the cellar door.

**TW Wines** *Back Ormond Rd, Gisborne; tel: (06) 868 6499; call for latest cellar door opening.* Recipients of 39 national and international medals for its Chardonnay grown by two of the country's best, Paul Tietjens and Geordie Witters, on the renowned 'Golden Slope'. Tours and tastings available.

**The Wharf Café Longbush Wines** *60 The Esplanade, Gisborne; tel: (06) 863 1285; www.gisbornewinecompany.co.nz; open daily 1000–1800.* This is a wine bar that shows off the wines of the vineyard. The restaurant and cellar are in a converted cargo shed and offer wines from most makers in the area, especially Longbush, Woodlands and Nicks Head.

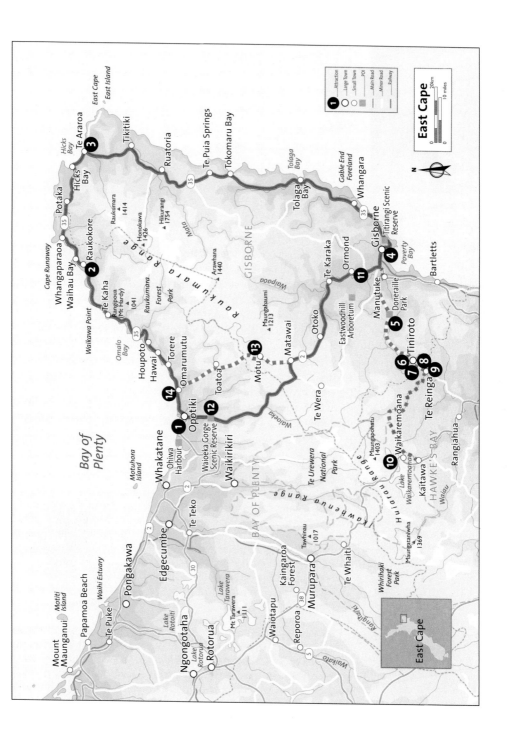

East Cape

# Lake Taupo

## Ratings

| | |
|---|---|
| Scenery | ●●●●● |
| Fishing | ●●●●● |
| Thermal spas | ●●●●● |
| Outdoor activities | ●●●● |
| Children | ●●● |
| Dining | ●●● |
| Heritage | ●● |
| Museums | ●● |

Lake Taupo covers some 619sq km, making it the largest lake in New Zealand. It was created by a huge volcanic eruption, and is now fed by a series of rivers, of which the largest is the Tongariro. Its outlet to the sea is the Waikato River, which is the country's longest inland waterway.

As long ago as the 1880s visitors came to enjoy the thermal baths that abound in the area. Then, following the example of American novelist Zane Grey, who thought it the best fishing spot on Earth, the anglers arrived. Lately Lake Taupo has become an important centre for watersports. The whole of the east and south coasts of the lake are dotted with holiday settlements but the west coast is still relatively inaccessible and is therefore a favourite retreat for anglers.

## TAUPO

ℹ **Taupo Visitor Centre** *Tongariro St;* tel: (07) 376 0027; fax: (07) 378 9003; email: taupo@ i-site.org; www. laketauponz.com

This town enjoys a spectacular setting – on the edge of the biggest lake in New Zealand and looking south across the lake to the snowcapped mountains of Tongariro National Park. This magical scenery was all created through volcanic activity. There were several monstrous Taupo eruptions, and those in AD 130 and AD 186 were reported in contemporary Chinese and Roman records. The last Taupo eruption is thought to have reached 50km in height, with volcanic rock blasted over an area of 7,000sq km. The eruption left a crater with a radius of 15km, which is now Lake Taupo.

Other cones in the area were also active at that time. Some of them still are. Within the Taupo volcanic zone there are three relatively active volcanoes – Tongariro, Ruapehu and Ngauruhoe. All three have erupted since European occupation, with Ngauruhoe erupting in one way or another more than 70 times, and Mount Ruapehu putting on a

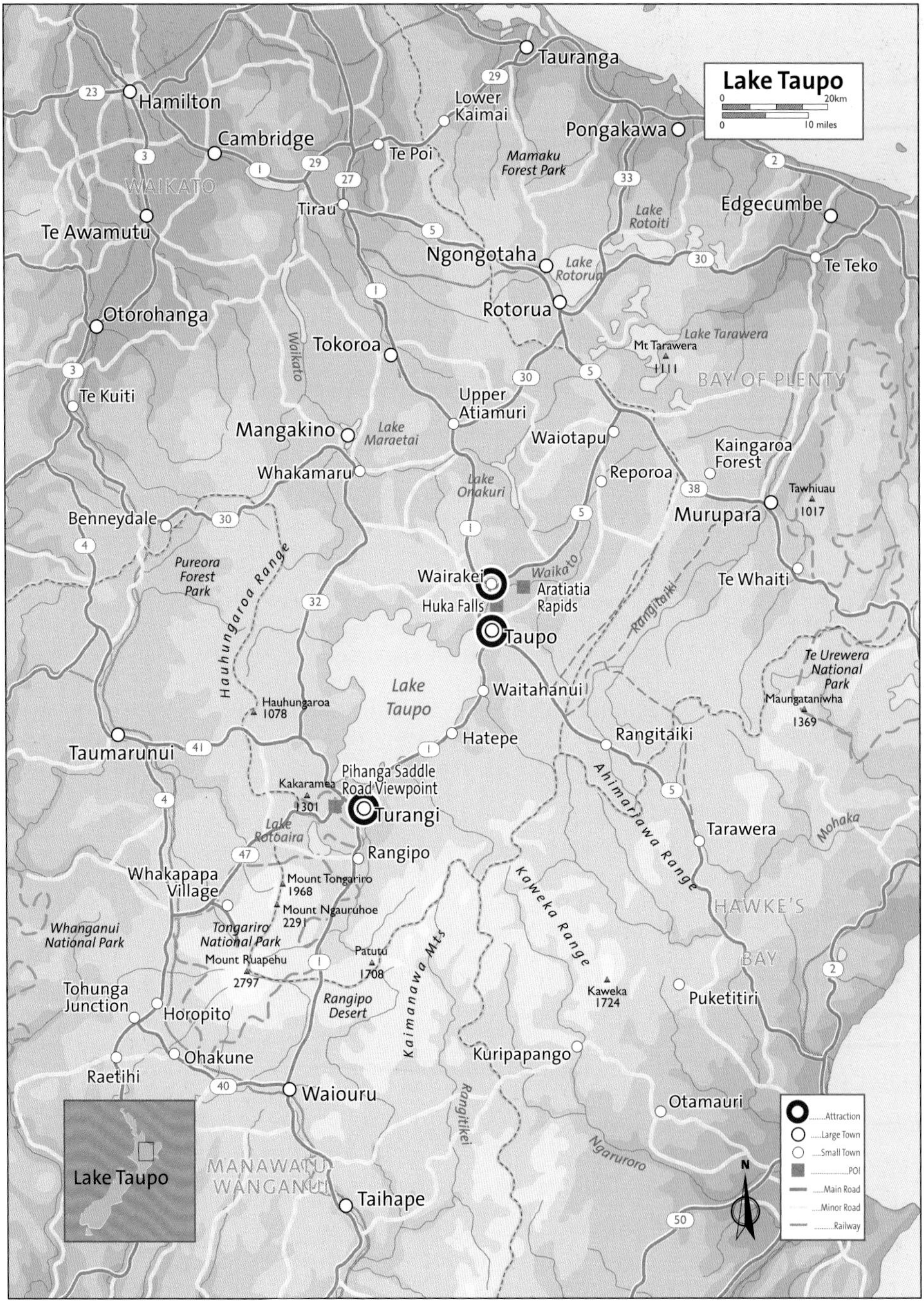

Lake Taupo

| | |
|---|---|
| 0 | 20km |
| 0 | 10 miles |

Tauranga
Hamilton
Lower Kaimai
Pongakawa
Cambridge
Te Poi
Mamaku Forest Park
Edgecumbe
WAIKATO
Tirau
Lake Rotoiti
Te Awamutu
Ngongotaha
Lake Rotorua
Te Teko
Otorohanga
Rotorua
Tokoroa
Lake Tarawera
Mt Tarawera
1111
BAY OF PLENTY
Te Kuiti
Upper Atiamuri
Mangakino
Lake Maraetai
Waiotapu
Kaingaroa Forest
Whakamaru
Lake Ohakuri
Reporoa
Tawhiuau
1017
Benneydale
Murupara
Pureora Forest Park
Waikato
Te Whaiti
Wairakei
Aratiatia Rapids
Huka Falls
Taupo
Te Urewera National Park
Maungataniwha
1369
Hauhungaroa Range
Lake Taupo
Hauhungaroa
1078
Waitahanui
Rangitaiki
Taumarunui
Hatepe
Pihanga Saddle Road Viewpoint
Kakaramea
1301
Turangi
Rangitaiki
Tarawera
Mohaka
Rangipo
Ahimanawa Range
Whakapapa Village
Mount Tongariro 1968
Mount Ngauruhoe 2291
Kaweka Range
HAWKE'S
Whanganui National Park
Tongariro National Park
Mount Ruapehu 2797
Patutu 1708
Rangipo Desert
Kaweka 1724
Puketitiri
BAY
Tohunga Junction
Horopito
Kaimanawa Mts
Kuripapango
Ohakune
Raetihi
Waiouru
Otamauri
Lake Taupo
MANAWATU WANGANUI
Rangitikei
Ngaruroro
Taihape

| | |
|---|---|
| ● | Attraction |
| ◎ | Large Town |
| ○ | Small Town |
| ■ | POI |
| | Main Road |
| | Minor Road |
| | Railway |

N

**Above**
Fishing in Lake Taupo

spectacular show in 1995 and again in 1996. As a by-product of this volcanic activity, Taupo became a fashionable spa in the 19th century. The most famous bath establishment was the **AC Baths** (*Spa Road; tel: (07) 377 3600; open daily 0600–2100*). The initials stand for Armed Constabulary and it was here that the soldiers stationed in Taupo from 1869, during the campaign against Te Kooti, relaxed at the end of a long march. The pool is kept at a steady 37°C, but there are private pools which are up to three degrees warmer. Smaller, but equally good, is **Taupo De Brett's Spa Resort** on SH5 (*open daily 0730–2100*).

For more on this period in the town's history, visit the **Taupo Regional Museum of Art and History**, which, although small, is extremely interesting (*in Story Place, near the visitor information centre; tel: (07) 376 0414; open daily 1030–1630*). Nearby is the old Court House, originally built in 1881 as a barracks for the Armed Constabulary, and the **Taupo Rose Gardens**, with over 500 bushes making a brave display when in full bloom in the summer.

There are many attractions in the area. At least three boats offer scheduled **cruises** on the lake. One is the vintage yacht *The Barbary*, which was once owned by the Australian film actor, Errol Flynn, and probably has a tale or two to tell. Typically the cruises last two to three hours. If time is a little tight, *Ernest Kemp* is a replica steamboat offering one-hour trips.

## Accommodation and food in Taupo

**Mole and Chicken $** *40 Taharepa Rd; tel: (07) 378 7843.* Traditional New Zealand cooking.

**Jolly Good Fellows $–$$** *80 Lake Tce; tel: (07) 378 0457.* Good atmosphere and lake views.

**L'Arte Café and Sculpture Garden $–$$** *225 Marapa Rd, Acacia Bay; tel: (07) 378 2962; www.larte.co.nz.* A bit hard to find, but well worth a visit.

Anchorage Resort Motel $$ *346 Lake Tce, Two Mile Bay; tel: (07) 378 5542; www.taupomotel.co.nz.* Lakeside with pool, spas and gym.

The Lotus Thai Restaurant $$ *137 Tongariro St; tel: (07) 376 9497; open daily 1200–2100; closed Tue.* Good Thai fare.

Taupo De Bretts Spa Resort $$ *Napier–Taupo Highway (SH5); tel: (07) 378 8559; www.taupodebretts.com.* Unusual in that it has thermal pools on site and is as much resort as accommodation. Only about 1km from the lake.

Terraces Hotel $$ *Napier–Taupo Highway (SH5); tel: (07) 378 7080; www.terraceshotel.co.nz.* Formerly De Bretts Hotel and first established in 1889, this renovated hotel on the edge of the town combines class and character. The added attraction is of course the Hot Springs and Spa only a short stroll away.

## Fishing in Lake Taupo and the Tongariro River

The first brown trout eggs were brought to New Zealand from Tasmania in 1868. Sixteen years after that, rainbow trout were introduced from California and the strain was established quickly throughout the country. Within 20 years brown trout between 10kg and 12kg were being caught. The rainbows averaged 4kg in 1910 and were preferred for their superior fighting ability.

From this arose the first great publicist of Taupo, the famous American writer Zane Grey. He fished the Taupo region for giant trout, collecting his experiences in a book called *Tales from a Fisherman's Log*, which has been frequently republished. Grey tells how his son caught 135 trout in 42 days, his brother 140 and Zane himself 87. All caught fish of around 4kg in weight, with son Romer topping them all with one weighing more than 7kg. The publicity created by this book attracted anglers from around the world.

Amazing fishing is still available, either on the lake itself or in the many small streams that run into the lake. Anglers require a Taupo trout fishing licence, purchased for a day, week, month or season. These are available at all sporting goods stores, dairies, service stations, motels, hotels and information centres.

The minimum legal size for any species in Lake Taupo, the Tongariro River and its tributary streams is 45cm. The average trout weighs about 1.5kg. The bag limit is three trout, irrespective of species, taken during the legal fishing hours of 0500–midnight. Nearly all rivers and streams in the district are restricted to fly fishing. There is no time when there is not excellent fishing somewhere in the lake, either from a boat or by casting from the shore.

Trout hatcheries are found throughout New Zealand because, while many of the lakes and rivers have plenty of food, many lack adequate spawning grounds. The rainbow trout of New Zealand are all descended from one shipment and are considered to be the only pure strain of rainbow trout left in the world. In a case of reverse export, the eggs from rainbow trout have been sent from one of the lake hatcheries back to their original California breeding grounds.

There are literally dozens of guides who can show you how and where to catch fish. The Taupo Launchmen's Association (*tel: (07) 378 3444; www.fishcruisetaupo.co.nz*), located at the Boat Harbour, has over 20 boats to choose from and the members are very experienced in making sure their guests land their full complement of fish, boasting an 80 per cent success rate. You can get your catch smoked and vacuum packed at one of the local smokehouses, ready to take home.

# TURANGI

**Turangi Visitor Centre** *Ngawaka Pl;* tel: (07) 386 8999; fax: (07) 386 0074; email: turangi@ i-site.org; www. laketauponz.com

Turangi was a small fishing village to the south of Lake Taupo when, in 1964, it was expanded to meet the needs of the Tongariro Hydro-electric Power Scheme, which draws on a range of rivers feeding down to Lake Taupo. The first new station was completed in 1973. A second station has been constructed underground. You can get details of this scheme from the Turangi information office.

The new town was also designed as a base for the forestry industry. It is built on the foothills of Pihanga, which rises to 1,325m behind the town in the Tongariro National Park. Nearby is the Tongariro River which is perhaps one of the most famous stretches of trout fishing water in the world. The **Tongariro National Trout Centre** (*3.5km south of Turangi on the SH1; open daily 1000–1600; tel: (07) 386 8085*) is run by the Department of Conservation as a factory for rainbow trout. Eggs are milked from the female trout, fertilised and developed. When they hatch, about a month later, they are sent on to other departmental stations and then released a year later.

There is a tremendous view over Lake Taupo if you drive up Highway 47 to the **Pihanga Saddle Road** viewpoint. Walkers should seek out the **Tongariro River Walkway** (*5.5km south of the town on the SH1*), originally created to give anglers access to the river and following a terrace above the river. The walk takes about $1^1/_2$ hours each way.

## Accommodation and food in Turangi

**Anglers Café $$** *Anglers Paradise Resort, SH41; tel: (07) 386 8980.*

**Brew Haus Bar & Restaurant $$** *Club Habitat, 25 Ohuanga Rd; tel: (07) 386 7492; www.clubhabitat.co.nz*

**Creel Lodge Motel $$** *177 Taupehi Rd; tel: (07) 386 8081; www.creel.co.nz.* Quiet riverside location.

# WAIRAKEI

Wairakei is both a town – although it could almost be considered a suburb of Taupo – and a park, set on the west bank of the Waikato River. The town is in the Waiora Valley, 10km north of Taupo in the middle of an area dedicated to producing geothermal power. This is the second-largest geothermal power installation of its kind in the world and the second ever to be set up. It is driven by the thermal activity from an active volcanic fault running from Mt Ruapehu through Taupo.

The geothermal power scheme taps a vast underground water system that has been heated by very hot rocks. The amount of power that can be obtained in this way has diminished somewhat in recent

years, and although ways have been found to improve the output, there are strong indications that this is a finite resource.

The Geyser Valley of Wairakei has been a tourist attraction for over a century, since the first holiday boarding house was established by Robert Graham, a former Superintendent of the Auckland Province. The valley is full of thermal activity and the Wipapa geyser spouts every 12 minutes or so. The best way to see all the sights of the area is to take the Huka Falls Tourist Loop, which will take you to all the main attractions.

First you will come to the **Huka Falls,** 2.5km south of Wairakei on the SH1. This is where the Waikato River suddenly squeezes into a chasm only 15m across. The water hurls itself over a ledge at a rate of 220,000 litres a second to stampede down 10m of rock in a torrent of foam – the word Huka means foam – into the basin below. The drop is not vertical – more a very steep ramp – but the effect is spectacular, with water blasting through at high velocity. There is a bridge across the falls and you can see the falls and rapids from several different vantage points on both sides of the river. There is also a 7km walk right down the bank of the river which ends at the Aratiatia Rapids.

If you want to see how bees make honey **The Honey Hive** (tel: (07) 374 8553; open 0900–1700) has hives with glass sides so you can spy on the bees working to keep the queen happy.

The Institute of Geological and Nuclear Sciences runs the **Volcanic Activity Centre** (*Huka Falls Loop Road; tel: (07) 374 8375; www.volcanoes.co.nz; open daily 0900–1700*). Here you can find out how geothermal forces are harnessed. The centre also gives an excellent account of vulcanology.

You can take trips down the river and to the base of the Huka Falls with Huka Falls Jet (*tel: 0800 485 253; www.hukafallsjet.co.nz*). Trips depart from the end of Huka Falls Rd (next to Prawn Park).

Practically next door, on the Huka Falls Loop Road, is the **Wairakei Prawn Park** (*30-min tours 1100–1600 on the hour*) where, in 20 minutes, you can find out more about prawns than you could ever want to know. The facility breeds giant freshwater prawns in a large pond using warm water from the Waikato River. You can get prawns barbecued on the spot, and these are the freshest, and probably the most flavoursome, prawns you will ever taste (*0900–1700; in the holiday season it would be best if you made a booking for it is, understandably, very popular: tel: (07) 374 8474*).

**Below**
Bungee jumping over the Waikato River near Taupo

Some 4km along the Karapiti Road, and only 5km from Taupo, is the aptly named **Craters of the Moon**, a wide valley full of steaming craters and pools. Walkways wend around this scene of desolation (*entry is free*). All of this is relatively new. It did not exist until the power station was opened in the 1950s, lowering the water level and exposing all of this activity.

The **Aratiatia Rapids** are 5km from town, on the Aratiatia Road, just off the SH5, and are well signposted. These rapids show the problems that arise when power needs come into conflict with conservation. The site had been recognised officially for half a century as 'at once the most beautiful and the most valuable location on the river'. That being the case, it was inevitable that, in 1957, the government authorised construction of a hydroelectric scheme that would have totally destroyed the rapids. In the end a compromise was reached. Now the rapids run at 1000, 1200, 1400 and, sometimes in the summer, at 1600. There is a warning siren, the water is turned on and the river comes smashing down through the rapids. The show lasts for about half an hour and there are lookout points along the river bank. **Rapids Jet** (*Rapids Rd; tel: (07) 378 5828; www.rapidsjet.com*) offer adrenalin-pumping trips up and down the river, taking in the base of the falls and various smaller rapids.

If that is not enough excitement, then the dreaded bungee jumping is available. You will find it ever-present in spots all over New Zealand – just like the measles. **Taupo Bungy** (*tel: (07) 377 1135; www.taupobungy.co.nz*) drops its customers from 50m above a bend on the Waikato River from a platform. Seniors over 65 years jump free. There is now a new variation called Baptism, where you plunge right into the water. There appears to be no end to this madness.

## Accommodation and food in Wairakei

**The Prawn Works Bar & Grill $$** *Huka Falls Rd; tel: (07) 374 8474; open only until 1700 most of the year.* Book ahead.

**Wairakei Resort $$** *SH1; tel: (07) 374 8021; www.wairakei.co.nz.* Spa pools and heated swimming pools.

# Suggested tour

**Total distance:** 305km.

**Time:** 5 hours' driving (excluding sightseeing).

**Links:** Manawatu (*see page 148*) lies immediately to the south.

A circuit that includes the area dominated by Lake Taupo starts at **Rotorua ❶** (*see pages 84–90*). You can go in either direction. Heading south on the SH5 you pass through Waiotapu, then the minute

**Above**
Waikato River trip

Golden Springs and then join the SH1 at **Wairakei ❷** before running into **Taupo ❸**, which is on the lake at the northeastern end. The SH1 then follows the lake shore to Wharewaka and Waitahanui before crossing a series of rivers which feed into the lake and ending up in **Turangi ❹**. This town marks the southern tip of the lake.

Coming up the other side of the lake on the SH41, join the SH32 to the east of the Hauhungaroa Range through the Pureora Forest Park. The SH32 goes through Whakamaru and then to **Tokoroa ❺**, which you can think of as the gateway to the Whakarewarewa Forest Park (*see page 88*). From there you drop back to Upper Atiamuri on the SH30 and then through Horohoro back to Rotorua.

## Also worth exploring

There are several back roads along the west side of Lake Taupo. These wander around to connect Acacia Bay and Kinloch before returning to join the SH32 in the Pureora Forest Park. These roads, which opened up a lot of the back country, were built when Sir Keith Holyoake was prime minister of New Zealand (1957 and again in 1960–72). It is, of course, purely coincidental that the Holyoake family holdings are centred on Kinloch.

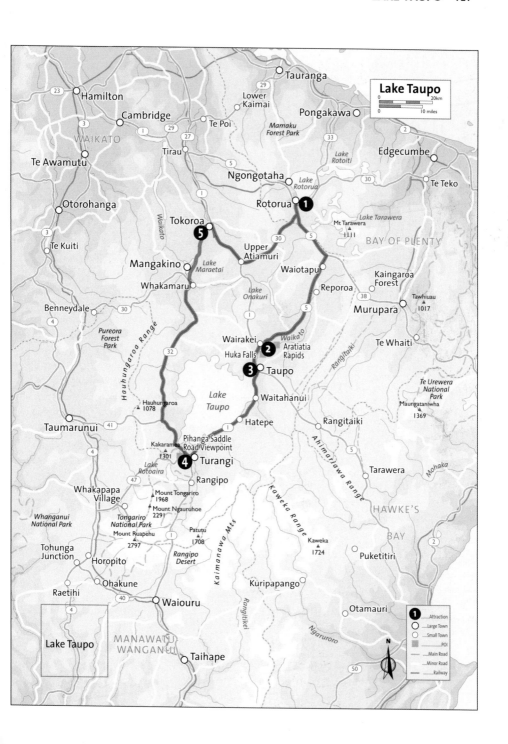

Lake Taupo

0        20km
0        10 miles

# Taranaki and Wanganui

## Ratings

| | |
|---|---|
| Mountains | ●●●●● |
| Scenery | ●●●● |
| Outdoor activities | ●●●● |
| Watersports | ●●● |
| Children | ●●● |
| Historic sights | ●● |
| Heritage | ● |
| Dining | ● |

The Taranaki area is almost the deserted corner of the North Island. What brings people there is the beauty and majesty of Mount Taranaki or, if you want to use the European name, Mount Egmont. But there is much more to the area than that. This clean and green region contains some of New Zealand's finest national parks. New Plymouth, the capital of Taranaki, is well worth a visit in its own right. The area's other major city, Wanganui, is one of the most picturesquely sited towns in New Zealand, and it gives you the Whanganui River as a bonus – a river that is worth an entire holiday of investigation in its own right.

## NEW PLYMOUTH

 **New Plymouth Information Centre** *Puke Ariki, 65 St Aubyn St; tel: (06) 759 6060; fax: (06) 759 6073; email: newplymouth@ i-site.org; www. newplymouthnz.com*

**Department of Conservation** *55A Rimu St; tel: (06) 759 0350.*

New Plymouth is a small but elegant town on the coast of Taranaki with a population of something under 50,000. It is on the junction of the SH3 and SH45 and is somewhat isolated as a city, but has a lively, prosperous, contented feel. The city lies on the northern side of the most beautiful mountain in New Zealand – Mount Taranaki, also known as Mount Egmont. The city is about 160km from Wanganui and has been the administrative capital of the New Plymouth district since 1989. It is at the centre of one of the biggest dairy regions in New Zealand, but it also has some petrochemical industry, based on oil and gas fields on land and offshore.

This area was much favoured by the Maori in pre-European times, but raids and local wars drove out many of the tribes, so that when the Europeans came the area was sparsely populated. The first European to settle in New Plymouth was Dickie Barrett, a colourful

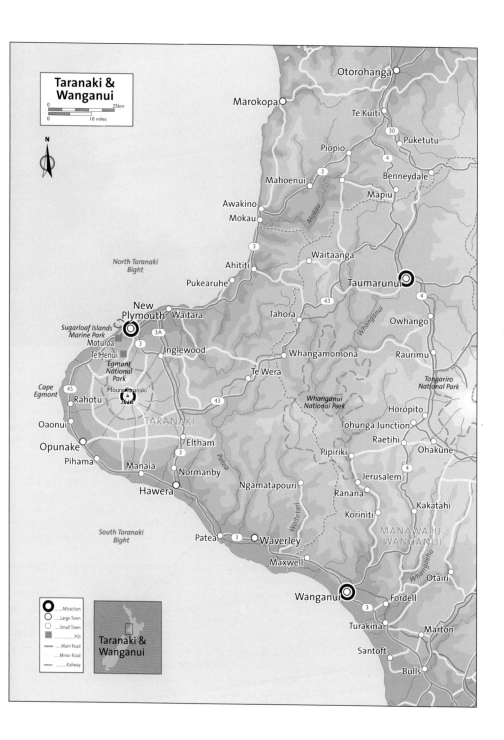

Taranaki &
Wanganui

0        25km
0    10 miles

N

Otorohanga

Marokopa

Te Kuiti

30

Puketutu

Piopio

4

Mahoenui

3

Benneydale

Mapiu

Awakino

Mokau

Waitaanga

Mokau

3

North Taranaki
Bight

Ahititi

Pukearuhe

Taumarunui

New
Plymouth    Waitara

Tahora

43

Owhango

4

Sugarloaf Islands
Marine Park

3A

Moturoa

3

Inglewood

Whangamomona

Raurimu

Te Henui

Egmont
National
Park

Te Wera

Tongariro
National Park

Cape
Egmont

45

Mount Taranaki
2518

43

Whanganui
National Park

Rahotu

TARANAKI

Horopito

Oaonui

Tohunga Junction

Eltham

Raetihi

Ohakune

Opunake

3

Pipiriki

4

Pihama

Manaia

Normanby

Jerusalem

Hawera

Ngamatapouri

Ranana

Kakatahi

Koriniti

MANAWATU-
WANGANUI

South Taranaki
Bight

Patea

Waverley

Maxwell

Otairi

Wanganui

Fordell

3

Attraction

Large Town

Small Town

POI

Main Road

Minor Road

Railway

Taranaki &
Wanganui

Turakina

Marton

Santoft

Bulls

**Above**
Taranaki (Mount Egmont),
viewed from New Plymouth

character who came in 1828 and married a local lady, Rawinia Waikaiua of the Ngati-te-Whiti. He also helped the locals to repel a Waikato invasion force.

The relationship between the Maori and the *pakeha* (Europeans) in the area was always troubled, and the colonists formed a militia in 1855. Misunderstandings and disagreements led to war in 1860. In that year New Plymouth became a military settlement and came under siege as the Taranaki campaigns got into their stride. It is difficult, at this distance, to rule on the single cause of the war, but it seems a Maori chief disputed a land sale, and the governor decided to proclaim martial law to drive the chief and his followers from their homeland. The war continued until 1881 when a formal peace was declared, so for more than ten years New Plymouth had a precarious existence as a military post.

The name New Plymouth was chosen for the province in 1853 but only five years later was changed to Taranaki. The history of the town can be read in some of the buildings. The oldest is the **Wesleyan Mission Girls School** at Moturoa. No one is quite sure when it was constructed, but it is very likely that it was built in 1869. That was shortly after oil was first found at Moturoa, at one end of Ngainotu Beach, in 1866. A small and very early oil field grew up here that produced petrol for more than a century, only closing in 1972.

You can argue as to which is the best municipal park in the country, but **Pukekura Park** (*Liardet Street*) is definitely a contender. It has been converted from wasteland into its current green loveliness mainly by volunteer labour. This process started in 1876. Two years later the dam was built to form the main lake. Poet's Bridge was built in 1884, the band rotunda in 1887, the Queen Victoria Diamond Jubilee fountain in 1897, the fernery in 1928 and the tea kiosk in 1931. Also within the park is a massive puriri tree, which is said to be over 2,000 years old. There is a splendid view from the tea kiosk of Taranaki, when it is not covered in clouds. The garden is floodlit on summer evenings.

Next to Pukekura is yet another green and pleasant area called **Brooklands Park**. This contains a natural amphitheatre seating over 16,000, with a lake in front of the stage to reflect the sound and the images. It was here, in the centre of the park, that the first resident magistrate, Captain Henry King, lived. You can still see what is left of his house – little more than the fireplace and chimney – from the original structure of 1843; the rest of it was burned down during the Maori Wars.

**The Gables** is the sole survivor of four colonial hospitals built by Governor George Grey between 1846 and 1848 with the aim of attracting the Maori people to make use of their medical facilities. It was originally sited on land now occupied by the New Plymouth Girls' High School. The idea did not work because in 1854 a chief died in the hospital from stab wounds, and the hospital was declared *tapu* (taboo). There may have been much sense in that decision, for the Gables was described as 'cold, draughty and inadequate' by no less a person than the first colonial surgeon.

Having failed as a hospital, it became a military command post during the Maori Wars, and later an old people's home. Early in the 20th century, it was purchased by local businessman Newton King and moved to its present location. In the 1930s, King's family gave the building, along with adjacent Brooklands Park, to New Plymouth. The Taranaki Society of Arts now uses it as a workshop and display premises (*open 1300–1600 at weekends and public holidays*).

The building of **St Mary's Church** started in 1842 and it was completed in September 1846, using rocks brought up from the beach. It is probably the oldest stone church in the country. Although it was originally a small building measuring 15m by 10m, it was solidly built and extensions were added between 1859 and 1861. During the Maori Land Wars of 1860–1 and 1863–6 the church was used in many different ways, including as a magazine. The original bell is still in use and hangs outside the church. Both the exterior and the interior are beautifully designed and the church contains the regimental colours of many of the European forces, as well as some Maori battalions.

At one time many of the buildings in New Plymouth boasted weatherboard cladding. This is now rare. One of the best remaining examples is the **Flight Family House** which is now used by New Plymouth Girls' High School as part of the school's art department. Until 1984 the building stood on Eliot Street but was then moved to its present position and most carefully restored. The house was built in

1868 by Josiah Flight who was, like the Lord High Everything Else in *The Mikado*, resident magistrate, collector of customs, provincial sub-treasurer, coroner, bank director and militia officer.

If you follow the Heritage Trail (a free Heritage Walkway brochure is available at the information centre, but it has a minuscule map so you will need a proper map of the town as well) you will come to the **Alpha Flour Mill** in Baines Terrace. This was the city's first mill and it was opened in February 1843 with millstones made from rocks taken from the beach. The Heritage Trail is a circular walk beginning at Pukeariki Landing, next to the Centre City Shopping Complex in Gill Street, and takes a leisurely two hours.

The first oil well in New Plymouth – and among the earliest in the world – was also named Alpha and it opened in 1865, primarily to produce gas. There is a **beam pump** at the end of Bayly Road, a relic of the Egmont Oil Well, which produced petrol from 1949–72.

The **Hen and Chickens** is a row of private homes, not open to the public, built as a group to accommodate the various branches of one family. Thomas and Grace Hirst started the row in 1864 by building a house for themselves called Willowfield. They added a further five houses for their son and four daughters. The houses are built to a basic plan but with individual variations. Hirst named the row York Terrace, but the nickname has stuck.

The excellent **Puke Ariki**, whose collection includes relics of the Polynesian migration, is a combined museum, library and visitor information centre for Taranaki.

Further out of town, **Te Henui** is a gentle signposted walk of about 3km starting at the Waiwaka Reserve and following the Te Henui stream through beautiful scenery. It passes the Pukewarangi *pa* site.

Some 29km from New Plymouth, on the Upper Carrington Road, is the world-famous **Pukeiti Rhododendron Trust**, set in the hills and consisting of 360ha of colourful rhododendron blooms – at their very best between September and November. Taranaki hosts an annual Rhododendron Festival in late October.

## West Country settlers

In 1841 the town was surveyed and settled by the Plymouth Company, a subsidiary of the New Zealand Company. The name is appropriate, as many of the new arrivals came from Devon and Cornwall, in the west of England. An obelisk in Pioneer Road overlooks the spot where, on 31 March 1841, the first Plymouth Company arrivals came ashore at Ngamotu Beach from the ship, *William Bryan*. The monument lists the pioneer ships. It is fascinating to note that when the monument was unveiled in 1911 no fewer than 43 of the original Plymouth Company immigrants were still alive to attend the ceremony.

**Above**
Maori heritage

The **Sugarloaf Islands Marine Park** is a protected marine area of some 8sq km, where you will see seals, dolphins and even humpback whales on their way to their breeding grounds. There are numerous species of bird, and over 70 different species of fish. The islands in the area are the remnants of an ancient volcano and were used in pre-European times as fortifications by and against marauding Maori tribes. The islands of Motomahanga, Moturoa, Mataroa, Paranaki and Motuotamatea were turned into forts with palisades, huts and water catchments. The best way to see them – you are not allowed to land on most – is on a cruise (try Chaddy's Charters and Sugar Loaf Café Cruise, which uses an old English lifeboat, *tel: (06) 758 9133; www.windward.co.nz*).

## Accommodation and food in New Plymouth

**Simply Read $** *81 Devon St West; tel: (06) 757 8667*. Café in a small bookshop.

**Arborio Restaurant $–$$** *St Aubyn St; tel: (06) 759 1241*. Situated within the Puke Ariki Museum and Library complex. A la carte dining with Italian influence.

**Amber Court Motel $$** *61 Eliot St; tel: (06) 758 0922; www. ambercourtmotel.co.nz*

**Flamingo Motel $$** *355 Devon St West; tel: (06) 758 8149 or 0508 352 646; www.flamingomotel.co.nz*

**André L'Escargot $$$** *37–41 Brougham St; tel: (06) 758 4812*. Very upmarket and very, very expensive French food. Licensed.

**The Nice Hotel $$$** *71 Brougham St; tel: (06) 758 6423; www. nicehotel.co.nz*. Boutique hotel well placed for the town centre with classy themed rooms and in-house restaurant.

# TARANAKI (MOUNT EGMONT)

**Mount Egmont or Taranaki?**

In 1986 the government ruled that both Mount Egmont and Taranaki may be used as equally valid names. As is very common throughout New Zealand, however, the Maori name of Taranaki is moving into favour as the name of choice.

Taranaki is one of the most beautiful mountains in the world. Certainly it is the most perfectly formed mountain in New Zealand. But, a confession: the author has never actually seen it clearly in its totality. Clouds and mist garland and hide the mountain, which only rarely reveals its beauty. Locals allegedly say that: 'When you can see Taranaki it is going to rain; when you can't see Taranaki it is raining already.' As this has been said of almost every mountain in the world it lacks originality but, in this case, has some considerable truth. The mountain is often in clouds, and, yes, it does frequently rain in the area. The vista is constantly changing, and you can well understand why the Maori imbued Taranaki with legend.

**Left**
Taranaki

**Right**
Walking in Egmont National Park

One story about the creation of Taranaki says that all the mountains of the North Island were originally gathered together in one place, and all of the mountains were male except for pretty Pihanga. As is always the way in these matters, the other mountains were constantly competing for Pihanga's attention. Eventually, two of them, Taranaki and Tongariro, had a punch-up which resulted in Taranaki being driven away towards the west coast – which is why Taranaki is where it is today.

Another, more prosaic, version says that Mount Taranaki is the youngest of three large volcanoes on the same fault line. It stands 2,518m high and, despite the fact that it has not erupted for some 350 years, is still considered dormant rather than extinct.

Captain Cook, sailing down the coast, sighted the peak in January 1770 and named it after the then Lord of the Admiralty, the Earl of Egmont. Cook noted that it is 'a very high mountain and in appearance is greatly resembling of the peak of Teneriffe' (sic).

The **Egmont National Park**, which is the second oldest national park in New Zealand, was created in 1900. It covers 33,534ha of land. The number of tracks across the park is quite remarkable, with 140km being available in total. If you are going to walk in the park, get the Department of Conservation booklet *Walks in the Egmont National Park* and the Egmont National Park Map (Infomap 273-09). If you are very fit and relatively experienced it is perfectly possible to climb to the summit of Taranaki and get back in one day. In winter you will need ice axes, crampons and ice-climbing experience. Even in summer the weather can be extremely changeable and it is important to check with the park rangers before setting off.

## The Taranaki Heritage Trail

One way of exploring the foothills of Mount Taranaki is to follow the Taranaki Heritage Trail. The trail is well signposted, with distinctive signs to direct you to each site and then, when you get there, more signs explaining exactly what you are looking at. The entire tour around the mountain is 238km, with more than half the route following the coast. Stopping and looking at each site along the way makes it into a full day's trip. The route can be taken in either direction and basically goes from New Plymouth to Inglewood, Stratford, Eltham, Hawera, Manaia, Opunake, Oakura and then back to New Plymouth.

# TAUMARUNUI

This small town sits astride the SH4, at the meeting of the Ongarue and Whanganui rivers. It is in the centre of what is known as King Country and is almost surrounded by national parks. To the northeast is the Hauhungaroa Range, which makes a barrier before Lake Taupo. To the southeast is Tongariro National Park and to the southwest is Whanganui National Park.

Taumarunui was one of the last places in the area to be settled by Europeans and indeed nothing much happened in the area until 1908. That was when the railway came to town. The railway was the North Island Main Trunk line, which linked Wellington to Auckland, a distance of 685km.

Although it was thought vital for the growth of the country, its completion was much delayed. Construction was held up because of the inhospitable terrain and because there were many Maori dissidents in King Country. Even to survey the line southward was immensely difficult and initially involved an armed force of Volunteer Engineer-Militia. The line entered King Country in 1885 and the two ends finally met near Makatote Viaduct near the middle of North Island, on 6 November 1908.

The biggest difficulty the railway faced was how to pull itself up on to the volcanic plateau, north of Mount Ruapehu. The engineer's answer was to make the line corkscrew up in the Raurimu Spiral, which comes up on a gradient of 1:50 and spirals through two tunnels which double the distance up the hill to just over 7km. This was a most extraordinary engineering feat and the experience of travelling the line is even more remarkable, as you glimpse the end of the train directly below the engine and proceeding in the opposite direction. Some 3km south of Taumarunui on SH4 is a **lookout** over the Raurimu Spiral. The visitor centre, downtown, has a model showing how it was constructed.

The town is now very quiet, with a population of only 5,500, but it serves as the entrance to the **Whanganui National Park**, noted for the Whanganui River, which comes charging down from Mount Tongariro via 239 rapids – enough to make canoeing a total excitement.

## Accommodation and food in Taumarunui

**Mohoe Motel $** *SH4, South Manunui; tel: (07) 895 8988; email: mohoe-motel@xtra.co.nz.* With licensed restaurant.

**Central Park Motor Inn $$** *Maata St; tel: (07) 895 7132 or 0800 283 030; www.central-park.co.nz.* Spa pools.

**Ruddies Place Café Restaurant $$** *Hakiaha St; tel: (07) 896 7442.*

**Zeebers Restaurant and Bar $$** *Cnr Hakiaha and Maata Sts, tel: (07) 895 7133.*

# WANGANUI

Wanganui is a town on the river called Whanganui. And no, that is not a spelling mistake. The river is spelled differently to the town. This was one of the most important early European settlements in New Zealand. And, indeed, it was one of the most prosperous. You can get a feel for this prosperity by viewing some of its mellow and elegant gardens. It became a city in 1924 and for a time was the largest provincial city in New Zealand. The peak year in its early history was probably 1926. After that its population declined and did not start to pick up steam again until after World War II. The city services a rich farming area and has a small port in the town of Castlecliff, at the mouth of the Whanganui River.

The river, which has played an important part in the development of the town, is the second longest in the North Island and runs for 290km. The river rises on Mount Ngauruhoe and drains some 7,380sq km. It is

**Above**
Wanganui town and
Whanganui River

**Above**
Victoria Avenue, Wanganui

fed by the Ongarue, Tangarakau and Ohura rivers. It is totally blocked to large ships because of a sandbar near Wanganui, but for small boats it is navigable for almost its entire length. For the Maori it was always an important means of communication. Forts – *pas* – were built almost all the way along the river bank.

Europeans started to arrive in the area in 1831, and among the arrivals was one Jim Rowe who is reputed to have traded mainly in preserved Maori heads. In a splendid piece of natural justice he later had his own head cut off and preserved by the Maori.

Originally the town was called Petre after Lord Petre, one of the directors of the New Zealand Company. But there were difficulties with the local Maori, who did not accept the terms of the land purchase, which was, to put it politely, somewhat dubious. On behalf of the New Zealand Company, Colonel William Wakefield gave the Maori some glasses, blankets, jew's harps, tobacco and a few trinkets. If you are willing to accept the colonel's very generous contemporary estimate, these were worth a total of £700. The Maori returned the compliment by presenting the colonel with 30 pigs and 10 tonnes of potatoes. Colonel William Wakefield insisted that he had accepted and paid for these gifts, and they had nothing to do with the land purchase which was, in his mind, £700 worth of tat in exchange for 16,000ha of land. This shoddy deal resulted in strife that lasted until 1848, when a new, and slightly more equitable, contract was eventually signed.

**Odorous name**

Some 38km to the southeast of Wanganui is the town of Marton. The original name of the area in which the town was sited was Tutaenui, the Maori word for dung heap. The townsfolk sensibly resolved in 1869 to change the name to Marton, which was the name of the English birthplace of Captain James Cook.

The best way to see Wanganui and the river estuary is to take the **Durie Hill elevator** (*open weekdays 0730–1800 and Sun 1000–1700*) on the other side of the Wanganui City Bridge. This was originally built in 1919 to provide a service for the residents of Durie Hill. There is a tunnel that goes into the hillside for about 200m. The tunnel is marked by a distinctively carved Maori gateway. From there an elevator rises 66m to the summit. If you feel energetic you can clamber up 176 steps to the top instead of taking the easy route. The **Memorial Tower** at the top of the hill (*open daily 0800–1800*) gives a fantastic view that takes in much of the north coast of the South Island, as well as Mount Taranaki and Mount Ruapehu.

Back in the centre of the city, Queen's Park is set out on a hill known to the Maori as Pukenamu and is the cultural centre of Wanganui. Nearby stands the Davies Public Library, with the Memorial Hall to one side, and the **Sarjeant Gallery** in front (*tel: (06) 349 0506; www.sarjeant.org.nz; open daily 1030–1630; public holidays 1300–1630*) which has a large collection of 19th- and 20th-century and contemporary art.

On the other side is **Wanganui Regional Museum** (*tel: (06) 349 1110; www.wanganui-museum. org.nz; open daily 1000–1630*). This museum opened in 1895 and was at one time the largest regional museum in the country, reflecting the importance of the town. It has a fine and intelligently displayed collection of Maori artefacts – probably the largest collection on permanent display in any New Zealand museum. Notable exhibits include the 23m war canoe, *Te Mata-o-Hoturoa*, dating from 1810, with bullets embedded in the hull. And, a splendid touch, the museum has ten articulated moa skeletons.

**Right**
Maori war canoe

Behind Queen's Park are the **Moutoa Gardens** where the first, infamous, and the second, more equitable, land agreements were signed. Originally this site was intended to be the market square. Local Maori insisted that the land was never included in either sale, and that it is still theirs. Interestingly, it is believed that the police have no power of arrest over Maori in the gardens. Perhaps that is why Moutoa Gardens were chosen as the scene of a major protest in 1995 by both Maori and *pakeha* over the way the then government intended to settle Maori claims. The peaceful occupation of the gardens lasted for four months. The matter was eventually settled in the High Court, but it did little to improve Maori–*pakeha* relations.

Near Queen's Park, on the west bank of the river, is a quay from which you can take trips up what the tourist board likes to call 'the

## Whanganui National Park

The major attraction of the Whanganui National Park is the Whanganui River, which snakes and weaves its way through some of the most picturesque scenery in New Zealand. Hire a canoe and explore this natural wonder or, alternatively, book a berth on the *Waimarie* and discover just why the Whanganui is the longest navigable river in the country.

For something more active, the trek along the Matemateaonga Walkway is highly recommended, though it takes four days to complete. The Mangapurua Track is equally impressive, runs for 40km and can be covered in three and a half days. A shorter walk is the 45-minute jaunt from the Mangapurua Landing to the Bridge to Nowhere.

Rhine of New Zealand'. The river is nothing like the Rhine, but it is very beautiful, and one of the best ways of exploring it is on the restored paddle steamers, the **Waimarie** or **MV Wairoa** (*tel: (06) 347 1863 or 0800 STEAMER; www.riverboats.co.nz*). The *Waimarie* was built in 1899, worked the river until 1952 and then sank before being recovered in 1993 and restored as a Millennium project. Likewise the MV *Wairoa* worked the river until 1955. It is said that the legendary explorer, Kupe, was the first to sail up the river in AD 950, though it was not until about 150 years later that the Maori began to settle in this area, when the river became an important route linking the coast to the interior.

The sporting centre of the city is **Cox Gardens** where Peter Snell set the world record for running a mile in 3 minutes 54.4 seconds in 1962. Above the gardens is a watchtower used by the Fire Brigade from 1800 onwards to keep an eye on the city. Now it houses the chimes for the town clock.

In Anaua Street, where the SH3 enters the city, is **Putiki Church**, also known as St Paul's Memorial Church, and one of the finest Maori churches in New Zealand. Built in 1937, the interior has some magnificent carving.

One of the town's finest gardens is **Virginia Lake** on St John Hill, 1.5km north of the city on the Great North Road. Settlers considered that the lake resembled Virginia Water, in Surrey, England.

### Accommodation and food in Wanganui

**Bushy Park Homestead $** *Rangitau East Rd, Kai Iwi, RD8; tel: (06) 342 9879; www.bushypark-homestead.co.nz.* Pleasant 1906 house set in 95ha.

**Rutland Arms $** *48–52 Ridgeway St (cnr Victoria St); tel: (06) 347 7677; www.rutland-arms.co.nz.* Large courtyard. Licensed.

**Anndion Lodge $–$$** *143 Anzac Pde; tel: (06) 343 3593; www. anndionlodge.co.nz.* Somewhere between a modern backpackers' lodge and a motel, and very well facilitated.

**Grand Hotel $$** *Cnr Hill and Guyton Sts; tel: (06) 345 0955; www.thegrandhotel.co.nz.* Heritage hotel and pub with in-house restaurant.

**Siena Motor Lodge $$** *355 Victoria Ave; tel: (06) 345 9009; www.siena.co.nz*

**Below**
Art Deco cinema in
Wanganui's Victoria Avenue

**Vega Restaurant $$** *49 Taupo Quay; tel: (06) 349 0078.* Converted warehouse overlooking the river.

# Hawke's Bay

## Ratings

| | |
|---|---|
| Scenery | ●●●● |
| Children | ●●●● |
| Vineyards | ●●●● |
| Outdoor activities | ●●● |
| Watersports | ●●● |
| Dining | ●●● |
| Museums | ●● |
| Heritage | ● |

This is one of the most attractive regions on the North Island, greatly appreciated by New Zealanders and lovers of Art Deco architecture. The Te Urewera National Park encompasses almost everything a visitor could ever want, from the staggeringly beautiful Lake Waikaremoana to a series of walks that range from a gentle half-hour ramble to serious three- and four-day hikes. Then there are the 30-odd major vineyards of the area, almost all of which welcome individual visitors. Finally there are the twin cities of Hastings and Napier (or the other way around if you prefer). Both flattened by a massive earthquake in 1931, they were rebuilt in a better and more elegant style. Both have friendly people, a close-to-perfect climate and tremendous charm, plus something else in the air that makes this a most pleasant area in which to spend some time.

## HASTINGS

ℹ️ **Hastings Visitor Information**
*Russell St North;*
*tel: (06) 873 5526; email:*
*hastings@i-site.org;*
*www.hastings.co.nz*

🎯 **Silver balls and red wine** One of the most popular sports in the area is petanque. Perhaps the reason for its popularity is that this is a wine growing area: petanque is the only sport you can play while still holding a wine glass.

Hastings is the sister city of Napier – and sometimes very much its rival. Together with Napier, Hastings has the fifth-largest urban population in New Zealand. It lies some 20km to the south of Napier on the Heretunga Plains in an area of very fertile country, with the result that the town is full of beautiful parks and gardens. In the 1931 earthquake the main street was totally destroyed and 93 people were killed. In Hastings this is known as the Hastings earthquake, definitely not as the Napier earthquake. As a result of the destruction, Hastings has (as does Napier) a fine collection of Art Deco and Californian-Spanish Mission-style buildings, erected after the earthquake. The visitor centre has full details of architectural trails.

The city is named after Warren Hastings, the first Governor-General of the East India Company. He was later tried for corruption in one of the scandals of the late 18th century. The early European history of the town may have had a touch of scandal about it as well. It started

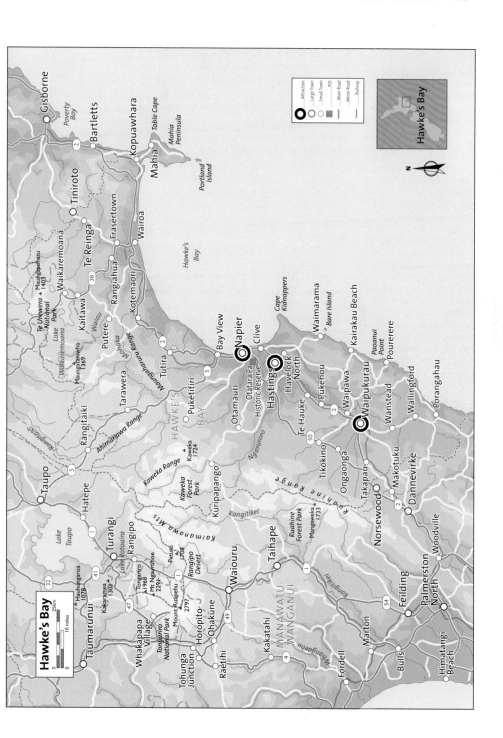

## Vineyard trails

There are many vineyards within easy reach of Hastings and Napier, mainly dotted around the southern end of the Ngaruroro River valley. Wine tours are run by **Grant Petherick Exclusive Wine Tours** (tel: (06) 876 7467; www.flyfishingwinetours.co.nz), **Bay Tours** (tel: (06) 845 2736; www.baytours.co.nz) or **On Yer Bike Winery Tours** (tel: (06) 879 8735; www.onyerbikehb.co.nz). To create your own tour (let someone else do the driving) you can get a free map from the Napier and Hastings visitor information centres. Every February, the Harvest Hawke's Bay Festival celebrates the latest wine crop.

in 1864 when a dozen settlers formed a syndicate, known as the Twelve Apostles. They purchased a large block of land called the Heretunga Block. One of the 12, Francis Hicks, later laid out the town. Fortunately he did not suggest that the town be named after him, or Hastings might have been Hicksville. It was later suggested that the purchase by the Twelve Apostles had been illegal. After investigation by a Royal Commission, the sale was confirmed, though reading about the original deal makes one wonder whether the legality was settled from the Maori or the *pakeha* point of view.

The Civic Square, at the centre of the town, is where you will find the **Hawke's Bay Exhibition Centre** (*on Eastbourne St; tel: (06) 876 2077*). This has a major collection of Maori works. For the children there is a splendid playground nearby called **Splash Planet** (*tel: (06) 873 8033*), a themed water park with a castle, a pirate ship and an elevated train. The playground is located within Windsor Park, which covers some 25ha and is accessed through Windsor Avenue.

Winemaking was introduced into the area by the Brothers of the Society of Mary, a French order of monks who introduced it in order to be able to make altar wines. That is the official story and it is, of course, totally accepted. Recalling those days is the **Mission Vineyard and Winery** at Greenmeadows (*Church Rd, Taradale; tel: (06) 845 9350; www.missionestate.co.nz; tours daily at 1030 and 1400*), the oldest winery in the country (although the building was moved to its present position at the end of the 19th century). The tours include tastings and cellar-door sales.

## Accommodation and food in Hastings

**Clearview Estate Winery $$** *Clifton Rd; tel: (06) 875 0150; www.clearviewestate.co.nz.* Lunches only. Classic cooking with great wines.

**Elmore Lodge Motel $$** *301 Omahu Rd; tel: (06) 876 8051; www.elmorelodgemotel.co.nz*

**Fairmont Motor Lodge $$** *1120 Karamu Rd North; tel: (06) 878 3850; www.fairmontmotorlodge.co.nz.* Double-sized spa baths.

**Peak House Restaurant $$** *Te Mata Peak Rd, Havelock North; tel: (06) 877 8663; www.peakhouse.co.nz.* On the slopes of Te Mata Peak, Havelock North, but be sure to book ahead and ask for a table by the window.

**Sileni Estate Vineyard $$** *2016 Maraekakahu Rd; tel: (06) 879 8768; www.sileni.co.nz.* One of the most architecturally stunning vineyards in the country, and a fine restaurant.

# NAPIER

**ⓘ Napier Visitor**
**Information**
**Centre** 100 Marine
Parade; tel: (06) 834 1911;
fax: (06) 835 7219;
email: info@VisitUs.co.nz;
www.VisitUs.co.nz

**Department of**
**Conservation Office**
Marine Parade;
tel: (06) 834 3111;
fax: (06) 834 4869; email:
napier-ao@doc.govt.nz

Napier has very much the appearance of a British seaside town of around, say, 1960. It has that distinct ambience, especially in the area of Marine Parade, the seafront boulevard that defines the town. You quite expect to see corpulent gentlemen with rolled-up trousers, braces and knotted handkerchiefs on their heads. The major difference between here and the UK is, of course, that Napier is almost invariably sunny, enjoying more than 2,350 hours of sun annually. This is marvellous for tourism and for the fruit growing and viticulture that are such a feature of this area.

The town was named after Sir Charles Napier, a 19th-century British military commander in India. Also adding some considerable style is the fact that, at the behest of the land commissioner of that time, many of the streets were given the names of literary figures. There can be little wrong with a city that names its streets after Shakespeare, Milton and Thackeray.

If you wish to explore the town's outstanding Art Deco architecture, your first stop should be the **Art Deco shop** (*163 Tennyson St; open daily 0900–1700; tel: (06) 835 0022; www.artdeconapier.com*), which is the headquarters of the Art Deco Trust. There is a daily **Art Deco walk**, of 90 minutes, at 1000, and an afternoon walk of 30 minutes at 1400. Perhaps better is to buy an inexpensive Art Deco walk map available from the visitor information centre. This allows you to design your own walk at your own pace.

**Right**
Art Deco buildings in Napier

**Bluff Hill Domain Lookout**

Overlooking Napier is Bluff Hill, a 3km-long feature of the landscape, which is also the name of a very highly desirable suburb. The Lookout here gives views along the coast in one direction as far as the Mahia Peninsula, and in the other to Cape Kidnappers. This was the name given by Captain Cook to the most prominent physical feature of the bay as he sailed by in 1769. The name came about when local Maori attempted to capture a young Tahitian from on board the *Endeavour*.

To understand Napier you first need to understand the earthquake of 3 February 1931, which brought total devastation to the town. One way of gaining a proper understanding of the earthquake is to visit the **Hawke's Bay Museum** (*9 Herschell St; tel: (06) 835 7781; www.hbmag.co.nz; open daily 1000–1800*). Here, two 20-minute videos show how it all happened and the terrible results (it is interesting to think that the videos last ten times longer than the actual earthquake itself). The museum also has an excellent gallery of Maori art, and tells extremely well the history of the Maori in the eastern North Island.

The heart of the city is **Marine Parade**, 2km long and bordered with Norfolk pines, which starts close to the museum, at the statue of *Pania of the Reef*, a legendary Maori siren, and continues past the open-air swimming pool to the port. Along Marine Parade you will find many attractions. First up, at the northern end heading south, is the **Ocean Spa Complex** (*tel: (06) 835 8553; open Mon–Sat 0600–2200, Sun 0800–2200*). It has hot pools, private spas, health and beauty therapies, and a café and gymnasium. Then there is **Marineland** (*tel: (06) 834 4027; www.marineland.co.nz; open daily 1000–1630, with dolphin shows at 1030 and 1400*). You may consider that dolphins kept in captivity for the entertainment of visitors is less than ideal, and prefer the fact that dolphins in the wild are available for inspection nearby, but the establishment also has Little Blue Penguins on show and plays a role in their conservation in the wild. You can take part in a feeding session for an extra charge. Finally there is the **Aquarium** (*tel: (06) 834 1404; www.nationalaquarium.co.nz; open daily*), a major oceanarium with seals, penguins, sea lions and dolphins. It even has divers hand-feeding the fish. If you are an experienced diver you can dive in and feed the sharks. And, yes, they do bite.

On the Springfield Road, 10km from the centre of Napier, is **Otatara Pa Historic Reserve** covering some 33ha, and with a lot of the original earthworks still visible. It has been the subject of a conservation programme that has included rebuilding the palisades and the ancestral figures which stand around the *pa*. It most vividly gives the impression of a fortified Maori village exactly as it was 100 years ago. After visiting it you will understand how very difficult they were to attack and how well suited they were to defence.

Just 40km to the north of Napier is the **Lake Tutira** bird refuge, sharing the same name as the district and the sheep station that once belonged to W H Guthrie-Smith, naturalist, author and founder of the refuge.

Still on the avian theme, there is a world-famous gannet colony 32km southeast of Napier, at **Cape Kidnappers**. The gannet here is the large white Australasian gannet (*Sula bassana serrator*), also known as the booby, which nests from November to February. The easiest way to visit the colony is to go by tractor-drawn trailer from Te Awanga, which takes you along the beach. After that there is a short climb and a walk to where the birds nest (*details from Gannet Beach*

Adventures; tel: 0800 426 638; www.gannets.com; or Gannet Safaris overland; tel: 0800 427 232; www.gannetsafaris.co.nz). The best time for viewing the gannets runs from some time in October to late April. Check at the visitor centre before you go to make sure the gannets are still there and have not gone walkabout.

Another, and slightly more energetic, way of viewing the birds is to walk along the beach from Clifton to the Cape. Along the way the strata in the cliff face reveal how the local landscape has been created over several hundreds of thousands of years. There are beds of sandstone, gravel, pumice and silt. One of the layers near Black Reef is called Maraetotara Sand and it contains over 100 different species of fossilised shells, including many extinct types.

## Accommodation and food in Napier

**Café Ujazi $–$$** *28 Tennyson St; tel: (06) 835 1490.* Arguably the best café in town.

**Edgewater Motor Lodge $$** *359 Marine Parade; tel: (06) 835 1148; www.edgewatermotel.co.nz*

**Fountain Court Motor Inn $$** *411 Hastings St; tel: (06) 835 7387; www.fountaincourt.co.nz*

**Sri Thai $$** *60 Bridge St, Ahuriri; tel: (06) 835 2299; from 1730 daily.* Licensed. Not authentic Thai – Moon Crispies was never a traditional Thai dish – but if you ask nicely they will create a proper Thai meal for you.

**Below**
Cape Kidnappers

**Thirsty Whale $$** *62 West Quay, Ahuriri; tel: (06) 835 8815.*

## The Hawke's Bay earthquake

The earthquake that devastated the Hawke's Bay area on 3 February 1931, measured 7.9 on the Richter scale, making it the biggest in New Zealand in recorded history. More than 600 aftershocks occurred in the following fortnight. The damage spread through Hastings and as far as Gisborne, but it was at Napier that the destruction was worst. Fire destroyed many of the buildings which had survived the initial earthquake and 258 people died in the Hawke's Bay area. All road and rail links were broken and the rescue work was hampered by the continuing tremors. It was the greatest natural disaster in New Zealand's history.

After the tragedy, Napier was built again almost from scratch. The old trams disappeared. Telephone wires went underground, where they belong. When the earthquake was over, the land around Napier was unbelievably more than 2m higher, and the sea had drained out of the Ahuriri lagoon. One beneficial result of the earthquake was the appearance of more than 40ha of new land, which was used for a new airport, among other things.

Architects redesigned the whole city. The style most of them used was Californian Art Deco in its many different forms. This may not be to everyone's taste, but it fits in with the climate and the location, and gives a feeling of that fantasy California that existed when the world was still innocent. Napier is only rivalled by Miami Beach for having the largest collection of Art Deco buildings in the world.

An appreciation of this unique art form within the city has, in truth, only surfaced in recent years. The Art Deco Trust was formed in 1986 and has been responsible for seeing that the buildings are maintained in the correct colours and without any unsightly additions. The town has begun to see what an attraction Art Deco is to visitors and now it is maintained in wonderfully good order. And, yes, before you ask, there is a McDeco McDonald's in Gloucester Street.

# WAIPUKURAU

**Visitor Information Centre** *Railway Esplanade; tel: (06) 858 6488; www.centralhawkesbay.com*

Waipukurau is 8km southwest of its sister town, Waipawa, and 50km southwest of Hastings. It is the larger of the twin towns. Both are farming centres founded in 1860 as private towns by two station owners. The two towns have always been rivals, and sometimes less than friendly ones. There was, for example, a major dispute over which town should have a telegraph office. Those disputes are now part of the past. The full name of the town means 'stream where the mushrooms grow' or possibly 'many floods'. It matters not. The locals do not even use the full name. They shorten it to the very ugly Waipuk.

You can see the town very clearly from Reservoir Hill (reached from Nelson Street off Reservoir Road), which used to have a major Maori *pa*. From this vantage point you can see how much the life of the town revolves around livestock. It is said that the sheep pens alone can hold a flock of 50,000. The time to see it in action is on Tuesday, which is sale day.

Just 35km south is a small township called **Porangahau**. It is about 3km from the sea, where there is a sandy exposed beach. This is not of the greatest interest to the traveller, but nearby is the range that is down in the record books as having the world's longest place name. A translation might be: 'The place where Tamatea, the man with the big knees, who sailed all around the land, played his nose flute to his loved one.' In this case, the loved one was his twin brother, who had been chopped down earlier in a nearby battle.

Is this name genuine? Fairly certainly it is, which is more than can be said for the Welsh entry that comes in at second place! Here it is in its full glory: **Taumatawhakatangihangakoauauotamateaturipukakapikimaungahoronukupolaiwhenuakkitanatahu.** A rather lengthy signpost can be found at the side of the road just south of Porangahau.

Waipawa is located 8km northeast of Waipukurau, on the northern bank of the Waipawa River, slightly to the northwest of where it joins with the Tukituki River. Waipawa became a county town in 1884 but is also now the administrative centre of Waipawa County, which includes

**Below**
Apple orchards in the Napier area

# Tongariro and Manawatu

## Ratings

| | |
|---|---|
| Scenery | ●●●●○ |
| Outdoor activities | ●●●○○ |
| Children | ●●●○○ |
| Watersports | ●●○○○ |
| Heritage | ●●○○○ |
| Dining | ●●○○○ |
| Historic sights | ●●○○○ |
| Museums | ●●○○○ |

The Manawatu River, which rises in the Ruahine Range, flows 160km through the Manawatu Gorge and across the plain into the Tasman Sea at Foxton Beach. The area from Palmerston North back to the Tararua and Ruahine ranges is full of scenic contrast. It has everything within a relatively small compass. There are volcanoes that have erupted in the last few years to warn people of their potential. There are areas of high scrub so desolate as to be like desert. In total contrast, there is also lush farming land. Palmerston North, the area's only city, is a university town with an appealing vibrancy. As a final and blessed bonus, between the Rangitikei area and Lake Taupo, there is the majesty of the Tongariro National Park, the first, and arguably the greatest, of the national parks of New Zealand.

## BULLS

 **Rangitikei Information Centre** *113 Bridge St; tel: (06) 322 0055; fax: (06) 322 0033; email: bullsinfo@rangitikei.com; www.rangitikei.com*

Bulls is a township 31km northwest of Palmerston North and 14km south of Marton. It is the oldest settlement in the northern Manawatu area and was originally known as Rangitikei. The town was founded by James Bull, who emigrated from England where he had been a woodcarver of some distinction (some of his work, for example, is in the House of Commons). He set up an inn and shop here in 1859 to serve the local farming population. The town was technically called Rangitikei, but the government accepted the reality and the name was officially changed to Bulls in 1872, which is what locals had called it from the start. It is often referred to as 'the only place in the world where you can get milk from Bulls'. The New Zealand sense of humour is perhaps subtly different from that of other nations.

The people of the town have taken up the idea of punning on the name with gusto – perhaps on the basis that nothing exceeds like

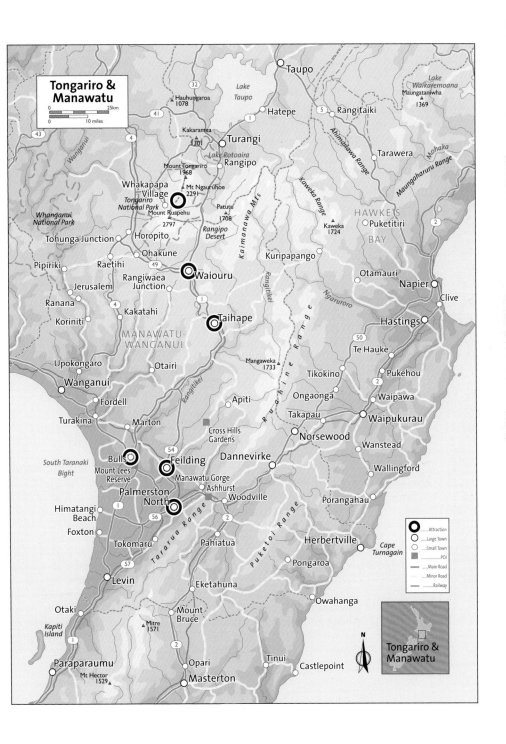

# Tongariro & Manawatu

0 _____ 25km

0 _____ 10 miles

Taupo

Lake Waikaremoana

Maungataniwha 1369

Lake Taupo

Hauhungaroa 1078

Hatepe

Rangitaiki

Ahimanawa Range

32

41

43

Wanganui

4

Kakaramea

1301

Turangi

Lake Rotoaira

Rangipo

Tarawera

Mohaka

Maungaharuru Range

Mount Tongariro 1968

Whakapapa Village

Tongariro National Park

Mt Ngauruhoe 2291

Mount Ruapehu 2797

Patutu 1708

Kaweka Range

HAWKES BAY

Kaweka 1724

Puketitiri

2

Whanganui National Park

Tohunga Junction

Horopito

Rangipo Desert

Kaimanawa Mts

Ohakune

Kuripapango

Pipiriki

Raetihi

Rangiwaea Junction

Waiouru

Rangitikei

Otamauri

Napier

Clive

Jerusalem

49

Ranana

4

Kakatahi

Koriniti

Taihape

Ngaruroro

Hastings

MANAWATU-WANGANUI

50

Te Hauke

Upokongaro

Otairi

Mangaweka 1733

Tikokino

Pukehou

Wanganui

Rangitikei

Apiti

Ongaonga

2

Waipawa

Fordell

Ruahine Range

Takapau

Waipukurau

Turakina

Marton

Cross Hills Gardens

Norsewood

Wanstead

Bulls

54

Feilding

Dannevirke

Wallingford

South Taranaki Bight

Mount Lees Reserve

Manawatu Gorge

Palmerston North

Ashhurst

Woodville

Porangahau

Himatangi Beach

1

56

Tararua Range

2

Herbertville

Cape Turnagain

Foxton

Tokomaru

Pahiatua

Puketoi Range

Pongaroa

57

Levin

Eketahuna

Owahanga

Otaki

Mount Bruce

Kapiti Island

Mitre 1571

1

2

Tinui

Castlepoint

N

Tongariro & Manawatu

Paraparaumu

Mt Hector 1529

Opari

Masterton

○ Attraction
○ Large Town
○ Small Town
■ POI
— Main Road
⋯ Minor Road
— Railway

excess. The cash machine (ATM) outside the bank has a sign telling us it is 'Cash-a-Bull'. The fire station has 'Extinguish-a-Bull'. The police station 'Const-a-Bull'. The visitor centre is 'Inform-a-Bull'. And so it goes on. This is one of the few towns in the world where you spend much of your time groaning at the puns.

The **Rangitikei River** passes the southern end of the town and is ideal for jet boating and for trout fishing (which here has an all-year-round season). The sea is only a quarter of an hour's drive away and the nearest beach is fine for swimming and surfing.

### Accommodation and food in Bulls

**Barrdroc Café and Petting Farm $** *115 Bridge St; tel: (06) 322 1594.* Has the added attraction of the petting farm.

**Bridge Motor Lodge $$** *2 Bridge St; tel: (06) 322 0894.*

# FEILDING

**Local hero**

Murray Ball (*see page 103*) was born in Feilding. Murray, the greatest cartoonist in New Zealand, is the creator of *Footrot Flats*, but perhaps more importantly to New Zealanders, he was also a rugby player who was almost selected for the All Blacks – and his dad did, in fact, wear the All Black jersey.

It is claimed that Feilding's design is based on that of Manchester in England. The main ground for the claim is the existence of two squares from which the main streets radiate. The reason for looking to Manchester as an inspiration is that Feilding was founded by the Emigrants and Colonists Aid Corporation, headed by the Duke of Manchester. The Corporation bought 43,000ha of uncleared land, known as the Manchester Block, for £75,000, and agreed to send 2,000 immigrants to the area over a five-year period. In return the government provided free passages and some guaranteed employment close to the town.

The block was selected by Lieutenant Colonel William Henry Adelbert Feilding, the son of the seventh Earl of Denbigh, who was one of the directors of the company. The first settlers arrived in 1874 and lived under very spartan conditions until they cleared the bush. The whole operation was intended to be a work of charity but, because it was run on very sound business lines, it actually returned a profit to its shareholders.

The town is now famous for its livestock sales, which take place every Friday in the yards which lie off Warwick Street and cover over 3ha. Outside the town are two quite splendid gardens. One is **Mount Lees Reserve** (*open daily*), which is 11km out of Feilding on the Ngaio Road, off the Mount Stewart Road. The other is **Cross Hills Gardens** (*Kimbolton; open Sep–Apr daily 1030–1700*), on the SH45, about 32km out of town. This is planted with an amazing range of rhododendrons and azaleas, which are at their best in October.

## Accommodation and food in Feilding

**Focal Point Cinema Coffee and Wine Bar** $–$$ *81 Manchester St; tel: (06) 323 0218.*

**Feilding Motel** $$ *7 Kimbolton Rd; tel: (06) 323 6837 or 0800 500 474.*

**Raceway Court Motel** $$ *Awahuri Rd; tel: (06) 323 7891; www. racewaycourtmotel.co.nz*

# PALMERSTON NORTH

**Palmerston North Visitor Centre** 52
*The Square; tel: (06) 350 1922; fax: (06) 350 1929; email: palmerstonnorth@i-site.org; www.manawatunz.co.nz*

**Department of Conservation** 717
*Tremaine Ave; tel: (06) 350 9700.*

Palmerston North is now the sixth-biggest city in New Zealand. The town was named after Lord Palmerston, UK Prime Minister when, in 1864, the British government bought a block of land from its Maori owners on which the town was laid out. In 1871, North was added to the name of the town to avoid confusion with another Palmerston, located midway between Dunedin and Oamaru in North Otago.

Palmerston North now services a large and fairly prosperous rural community but it is also home to New Zealand's second-largest university, Massey University, originally founded as an agricultural college in 1926 and raised to full university status in 1963. There are a number of educational and research establishments within Palmerston North and, as a result, it calls itself 'Knowledge City'. Apart from the university there is also Manawatu Polytechnic and the privately owned and run International Pacific College. Then there is the College of Education, specialising in training teachers.

As a result, a quarter of the residents in this city are aged between 15 and 24. In the summer months, December until March, most students leave town, which makes Palmerston North a somewhat dull city.

When the bush was originally cleared for the town, a 6.8ha square was set aside to be the commercial heart of the city. This farsighted action still has a powerful effect on the city. For a time the square was the site for the railway station, but in 1963 the railway was removed and the square returned to the original idea of a spacious garden shaded by trees. Now part of the square has been taken over by the **Civic Centre** but it still retains its charm. You can climb to the top of the Civic Centre to get a bird's-eye view of the whole of Palmerston North. Opposite is the visitor centre (*open daily 0900–1500*).

Within the square is a fountain created for the coronation of Edward VII – known wittily as Edward the Caresser – and a statue of the local chief, Te Awe Awe, who fought on the government side in the Land Wars.

The university, which is so important to the style and atmosphere of Palmerston North, was named after the Prime Minister William Ferguson Massey, who led the country from 1912 until his death in 1925. There is a good view of the campus from the **Munro Lookout**.

This is a memorial to C S Munro, who set up New Zealand's first Rugby football club and who therefore, in New Zealand terms, is a truly great person.

When you are in Palmerston North it is mandatory that you visit the **Rugby Museum** (*87 Cuba St; tel: (06) 358 6947; www.rugbymuseum.co.nz; open Mon–Sat 1000–1600, Sun afternoon only*). When you visit the rest of New Zealand and you mention that you have been to Palmerston North, you will immediately be asked if you went to the Rugby Museum. Of course you went to the Rugby Museum. Are you some insensitive clod who doesn't understand the finer things of life? It is that important. Pop into the museum if only for a few minutes just so that you can say you have been there. It contains a range of memorabilia of the game played in heaven. There are also videos of famous international games, which the All Blacks invariably win, normally with astronomical scores.

**Te Manawa Science Centre and Manawatu Museum** (*396 Main St; tel: (06) 355 5000; www.temanawa.co.nz; open daily 1000–1700*) was opened in 1994 and has brought together under one roof both the original museum and the science centre. Among the best parts of the museum are the Maori galleries. The museum also includes within its complex a house built by one of the first European settlers, a one-room schoolhouse dating from the start of the 20th century, a reconstruction of a local forge and a reconstruction of the city's first store. In the science centre are interactive exhibits, moving displays and an earthquake simulator – enough to keep children, and their parents, amused all day.

What used to be the **Manawatu Art Gallery**, now part of Te Manawa, is quite exceptional and was created, like so many of New Zealand's present public galleries, through the initial efforts of an enthusiastic arts society. In this case it was the now-defunct Manawatu Society of Arts which in 1956 decided to form an incorporated society to raise funds for a gallery. Works owned or on loan include some by James Nairn, Rita Angus, Frances Hodgkins, Edward Fristroin, Mina Arndt and T A McCormack, while more contemporary figures, like Colin McCahon, Toss Woollaston, Pat Hanly and Michael Smither, are represented in depth by major works and sizeable drawing collections. It is a most remarkable effort.

Palmerston North is a city made for strolling. The **Esplanade** is near the road to Shannon and forms a park that runs along the shore of the Manawatu River, with everything from a rose garden to a miniature railway. The **Riverside Walkway** runs through the Esplanade park for 10km up the river.

On the opposite, southern, bank of the river is the spacious and leafy **Massey University campus**. The campus is 3km south on the SH57 road to Shannon, and is well worth a visit just to see how pleasant a university can be when it is designed properly.

The **Manawatu Gorge** is some 16km out of town, on the road to Woodville. The road that passes through the gorge was built in 1871 and is an example of great construction skills exercised under arduous conditions. At times workmen hung from ropes from the clifftop in order to cut a way through.

Also of great allure is the small forest of wind turbines that straddle the Tararua range east of the city. These are part of the ever-growing **Tararua Wind Farm**. You can access them from Ashhurst, north on the SH3. Follow signs into the hills to a purpose-built viewpoint below a working turbine.

**Himatangi Beach** is 38km west of Palmerston North on the SH56 and extends for 10km. In the summer it is heavily used by the inhabitants of the city, but the rest of the time it is fairly deserted. In truth the sand is grey rather than golden, but this does not deter the hordes of summer holiday sun-worshippers.

Some 20km south of Palmerston North on Highway 57 is the **Tokomaru Steam Engine Museum** (*tel: (06) 329 8867; open daily*), which has a group of working steam engines, some of them over a century old. There is an occasional live steam day when a steam train runs on the lines – magic if you are an unabashed train enthusiast.

**Air Force experience**

The Ohakea Wing Museum, home of the now defunct New Zealand Air Force, is just 10 mins from Palmerston North on the SH1 (*tel: (06) 351 5020*).

## The railway comes to town

When the first clearing of land began in the 1860s, the main products of the Manawatu region were flax and timber. The production of flax in the low-lying basin that characterises the lower reaches of the Manawatu River continued until recent times. Timber was shipped downriver to Foxton and was later transported by a wooden tramway connecting the two townships. This was replaced in 1876 by a steam railway.

For a while there was a lively rivalry between the two towns of Foxton and Palmerston North for leadership of the area. This was settled when the railway from Wellington bypassed Foxton and, instead, came to Palmerston North. The result of that decision is that, while Palmerston North is still vibrant and expanding, Foxton has settled down as a quiet backwater.

## Accommodation and food in Palmerston North

Café Cuba $–$$ *236 Cuba St; tel: (06) 356 5750.* Good vibe.

Alpha Motor Inn $$ *Cnr Broadway and Victoria Aves; tel: (06) 357 1129; www.alphamotorinn.co.nz.* Central and quiet with a reasonable licensed restaurant.

Aubyn Court Motorlodge $$ *360 Ferguson St; tel: (06) 354 5757; www.aubyncourt.co.nz.* Near the university.

Déjeuner $$ *159 Broadway Ave; tel: (06) 952 5581.* Upmarket French restaurant, but with New Zealand wines.

Elm Café and Brasserie $$ *283 Fitzherbert St; tel: (06) 355 4418.* Away from the centre with good à la carte and Tuscan-style aesthetic.

Spostato $$ *213 Cuba St; tel: (06) 6952 3400.* Best Italian option.

Supreme Motor Lodge $$ *665 Pioneer Highway; tel: (06) 356 5265 or 0800 112 211; www.supremeaccom.co.nz.* Heated indoor swimming pool and gym.

# TAIHAPE

Taihape is first and foremost a railway town. It is set, however, in some stunningly beautiful countryside and has always been a magnet for landscape artists. The town is 33km southeast of Waiouru and lies along the Hautapu River, 11km above its confluence with the Rangitikei. Taihape was founded in 1894 as a coaching station on a track leading east to Hastings and was originally known as Otaihape, a Maori word meaning the 'abode of Tai the hunchback'. At the end of the Land Wars of 1881 it was at last possible to drive a railway right through the heart of North Island without meeting armed opposition. Settlers arrived here in 1894 simply because there was work available.

**Right**
View from the Whakapapa
Ski Field

**Rangitikei Information Centre** 90 Hautapu St; tel: (06) 388 0604; fax: (06) 388 1919; email: taihapeinfo@rangitikei. govt.nz; www.rangitikei.com

There is not much to see in Taihape itself. When a town calls itself the 'Gumboot Capital of New Zealand' it is plainly a little desperate. All its attractions are in the surrounding countryside. Adrenaline junkies (and spectators) should head for the **Gravity Canyon** complex 20km east of Taihape (*follow signposts 7km south of the town off SH1; tel: (06) 388 9109 or 0800 802 864; www. gravitycanyon.co.nz*). The company makes admirable use of the 82m Mokai Gorge and former Mokai Suspension Bridge, with several mind-bending, laundry-creating activities on offer, including the ubiquitous 'Bungy', the freefall 'Swing' and, at 1km, the longest 'Flying Fox' in the country. Need one say more?

## Accommodation in Taihape

**River Valley Lodge $** *Beside the Rangitikei River; tel: (06) 388 1444; www.rivervalley.co.nz.* Excellent range of accommodation and activities including rafting and horse trekking.

**Taihape Motel $** *Cnr Kuku and Robin Sts; tel: 0800 200 029; email: taihapemotels@paradise.net.nz*

**Aspen Court Motel $$** *Mataroa Rd; tel: (06) 388 1999; www.aspencourt.co.nz*

# TONGARIRO NATIONAL PARK

**The Visitor Centre** at Whakapapa Village has some splendid displays and information about the park. The centre is open every day (tel: (06) 892 3729; www.whakapapa.co.nz, www.doc.govt.nz).

**Mountain safety**

The weather in the park is extremely changeable all year round. If you are walking or camping, get the latest weather and track information before you leave and, where appropriate, register at the visitor centre.

In 1887, Te Heuheu Tukino IV, chief of the Tuwharetoa tribe, gave what was to become the Tongariro National Park to the people of New Zealand. It was a most amazing and munificent gesture and was the start of the growth of national parks in New Zealand.

The original size of the park was 2,600ha, although Tongariro now covers a total of 78,651ha. It has been declared a World Heritage Site by UNESCO and contains the peaks – sacred to the Maori – of Tongariro, Ngauruhoe and Ruapehu. It is an all-season park in that the Mount Ruapehu ski fields are a major attraction in winter, and the numerous trails and tracks are used by casual visitors and serious hikers in summer.

The park has more than enough walks to keep you happily occupied for several weeks. They range from a ten-minute saunter to a five-day tramp. Many of the walks start near **Whakapapa Village**. For those who are fit and seek a challenge, the three big one-day walks are the Tongariro Crossing, Ngauruhoe Summit and Ruapehu Crater. In the summertime these are within the grasp of most serious walkers. In the winter, the situation is totally different: they should not be attempted except by experienced mountaineers, properly equipped and preferably led by a guide.

The most famous walk in the park is the **Tongariro Crossing**, which runs for 17km, past ancient lava flows, an active crater and the beautiful **Emerald Lakes**. The walk can be done in something under

**Left**
Looking towards Mount Ngauruhoe

**Explosive reminder**

In 1996 Mount Ruapehu erupted as a reminder that New Zealand, and specifically the Tongariro National Park, is part of the Pacific Ring of Fire – a series of active volcanoes set around the Pacific Plate.

eight hours and there are several operators who will deliver you to the start and pick you up from the end. On a clear day, however, don't expect much solitude!

The climb to the summit of **Ngauruhoe** is a 16km return journey. It follows the same route as the Tongariro Crossing until you reach a saddle at the base of Ngauruhoe. Here you branch off to climb Ngauruhoe. The mountain looks somewhat like Mount Fuji in Japan. When you get to the summit, you have a splendid view of the still-active crater, which last erupted in 1975. You will, of course, need a full set of maps and advice from the park rangers before you set off.

You can join a guided walk to climb to **Mount Ruapehu's crater**. Organisers include Ruapehu Alpine Lifts; during the summer months they leave from the base of the Whakapapa Ski Field at around 0930 (*tel: (06) 892 3738*).

**Mount Tongariro**, at 1,968m, is the lowest of the three mountains within the park. It still has a number of craters, fumaroles, mud pools and hot springs on the northern slopes, warning that it could, at some unspecified time in the future, erupt.

# WAIOURU

Waiouru is the New Zealand Army's main training base. The town has always had the reputation of being cold, bleak and barren – the ideal place, indeed, for an army training camp. The chill, in anything but high summer, comes from the fact that the town is located at 813m above sea level (the town's railway station, at 814m, is the highest in the country). Surrounding the town are hundreds of square kilometres of largely uninhabited, relatively barren countryside, ideal for manoeuvres and training. This area has bitterly cold winters and dry, dusty, hot summers – a type of climate rarely found in New Zealand.

The town is on the edge of the Tongariro National Park and, despite the distinctive chill in the air, it is a most impressive place – not beautiful and lush, but handsome in a stark sort of way. Starting 10km north of the town, and running north towards Lake Taupo, is a section of the SH1 known as the **Desert Road**. It is not true desert, but a reasonable facsimile, for there is little rain, and the strong winds and loose sand and gravel means that there is very little plant life, apart from occasional tussocks.

The main reason for going to Waiouru is to see the splendid **Queen Elizabeth II Army Memorial Museum** (*tel: (07) 387 6911; open daily 0900–1630, and you can get a cup of tea and a snack on the premises*). Through a series of fine displays it gives a very real idea of army life over the years. There is an extensive range of military machinery exhibited with enough to satisfy the keenest enthusiast, including uniforms and dioramas of famous battlefields.

## Suggested tour

**Total distance:** 215km.

**Time:** 4 hours' driving (excluding sightseeing).

**Links:** Lake Taupo (*see page 112*) lies immediately to the north.

From **PALMERSTON NORTH** ❶, the SH3 goes close by **FEILDING** ❷ to **BULLS** ❸. Here the SH1 starts to follow the Rangitikei River up through Hunterville, Ohingaiti and Mangaweka to **TAIHAPE** ❹, and then through Hihitahi to **WAIOURU** ❺.

From Waiouru it is possible to make a circuit of the **TONGARIRO NATIONAL PARK** ❻, and to make some small side excursions into

**Below**
Mount Ngauruhoe from the air

# Wairarapa and Kapiti Coast

## Ratings

| | |
|---|---|
| Vineyards | ●●●●● |
| Scenery | ●●●●○ |
| Outdoor activities | ●●●○○ |
| Children | ●●●○○ |
| Watersports | ●●○○○ |
| Museums | ●●○○○ |
| Heritage | ●○○○○ |
| Dining | ●○○○○ |

Wairarapa residents consider the area to be one of the least-known, least-visited districts in New Zealand. That may well once have been true, but since the rise in the popularity of Martinborough wines the number of visitors coming here has increased tremendously. The area is also a relief valve for Wellington. City dwellers head up the SH1 in search of the Kapiti Coast, which has a special charm all of its own.

It used to be the case that the Wairarapa area came alive only once a year, in March, when the Golden Shears Shearing Competition – the Olympics of sheep shearing – was held in Masterton. Now it has become a year-round destination and facilities for tourists in the region are improving almost by the month.

## LEVIN

**ⓘ Horowhenua Visitor Centre** *SH1;* tel: *(06) 367 8440; fax: (06) 367 0558; email:* levin@naturecoast.co.nz; www.naturecoast.co.nz

Levin sits on the junction of the SH1 and the SH57, 57km southwest of Palmerston North and 95km north of Wellington. It was founded in 1889 and owes its origin to the construction of the Wellington to Palmerston North Railway. The fertile plain on which it stands was a major north–south highway for the Maori in pre-European times, and many major battles were fought for control of the area. This continued almost until the arrival of the Europeans.

The site of the new town was surveyed in 1888 and subdivisions sold from 1889. Originally named Tautoka, the name was changed to Levin in honour of William Hort Levin, one of the founder-directors of the Wellington–Manawatu Railway Company, to which the new town owed its existence.

The town (population 16,000) now has distinct signs of a split personality. On the one hand it is a horticultural centre, serving a market-gardening and dairy district. As you drive there you will pass

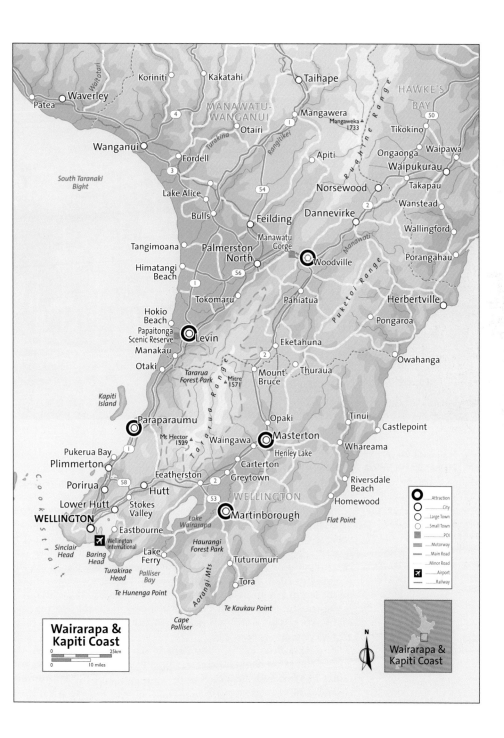

Koriniti  Kakatahi  Taihape

Waverley
Patea

MANAWATU-
WANGANUI
Otairi
Mangawera
Mangaweka ▲
1733

HAWKE'S
BAY
50

Tikokino

Wanganui
Fordell
Turakina
Rangitikei
Apiti
Ongaonga  Waipawa
Waipukurau
Takapau

South Taranaki
Bight
Lake Alice
54
Norsewood
Wanstead

Bulls  Feilding  Dannevirke
2
Wallingford

Tangimoana
Palmerston
North
Manawatu
Gorge
Manawatu
Woodville
Porangahau

Himatangi
Beach
56
1
Tokomaru  Pahiatua
Herbertville
Pongaroa

Hokio
Beach
Papaitonga
Scenic Reserve
Manakau
Levin
Eketahuna
Owahanga

Otaki
Tararua
Forest Park
Mitre
▲1571
Mount
Bruce
Thuraua

Kapiti
Island

Paraparaumu
Mt Hector ▲
1529
Waingawa
Opaki
Masterton
Tinui
Castlepoint
Whareama
Henley Lake

Pukerua Bay
Plimmerton
1
Carterton
Featherston
58
2
Greytown
Riversdale
Beach

Porirua
Hutt
WELLINGTON
Homewood

Lower Hutt
Stokes
Valley
53
Martinborough
Flat Point

WELLINGTON
Lake
Wairarapa
Eastbourne
Wellington
International
Haurangi
Forest Park

Sinclair
Head
Baring
Head
Lake
Ferry
Tuturumuri

Turakirae
Head
Palliser
Bay
Tora

Te Hunenga Point
Aorangi Mts
Te Kaukau Point

Cape
Palliser

Cook Strait

**Wairarapa &
Kapiti Coast**
0          25km
0      10 miles

O ....Attraction
O ....City
O ....Large Town
O ....Small Town
■ ....POI
....Motorway
....Main Road
....Minor Road
✈ ....Airport
....Railway

N

**Wairarapa &
Kapiti Coast**

dozens of roadside stalls selling fresh fruit, vegetables and wild flowers. On the other hand it is also a centre for clothing factories, and there are many factory shops in the town selling discount clothing.

Nearby is the **Tararua Forest Park**. This is generally a very rugged area and suitable only for experienced walkers. However, there are some short walks from Levin which give you a taste of the area. The nearest is perhaps the **Mount Thompson Track**, which will take you two to four hours and climbs one of the small peaks in the range. The walk begins 10km south of Levin just past the Pamatewaewae car park on the North Manukau Road, which is itself a turning off the SH1.

Within the town is **Lake Horowhenua**, a pleasant boating and picnic spot. There are two islands in the lake which have been artificially built to create a *pa*.

Some 8km from Levin is the **Papaitonga Scenic Reserve**, on the lake of the same name. There are also the softly sloping sands and dunes of **Waiterere Beach**. Nearby is the wreck of the sailing ship *Hydrabad*, blown ashore in 1878.

# MARTINBOROUGH

**Visitor Information Centre** Kitchener St; tel: (06) 306 5010; fax: (06) 306 8033; email: martinborough@i-site.org; www.wairarapanz.com

The layout of the centre of Martinborough is not like that of a normal New Zealand country town. The reason is that Sir John Martin designed it in the 1870s to show his loyalty to the Old Country. The central part is a representation of the Union Jack, with the streets radiating from the centre like bars on the flag. To add an exotic flavour, the streets were named after various places that Sir John had visited on his world tour. Thus you find in the middle of this small country town – population much less than 2,000 – streets with names like Venice, Dublin and New York.

You can trace all of this in the **Colonial Museum** on The Square, the dead centre, as it were, of the flag (*open weekends and daily during school holidays 1400–1600*). This 1894 building originally housed the town library and reopened as a museum in 1979.

Though a small town, Martinborough has lately come to glory. The reason is that Wairarapa has become well known as a wine-producing area. Indeed, it could be claimed that some of the best Sauvignon Blanc in the world is grown in some of the local vineyards – and about 20 of them are in the vicinity of Martinborough. With few exceptions the vineyards can be visited and offer cellar-door sales (but note that they all add an ominous warning – while stocks last; the inhabitants of Wellington know their wines and come to Martinborough on wine shopping expeditions).

Toast Martinborough Wine, Food and Music Festival is on the third Sunday in November each year (*tel: (06) 306 9183; www. toastmartinborough.co.nz*).

**Left**
Colonial architecture in Martinborough

## Vineyards in the Martinborough region

Note that there is an excellent guide to New Zealand wines on the internet on *www.nzwine.com*

**Alana Estate** *Puruatanga Rd; tel: (06) 306 9784; www.alana.co.nz*

**Ata Rangi Vineyard** *Puruatanga Rd; tel: (06) 306 9570; www.atarangi.co.nz*

**Canadoro Wines** *New York St; tel: (06) 306 8801.*

**The Claddagh Vineyard** *Puruatanga Rd; tel: (06) 306 9264; www.claddagh.co.nz.* Tastings by prior appointment.

**Dry River Wines** *Puruatanga Rd; tel: (06) 306 9388; www.dryriver.co.nz.* Visits by prior appointment.

**Gladstone Vineyard** *tel: (06) 379 8563; www.gladstone.co.nz.* About halfway between Martinborough and Masterton, this vineyard won the trophy for the best Sauvignon Blanc in New Zealand – and that is saying something – with its 1993 vintage. It positively encourages visits between September and June, 1100–1700.

**Above**
Martinborough vineyard

**Margrain Vineyard** *tel: (06) 306 9292; www.margrainvineyard.co.nz.* Café and excellent accommodation.

**Martinborough Vineyard** *Princess St; tel: (06) 306 9955; www.martinborough-vineyard.co.nz; open throughout the year 1100–1700.* Well known for Pinot Noir and Chardonnay.

**Muirlea Rise** *tel: (06) 306 9332.* Cellar-door sales Fri–Mon all year.

**Nga Waka** *tel: (06) 306 9832; www.ngawaka.co.nz; open weekends.*

**Palliser Estate** *Princess St; tel: (06) 306 9019; www.palliser.co.nz; open daily 1030–1600.*

**Te Kairanga Wines** *tel: (06) 306 9122; www.tkwine.co.nz; open daily 1100–1800.* Guided tours at weekends.

**Winslow Wines** *tel: (06) 306 9710; open daily 1000–1700 (weekends in winter).* Cellar sales.

## Accommodation and food in Martinborough

**The Old Winery Café $** *Margrain Estate, corner Ponatahi Rd and Huangarua Rd; tel: (06) 306 8333; open daily for lunch in summer, Fri and Sat dinner; winter Thu–Sun for lunch, Fri and Sat dinner.* One of the most popular.

**Pukemanu Tavern and Steak House $** *The Square; tel: (06) 306 9606; open Mon–Sat 1000 till late, Sun 1100.*

**Claremont Motel and Apartments $$** *8 Regent St; tel: (06) 306 9162; www.theclaremont.co.nz.* Massive garden with views.

**Peppers Martinborough Hotel $$** *The Square; tel: (06) 306 9350; www.peppers.co.nz.* Historic 1882 Martinborough Hotel offers character and sophistication. Elegant, luxurious, en-suite rooms.

**Est Winebar and Eatery $$$** *8 Memorial Square; tel: (06) 306 9665.*

# MASTERTON

**ⓘ Visitor Information Centre** *Cnr Bruce and Dixon Sts; tel: (06) 370 0900; fax: (06) 378 8451; email: info@wairarapanz.com; www.wairarapanz.com*

The Wairarapa coast is some of the most remote and rugged in the North Island. A drive to **Castlepoint** from Masterton or Cape Palliser from Martinborough is highly recommended. If you decide to stay in Castlepoint try the **Castlepoint Holiday Park and Motels $–$$** *(tel: (06) 372 6705; www.castlepoint.co.nz).*

Masterton came about as a result of a brave experiment to give the working class a chance. The first European explorers came here around 1841 and soon there were smallholders farming sheep along the coastline. These were effectively illegal holdings.

The New Zealand Company had no interest in small farmers. Indeed, it was only interested in amassing large properties that could be bought by people of wealth, breeding and discernment. That is, directors of the New Zealand Company and their friends and acquaintants. But in the Wairarapa the company's grand plan fell apart.

In this area the farmers, led by Joseph Masters – a man known for his aggressive approach to solving problems – got together and formed the Small Farms Association. The idea of the association was to make land available for sale in parcels small enough to be sold at prices that poorer migrants could afford. The association petitioned Governor Grey, who was sympathetic to the idea and helped carry the day. Two town sites were chosen; one was called Masterton in honour of Joseph Masters and the other Greytown, 23km further south, in honour of Governor George Grey.

Did this mean that the two towns then went forward in peaceful harmony? It does not happen like that in real life. The two towns were bitterly jealous of each other and the fight for pre-eminence was eventually settled when the railway came up the valley to Masterton and bypassed Greytown.

Masterton now has a population of something under 20,500 and serves a rural community of around 5,000. The district extends from the Tararua Range across a plain of rich farmland. There were some who dreamed that the town might become something much more

**Above**
Suspension bridge over the
Waiohine River, Tararua
Forest Park

significant. The Canterbury Christian Society, a subsection of the New
Zealand Company, considered establishing a church settlement in the
Wairarapa. Instead it chose a site on the South Island – which became
today's city of Christchurch.

It used to be said of Masterton that the town lay somnolent for
eleven months of the year, springing into life in March. Masterton is
where the international Golden Shears event was born and is held to
this day. It is the most important sheep-shearing event in the world.
Anyone who is even asked to compete in this event is already
considered one of the best shearers in the world.

Masterton continues to be electrified by the Golden Shears – until
you have seen a gun shearer strip a sheep without a cut or a ridge in
under a minute you cannot appreciate the skills and strength involved
– but there are now other attractions, albeit fairly low-key.

For children there is **Queen Elizabeth Park**, on Dixon St, with its
shaded gardens, small deer farm and boats to hire. There is even a
miniature railway running through the park that has both a steam and
a diesel engine. This operates throughout the summer, as well as at
weekends, on public holidays and school holidays (*1300–1600*). The
park was the site of the district's first vineyard, planted in 1878. The
**Aratoi Wairarapa Museum of Art and History** (*Bruce Street; tel: (06)
370 0001; www.aratoi.co.nz; open daily 1000–1630*) has art exhibitions
and historic collections. Alongside Aratoi is the new **Shear Discovery
National Shearing and Woolhandling Museum** (*tel: (06) 378 8008;
www.sheardiscovery.co.nz; open daily 1000–1600*). Created in two
relocated former woolsheds, it offers 'a fine round-up' of the shearing
and weaving process and showcases the champions of the prized
annual Golden Shears contests.

Worth looking at is **Victoria Street**, which contains a fine representation of the wooden domestic architecture of New Zealand of the late 1870s – for that is when No 30 was built – and of the early 1960s.

East of Masterton is the artificial **Henley Lake**, a pleasant spot with walking tracks around the lake and along the adjacent river.

Masterton is the nearest town to the **Tararua Forest Park**, which has a wide range of walks suitable for all levels. Most walks start at **Holdsworth**, where there is a ranger on duty. Note that weather conditions can change rapidly and you need to be properly equipped. The ranger will advise you, or you can get more information from the visitor information centre.

Some 30km north of Masterton is the **Pukaha National Wildlife Centre** (*tel: (06) 375 8004; email: info@mtbruce.org.nz; open daily 0900–1630*) at Mount Bruce, founded in 1962. This is home to a large collection of native and endangered bird species. It has an informative audiovisual programme and a series of aviaries. There is also a nocturnal house with kiwis, tuataras and lizards. You follow an excellent guide who takes you by a walkway past all of the sights of interest. It even has a printed twitcher's list so that you can tick off all the birds that you see. Of those, the takahe and the kokako are still in imminent danger of extinction.

## Accommodation and food in Masterton

**Café Cecille $** *in the heart of Queen Elizabeth Park (eastern end of Park Ave or from Memorial Dr, off Dixon St); tel: (06) 370 1166.* Lunch or dinner.

**Chanel Court Motel $** *14–16 Herbert St; tel: (06) 378 2877; www.chanelcourtmotel.co.nz*

**Café Strada $$** *232 Queen St; tel: (06) 378 8450.*

**Discovery Motor Lodge $$** *210 Chapel St; tel: (06) 378 7745 or 0800 188 515; email: info@discovery.co.nz.* Studio suites with considerable style.

**Hackneys @ Homebush $$** *10 Homebush Rd; tel: (06) 370 1909.* Old house with panelled dining room.

**Masterton Motor Lodge $$** *250 High St; tel: (06) 378 2585; www.masterton-motorlodge.co.nz.* Swimming pool, tennis courts, 4ha gardens.

# PARAPARAUMU

ℹ **Paraparaumu Information Centre** *Coastlands Pde; tel/fax: (04) 298 8195; www.naturecoast.co.nz*

Paraparaumu, about 45km from Wellington, is the biggest resort on the Kapiti Coast, and the centre of one of the fastest developing regions of New Zealand. The town and administration are on the main highway, where you will find the **Southward Car Museum** (*open daily 0900–1630*), considered to be the largest and most varied collection of its kind in the southern hemisphere.

**Kapiti Island**
You can book a day-
trip to Kapiti Island
through Kapiti Tours
(*tel: 0800 527 484;
www.kapititours.co.nz*) or
the Maori owned and
operated Kapiti Island
Alive Nature Heritage
Tours (*tel: (06) 362 6606;
www.kapitiislandalive.co.nz*).

Most visitors are more interested in the Paraparaumu Resort, 3km from the town, with its long safe beach, and a sea view that takes in the densely forested **Kapiti Island**. The island, with dramatic cliffs on the side away from the shore, was at one time a major Maori stronghold and later the site of seven whaling stations. It is about 2km wide and 10km long and was declared a nature reserve in 1897.

The Department of Conservation now allows day-trips but only for 50 people a day and only from Wednesday to Sunday (you need a permit from the Department of Conservation to visit the public land on the north end). From December to March your chances are less than good. Some days are booked up a year in advance. The rest of the year you will need to give at least a day's notice, preferably more.

Is it worth it? If you are a bird spotter, then this is avian heaven. There are three walks over and around the island and if you take your time and don't make loud noises and sudden movements you will see an immense variety of birds, many of them rare or threatened species.

## Accommodation in Paraparaumu

**Copperfield Seaside Motel $$** *7–13 Seaview Rd; tel: (04) 902 6414; www.seasidemotel.co.nz.* Two minutes from the beach.

**Ocean Motel $$** *42 Ocean Rd; tel: (04) 902 6424; www.oceanmotel.co.nz*

**Raumati Sands Resort $$** *4–8 Matatua Rd, Raumati Beach; tel: (04) 299 0155; www.raumatisands.co.nz.* A little out of town but worth the inconvenience.

# WOODVILLE

**Tararua Visitors
Information
Centre** *42 Vogel St;*
tel: *(06) 376 1023;*
fax: *(06) 376 1023; email:*
*info@tararua.com*

The town was originally known as The Junction and that is precisely what it is – the junction for the road and railway from Wellington. It is 28km east of Palmerston North and was once roughly at the centre of the Seventy Mile Bush. It became known as Woodville because of its situation in the dense heart of the forest. Now most of the bush has gone and the town remains as a service centre for the surrounding farming area.

Gottfried Lindauer, renowned for his portraits of 19th-century Maori, spent his later years in Woodville. His **headstone** can be seen in the cemetery.

The town park, in Ormond Street, has picnic tables, a playground, toilets and plenty of shade. For a more rural spot head out of Woodville towards Palmerston North. Just before the Manawatu Gorge, cross the bridge and drive a short distance along Ballance Road to find another quiet picnic area.

One of the best ways of exploring the **Manawatu Gorge** is on horseback. You get the fresh air, a great view and it is the horse that

**Right**
Jet boating, Manawatu Gorge

has to mind where it puts its feet. If you have not ridden before, try wearing tights under your jeans to protect your legs from chafing. That goes for men as well. **Timeless Horse Treks** in Pahiatua, Woodville (*tel: (06) 376 6157; www.timelesshorsetreks.co.nz*) operates through bush and river scenery.

## Accommodation and food in Woodville

**New Central Motor Inn and Hotel $** *63 Vogel St; tel: (06) 376 5282.* This is also a pub.

**Ormond Street Motel $** *45 Ormond St; tel: (06) 376 5638; www.ormondstmotel.co.nz.* Very quiet garden setting.

**Lindauer Restaurant $$** *50 Vogel St; tel: (06) 376 5440; open daily from 1100 till late.* Large, family-style restaurant. Licensed and BYO.

### Old and New St Paul's

Just a block away is **St Paul's Cathedral**, which was finished in 1998 and is not universally admired for its architecture. To see architecture at its best you need to visit **Old St Paul's**, one street down, which is built in wood and is one of the most beautiful churches in New Zealand. The church was consecrated on 6 June 1866. It served as the cathedral for the city until the new cathedral opened. At one stage the idea was to pull down this wonderful building, but government intervened. It first put a conservation order on the building and then restored it to its elegant original form. Now ecumenical, it is used for weddings, funerals and other services (*open Mon–Sat 1000–1700, closed Sun*).

### Te Papa Museum

In the heart of Wellington, on a superb waterfront site, stands **Te Papa Tongarewa**, opened in 1998 as the National Museum of Art, History and Maori Culture (*tel: (04) 381 7000; www.tepapa.govt.nz; open daily 1000–1800, late night Thu*). The museum incorporates the National Art Gallery which was originally set up in Wellington in 1936 as a direct lineal descendant of the New Zealand Academy of Fine Arts, established in 1889.

**Below**
Old St Paul's

⚫ Contrary to what you might expect, the nightlife of Wellington is excellent and an unbiased observer might conclude it is superior to that of Auckland. **Courtenay Place** is a good central focus, with bars, cafés, restaurants and clubs. The city has four professional theatre companies of a very high standard, the New Zealand Symphony Orchestra, the Wellington Sinfonia, the Wellington Opera Company and the Royal Ballet Company. There is something happening every night of the week, so check with the visitor centre, which can tell you what is available and arrange the tickets.

Te Papa – 'our place' in Maori – has state-of-the-art interactive displays bringing the history of the area, and the whole of New Zealand, to life. The top floor has an area devoted to Maori history, including a number of Maori buildings and a war canoe, and other exhibits charting New Zealand's history.

Two floors below, there are areas given over to New Zealand's great natural resources and wildlife. Among the hands-on interactive displays is one that allows you to experience varying degrees of seismic shock. The wildlife sections are dominated by reconstructions of a blue whale and the huge but extinct moa bird. An outdoor trail takes you past examples of New Zealand's native foliage.

The museum also hosts its fair share of temporary national and international exhibitions. One of the most popular it has ever staged was, not surprisingly, the *Lord of the Rings* exhibition in 2003.

### Penguin alert

The coast road out of Wellington continues past marinas and waterfront properties and on to a more exposed area of volcanic rock with the warning that penguins may be crossing. Many local residents proudly have penguins nesting under their houses.

# Miscellaneous sights

Located on Queen's Wharf, the **Museum of Wellington City & Sea** is housed in a restored bondhouse owned by the Harbour Board. It has a wide range of magnificent ship models, as well as figureheads and other mementoes. The **Cricket Museum** in Old Grandstand, Basin Reserve (*tel: (04) 385 6607; www.museumofwellington.co.nz; open daily 1000–1700 in summer and weekends 1030–1530 in winter*), beneath the old grandstand, is well worth a visit if you are serious about the game.

**Wellington Zoo** is at Manchester Street, Newtown, about 4km from the centre of the city (*tel: (04) 803 0777; open daily 0930–1700*). This began life in 1906 with a tame lion from a circus. Now it has a wide range, including native species. The zoo is trying hard to move to a more naturalistic display and is involved in several conservation and 'animal encounter' programmes.

There are several beaches within easy reach of the city centre. Perhaps the most attractive is **Days Beach** on the east side of the harbour, backed by Williams Park, a native bush area. You can get there by sea after a pleasant 20-minute ride on the *Dominion Post* East by West Ferry from Queen's Wharf.

# Marlborough

**Ratings**

| | |
|---|---|
| Scenery | ●●●●● |
| Dining | ●●●●○ |
| Watersports | ●●●●○ |
| Children | ●●●●○ |
| Outdoor activities | ●●●○○ |
| Vineyards | ●●●○○ |
| Museums | ●●○○○ |
| Heritage | ●○○○○ |

The northern end of the South Island is one of the most pleasant spots on Earth. It has a little of everything, and all of it is of the best of its kind. Nelson, the area's main city, is one of the sunniest spots in New Zealand and is also well designed and full of parks. Blenheim, the other major town, is at the centre of the greatest vine-growing area of New Zealand. From the ferry landing at Picton you can get along the Queen Charlotte and Marlborough Sounds, two of the great scenic areas of New Zealand. Across to the far side, towards the west, is the Abel Tasman Park, and beyond that the wonders of the Kahurangi National Park, the Wakamarama Range and Farewell Spit. All of this is within a reasonably sized area that is easy to explore, easy to navigate, and full of joys and splendid surprises.

## ABEL TASMAN NATIONAL PARK

ℹ The gateway to the park is Motueka, and you can get more information from the **Department of Conservation** Cnr King Edward and High Sts, Motueka; tel: (03) 528 1810; fax: (03) 528 8111; email: MotuekaAO@doc.govt.nz

The park covers an area of 22,350ha, and is a very popular destination in the height of summer, attracting large crowds of day visitors. Visually, the park enjoys the contrasting colours of golden beaches, blue water and green bush and forest; it is full of wildlife. The area was proclaimed a National Park in 1942. Within the park there are many huts for campers but there are also camping grounds just outside the park at both Marahau and Totaranui. There is a popular 51km coastal walk around the park which is one of the Great Walks of New Zealand, and a more strenuous inland walk. You can get more information about the walks, and the huts available, at the Department of Conservation and the information centres. The full tramps are seriously long walks, but there are many others which take anything from one to three hours. Several guided tours can also be arranged, either by boat, walking or kayaking (*tel: (03) 528 2027 for details*).

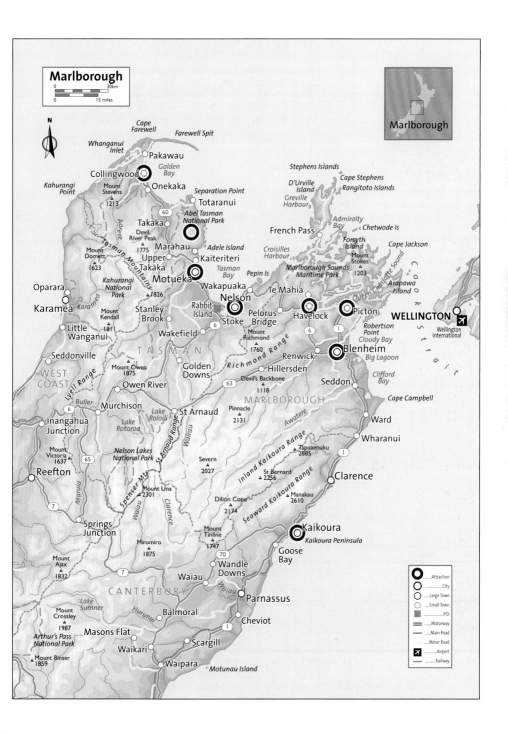

# Marlborough

0 ___ 30km
0 ___ 15 miles

N

Marlborough

Cape Farewell
Farewell Spit
Whanganui Inlet
Pakawau
Golden Bay
Collingwood
Kahurangi Point
Mount Stevens
1213
Onekaka
Separation Point
Stephens Islands
Cape Stephens
D'Urville Island
Rangitoto Islands
Greville Harbour
Totaranui
60
Abel Tasman National Park
Takaka
Devil River Peak
1775
Marahau
Adele Island
French Pass
Admiralty Bay
Chetwode Is
Forsyth Island
Cape Jackson
Mount Domett
1623
Upper Takaka
Kaiteriteri
Croisilles Harbour
Pepin Is
Mount Stokes
1203
Kahurangi National Park
1826
Motueka
Wakapuaka
Tasman Bay
Marlborough Sounds Maritime Park
Arapawa Island
Oparara
Karamea
Karamea
Stanley Brook
Rabbit Island
Nelson
Te Mahia
Havelock
Picton
WELLINGTON
Mount Kendall
1811
6
Stoke
Pelorus Bridge
6
Robertson Point
Cloudy Bay
Wellington International
Little Wanganui
Wakefield
Mount Richmond
1760
Renwick
1
Blenheim
Big Lagoon
Seddonville
Mount Owen
1875
Golden Downs
Richmond Range
Hillersden
Clifford Bay
WEST COAST
Lyell Range
Owen River
63
Devil's Backbone
1118
Seddon
Cape Campbell
Buller
6
Murchison
Lake Rotoiti
St Arnaud
Pinnacle
2131
MARLBOROUGH
Awatere
Ward
Inangahua Junction
Lake Rotoroa
Wairau
Wharanui
Mount Victoria
1637
65
Nelson Lakes National Park
St Arnaud Range
Severn
2027
Inland Kaikoura Range
Tapuaenuku
2885
1
Reefton
Maruia
Spenser Mts
Clarence
Mount Una
2301
St Bernard
2256
Seaward Kaikoura Range
Clarence
Springs Junction
Dillon Cone
2174
Manakau
2610
7
Miromiro
1875
Mount Tinline
1747
Kaikoura
Kaikoura Peninsula
Mount Ajax
1832
70
7
Wandle Downs
Goose Bay
Waiau
Parnassus
CANTERBURY
Waiau
Lake Sumner
Mount Crossley
1987
Hurunui
Balmoral
Cheviot
1
Arthur's Pass National Park
Masons Flat
Waikari
Scargill
Mount Binser
1859
Waipara
Motunau Island

Attraction
City
Large Town
Small Town
POI
Motorway
Main Road
Minor Road
Airport
Railway

## Accommodation and food in Abel Tasman National Park

**Abel Tasman Marahau Lodge $$** *Marahau Beach Rd, Marahau; tel: (03) 527 8250; fax: (03) 527 8258; email:robyndon@abeltasmanmarahaulodge. co.nz*

**Ocean View Chalets $$** *Marahau Beach Rd, Marahau; tel: (03) 527 8232; fax: (03) 527 8211; email: info@accommodationabeltasman.co.nz*

# BLENHEIM

**ⓘ Visitor Information**
*Railway Station, Sinclair St; tel: (03) 577 8080; fax: (03) 577 8079; email: blenheim@ i-site.org; www. destinationmarlborough.com*

**Below**
The wide-open spaces of the Abel Tasman National Park

The largest town in the Marlborough region is built on sunshine and good soil, which results in excellent wine. History suggests that the entire plain of 26,500ha was bought from the local Maori around 1830 by Captain John Blenkinsopp, a whaling captain. His widow sold the deeds on to the New Zealand Company in 1839. In fact, all that the Captain had arranged was the right to get water and wood from Cloudy Bay, for which rights he handed over a ship's cannon. The deeds he drew up were parsimonious with the truth, but the local Maori chiefs – Blenkinsopp was married to one of their daughters – did not read English and stamped the deed. He sold it on to a solicitor in Sydney for £200 while his widow sold a copy to Colonel William Wakefield of the New Zealand Company for £200. Inevitably the Maori found out how they had been duped and tore up their copy of the deed.

## Terminology

The word 'tramp' refers, in New Zealand, not to a person of dubious virtue, nor to a homeless wanderer; it is rather the term used to mean a serious hike (as opposed to a casual walk that needs no special planning) – a useful addition to the vocabulary.

The settlers disregarded all of this and started surveying the land. In a demonstration of great restraint the local Maori took the pegs, strings, huts and other paraphernalia and destroyed them. The settlers decided to arrest the chiefs. There was a confrontation and 22 Europeans and 6 Maori were killed in what was known as the Wairau Affray. After that, no decisive action was taken on either side, but Governor Grey decided to renegotiate and paid the Maori £3,000 for a largish block of land in 1847.

The first building was almost certainly a combined pub and store. It was 'the resort of all the disorderly characters'. As always, what triggered a major influx to the area was the discovery of gold in 1864. Blenheim was named after the Battle of Blenheim of 1704, in which the Duke of Marlborough had defeated the French. In truth it was not a great battle but it was made much of in England.

Blenheim now has a population of around 25,000. Set on the Wairau Plains, it was very much a sheep farming area in its original incarnation. Now it is, above all else, a wine capital. Visitors should avoid getting into an argument over whether the wineries that surround Blenheim produce the best wine in New Zealand. Feelings get hurt. Tempers are roused. If you are prepared to state that Blenheim produces some of the best white wines in the world, then everyone will be satisfied.

The first vines were planted here in the 1970s when someone realised that the high annual rate of sunshine, the long summers and the low autumn rainfall would permit the growing of excellent grapes. Nowadays many of the grapes produced in this area find their way to North Island wineries to be blended with other grapes to make a given vintage. This is a fact not widely publicised.

The town itself is not a major attraction but it contains several pleasant gardens, giving Blenheim room to breathe. In the centre is **Seymour Square** with a spectacular fountain and extensive gardens. It also contains what is claimed to be **Blenkinsopp's cannon**, with which he purchased the Wairau.

On the other side of the Taylor River, over a footbridge, is **Pollard Park**. This covers an area around the spring-fed Fulton Creek and has a duck pond. Both of them are beautifully cared for and full of elegant flower arrangements and native plants.

The **Brayshaw Historic Museum Park** is 2km east of the centre of town and shows old farming equipment – more than you would believe – and relocated colonial buildings which re-create a late 19th-century streetscape. It also contains the Marlborough Historical Society's Museum and Archives collection. Five kilometres to the south of town, on the SH1, is the **Riverlands Cob Cottage**, a mud-walled and shingle-roofed pioneer house dating from the 1860s, furnished in the style of the period.

Just outside Blenheim is the **Wither Hills Walkway**. This network of paths allows you to view the whole of Blenheim and the Wairau

# Blenheim's world of wine

There are over 40 wineries in the Blenheim area, ranging from the biggest producers in New Zealand to very small vineyards. The size of the vineyard is no indication of the quality of the wine. You can get all the information you need from the information centre on the High Street: it has details of wine tours and a copy of *The Wines and Wineries of Marlborough*, which allows you to set up your own itinerary. Bear in mind that whoever does the driving cannot taste the wine. That is an inviolable rule.

Most of the major wineries are between Blenheim and Renwick. The area is famous for its Sauvignon Blanc, but also for its Chardonnay. As a complement to the wine there is now a movement to provide a wide variety of gourmet food. All of this comes together in the Marlborough Wine and Food Festival, which is held in early February every year.

Many people try to visit the vineyards as if it were some sort of collection race, with a prize for visiting the most. This is not the way to do it. If you get to three or four in a day, that is about enough – especially if you are sampling the wines as you go.

You may be tempted to join an organised winery tour to give the driver a break and let him or her taste the wine. In fact, it is a less than felicitous idea. You will find that organised tours move rapidly from vineyard to vineyard without allowing time for that serene contemplation that is so essential to the enjoyment of good wine. Also, the wineries view a busload of happy sampling – but not buying – tourists with something rather less than total enthusiasm, and may therefore not give of their best. Vineyards are much more welcoming towards two or three visitors who appear to be serious seekers after truth and beauty. Below are details of some of the wineries that welcome visitors of the right sort.

**Allan Scott Wines** *Jackson Rd; tel: (03) 572 9054; www.allanscott.com. Open daily 0900–1700.* Has the excellent Twelve Trees Vineyard restaurant on the premises (*tel: (03) 572 7123 for reservations*).

**Cloudy Bay** *Jackson's Rd; tel: (03) 520 9140; www.cloudybay.co.nz. Open daily 1000–1600.* The Sauvignon Blanc and the Chardonnay produced by this vineyard have been called two of the greatest white wines to come out of New Zealand, and possibly two of the greatest white wines in the world. Equally, there has been a consistent campaign to suggest this is not so. Nailing colours to the mast, the author will say that Cloudy Bay Sauvignon Blanc is the greatest white wine in the world, no risk and no argument. Try it for yourself and see if you agree. The Cloudy Bay bubbly, 'Pelorus', is also absolutely delicious.

**Framingham Wine Co** *Conders Bend Rd, Renwick; tel: (03) 572 8884; www.framingham.co.nz.* Prize-winning Riesling and a beautiful rose garden.

**Fromm Estate** *Godfrey Rd; tel: (03) 572 9355; www.frommwinery.co.nz. Open daily Oct–Apr 1100–1700; May–Sep 1100–1600.* Quality range of varieties, from Pinot to Riesling.

**Highfield Wineries** *Brookby Rd; tel: (03) 572 9244; www.highfield.co.nz. Open daily 1030–1700.* Looks like a vineyard in Tuscany with its tower. Offers tastings with *tapas*, for which you pay, but this is the best way to do it (*tel: (03) 572 8592 for restaurant reservations*).

**Hunter's** *Rapaura Rd; tel: (03) 572 8489; www.hunters.co.nz. Open weekdays 0930–1630, Sun 1130–1530.* Broad range of wines, including the outstandingly popular Sauvignon Blanc, but here you pay a nominal fee for tastings. The restaurant, of a high international standard, is open for both lunch and dinner (*tel: (03) 572 8803*).

**Johannesdorf Cellars** *Koromiko; tel: (03) 573 7035.* Underground cellars, free tastings and cellar-door sales.

**Montana Brancott Winery** *Marlborough, on the SH1, 5km south of Blenheim; tel: (03) 578 2099; www.montana.co.nz. Open daily 1000–1630.* The Big Cheese of local winemakers. One of the oldest – originally established in 1924 near Auckland – certainly the largest, supplying about 40 per cent of the country's wine, and totally commercial, but still producing some lesser-known great wines which you can try here.

**Ponder Estate** *New Renwick Rd; tel: (03) 572 8642. Open Oct–May only, Mon–Sat 1100–1700.* Does olive oil as well as wines, including its award-winning Pinot Noir.

**Seresin Estate** *Bedford Rd, Renwick; tel: (03) 572 9408; www.seresin.co.nz. Open daily in summer 1000–1630, winter by appointment only.* A strong body of opinion has it that the Sauvignon Blanc and Chardonnay produced here are the definitive wines of the area.

**Stoneleigh** *Main Rd South; tel: 0800 503 000; www.stoneleigh.co.nz.* Very distinctive and individual wines.

**Wairau River Wines** *Cnr SH6 and Rapaura Rd; tel: (03) 572 7950; www.wairauriverwines.com. Open daily 1000–1700.* Free tastings, good lunches.

**Below**
The Allan Scott Winery

Valley. At one time this was a fairly barren area but it has been replanted and is now a most elegant nature reserve with groups of short well-signposted walks. You could probably do a complete circuit of the park in something less than three hours. The entrance to the walkway is off Taylor Pass Road, about 7km from the town centre.

The Richmond Range of mountains is around 26km southwest of Blenheim, and the Department of Conservation has some excellent leaflets showing the facilities and the walks in the area. You can get these leaflets at the visitor information centre. The peak of the Richmond Range is **Mount Richmond**, which is 1,760m high. It is not a tough climb to the top and many people do it as a day-trip from Blenheim. There are several ways to get to the summit including the Top Valley route, which is only 7.5km.

## Accommodation and food in Blenheim

Some of the best food is, of course, served at the vineyards listed on pages 188–9.

**Raupo Riverside Café $–$$** *2 Symons St; tel: (03) 577 8822; open daily 0700–1900.*

**Aorangi Manor $$** *193 High St; tel: (03) 578 2022; fax: (03) 578 2021; email: relax@193aorangimanor.co.nz; www.193aorangimanor.co.nz*

**Colonial Motel $$** *66 Main St; tel: (03) 578 9284; fax: (03) 578 2233.*

**Below**
Marlborough wine country

**D'Urville Wine Bar & Brasserie $$** *52 Queen St; tel: (03) 577 9945; open daily for breakfast and dinner, Mon–Fri for lunch.* Fresh local

produce, great selection of local wines. Also has classy accommodation.

**Phoenix Motor Inn** $$ *174 Middle Renwick Rd; tel: (03) 577 9002; www.phoenixmotorinn.co.nz*

# COLLINGWOOD

**Visitor Information Centre** *Golden Bay VIC, Willow St, Takaka; tel: (03) 525 9136; www.nelsonnz.com*

**Golden Bay** marks the start of the **Heaphy Track**, which goes through the Kahurangi National Park for 77km to Kohaihai Bluff. This is one of the Great Walks of New Zealand.

Collingwood's early growth is not unrelated to the discovery of gold in the area in 1843 – though this petered out in 1859, when the town's population dropped from 2,000 to a few dozen. The find was enough reason to rename the sea in front of the town the Golden Bay. At the time of this small gold rush there was even talk of making the town the new national capital. Originally it was called Gibbstown after the first settler in the district, but with aspirations of grandeur the name was changed to Collingwood, after Nelson's second in command at the Battle of Trafalgar.

Outside the town is **Farewell Spit**, which extends to the east of Cape Farewell for 24km. The Cape and the Spit were named by Captain Cook as he left for Australia at the end of his first visit in March 1770. The Spit can be visited only by means of a conducted tour, which is well worth doing, especially if you are a bird lover. Book with the Farewell Spit Tours (*tel: 0800 808 257; www.farewellspit.com*).

Measuring about 500m at its widest, the Spit consists of some of the largest sand dunes in the world, reaching up to 25m in height. The Spit is a wildlife refuge for the protection of birds, specifically the bar-tailed godwits and other migratory species that spend the summer here before moving on to Siberia and Alaska.

All of this lies within the **Kahurangi National Park** which was designated in 1996 and covers some 456,000ha and a range of landforms. It includes the western side of the Wakamarama Range, the side away from Collingwood and Farewell Spit. More than half of New Zealand's plant species can be found here, 67 of which exist nowhere else in the country. Over 100 native bird species have been recorded here, including the great spotted kiwi, blue duck and rock wren.

## Accommodation and food in Collingwood

**Collingwood Beachcomber Motels** $ *Haven Rd; tel: (03) 524 8499; fax: (03) 524 8599; email: goldenbaybeds@paradise.net.nz*

**Courthouse Café** $ *Corner of Gibbs and Elizabeth Sts; tel: (03) 524 8025.*

**Skara Brae B&B and Motels** $$ *Elizabeth St; tel: (03) 524 8464; www.accommodationcollingwood.co.nz.* Peaceful, garden setting.

# HAVELOCK

**Tourist Information**
**Rutherford Travel** *46 Main Rd; tel: (03) 571 6090; www.rutherfordtravel. co.nz, www.havelocknz.com*

**Foxy Lady Cruises**
*Tel: (03) 574 2564; www.foxylady.co.nz*

**Affinity Cruises** *Tel: (03) 572 7223; www. affinitycruises.co.nz*

Havelock has several claims to fame. First it is the best place from which to explore the Marlborough Sounds, and second it is where the produce from the 200 mussel farms within the Sounds is taken to be processed. It calls itself the Greenshell Mussel Capital of the world, which is not a title that anyone would seriously want to challenge. These mussels are the type known as New Zealand green-lipped mussels – *Perna caliculus* – and they are of a superior flavour to those found in most other waters.

It is therefore understandable that one of the great attractions of the town is a restaurant. This is very possibly the best seafood restaurant in New Zealand. It is called The Mussel Boys and you can have mussels either as 'steamers' (mussels in the whole shell) or 'flats' (mussels on the half shell). In their simplest and best form they are delivered in a handleless saucepan and you use the shells as tweezers to drag out the flesh. The café is totally unpretentious with wooden tables and stools. Knives and forks are not normally supplied. Wine is available. You go there for the mussels, done as simply as possible – a great saucepan full of them. A totally magical experience.

The other great attraction is to ride on one of the launches that take a day-long trip delivering mail and provisions to the farmers and campers in the Sounds. The Pelorus Mail Boat departs from Havelock Marina (*0930 every Tue, Thu & Fri; tel: (03) 574 1080; www.mail-boat.co.nz*). There are also trips to the Tennyson Inlet and other places. Check them out with Marlborough Travel (*tel: (03) 577 9997*) or HavelockNZ (*tel: (03) 571 6090*).

## Accommodation and food in Havelock

**Chartridge Park $** *SH6 (3km south of Havelock); tel: (03) 574 2129.* Excellent low-key little motor park with two great-value cabins. Small camp kitchen. Book ahead.

**Havelock Garden Motel $** *71 Main Rd; tel: (03) 574 2387; fax: (03) 574 2376; www.gardenmotels.com*

**Mussel Pot Restaurant $** *73 Main Rd; tel: (03) 574 2824; open 1100–2100 in summer, 1100–1900 in winter.*

# KAIKOURA

The name Kaikoura literally means 'meal of crayfish', an appropriate name, for Kaikoura is world famed for the variety of marine mammals that can be seen from the shore or, even better, by boat. The two-hour drive from Picton along the Christchurch road passes along a scenic route that hugs the coast most of the way. The town itself has a population of 2,500 and sits on a peninsula jutting out from the

**Above**
Mural at Kaikoura

**ℹ Kaikoura Visitor Centre** *Westend; tel: (03) 319 5641; fax: (03) 319 6819; email: kaikoura@ i-site.org; www.kaikoura. co.nz.* Keeps a blackboard continuously updated with information about activities in the area. Infinitely helpful.

🎧 The following operators specialise in different aspects of the marine attractions of Kaikoura. **Whale Watch Kaikoura** *Railway Station,* tel: *(03) 319 6767.* Trip takes 3¹/₂ hours. There are four trips daily. **Seal Swim Kaikoura** Tel: *(03) 319 6182.* **Dolphin Encounter** *96 The Esplanade; tel: (03) 319 6777.* **Wings Over Whales** *Peketa Airfield; tel: (03) 319 6580.* 30-minute flight. **Kaikoura Helicopters,** *Railway Station; tel: (03) 319 6609.*

rugged coastline. In the 19th century, whaling stations along this coast used the cliffs as lookouts. You can see relics of those days in the **Kaikoura Museum**. The town itself is not attractive. It has developed along the Esplanade like a very bad English seaside town. This matters not, because one does not go there to see the attractions of the town itself, but those off the coast, along the shoreline, and in the sea.

Off the peninsula is a complex underwater system, with deep water, providing a rich feast of marine organisms. This attracts an almost unparalleled range of **sealife**. First and foremost there is the giant sperm whale, which was once close to extinction and now can be viewed nearly all year around. Then, from October to April, the dolphins arrive in pods several hundred strong. The New Zealand fur seal makes an appearance, as well as a wide range of sea birds and fish.

It is possible to go swimming in wet suits with the dolphins and the seals, and the scuba diving is superb. However, what most people come here for is to see the whales and the dolphins and they can do this either from the coast, from a cruise boat or light aircraft or, if they are seriously wealthy, from a helicopter.

## Accommodation and food in Kaikoura

**Kairoura Top 10 Holiday Park $** *34 Beach Rd; tel: (03) 319 5362; www.kairouratop10.co.nz*

**Panorama Motel $** *266 The Esplanade; tel: (03) 319 5053; email: panoramamotel@xtra.co.nz; www.panoramamotel.co.nz.* Great sea views.

**Blue Seas Motel $$** *222 The Esplanade; tel: (03) 319 5441; fax: (03) 319 6707; email: blue.seas@xtra.co.nz; www.blueseasmotel.co.nz*

# MOTUEKA

ℹ **Motueka Visitor Information** *Wallace St; tel: (03) 528 6543; fax: (03) 528 6563; email: motueka@i-site.org; www. abeltasmangreenrush.co.nz*

Motueka is located on the coast of the Tasman Bay. Its name means 'wood hens in a grove of trees' or, in some versions, 'eight crippled wood hens' – crippled perhaps because of over-indulgence – for this is also the centre of the New Zealand hop industry which is essential to the beer with which New Zealand wins prizes all over the world.

The Europeans arrived here in the 1840s. One of the earliest relics is the **Te Ahurewa Maori Church**, which was built in 1897, a simple but moving structure (*Pah St, opposite the Post Office*).

One lady settler wrote of Motueka: 'The climate is delightful. It has neither the rains of Auckland nor the winds of Port Nicholson. The waters abound in fish of excellent quality, and the land with birds, pigeons, quails, wild duck and parrots.' If you want to see birds now, just drive out of the town, by way of Staple Street, to the **Motueka Sandspit**, which has an immense variety of sea birds – and the view is quite remarkable.

**Above**
Nelson's modern cathedral

### Accommodation and food in Motueka

Abel Tasman Motel $ *45 High St; tel/fax: (03) 528 6688; email: stay@abeltasmanmotel.motueka.co.nz; www.motuekamotel.co.nz*

Equestrian Lodge Motel $ *Tudor St; tel: (03) 528 9369; fax: (03) 528 6369.*

Motueka Garden Motel $ *71 King Edward St; tel: (03) 528 9299; fax: (03) 528 6284; www.motmotel.co.nz*

Bakehouse Café $$ *21 Wallace St; tel: (03) 528 6111.*

# NELSON

**ⓘ Nelson Visitor Information Centre** *Cnr Trafalgar and Halifax Sts; tel: (03) 548 2304; fax: (03) 546 7393; email: nelson@i-site.org; www.nelsonnz.com*

Nelson is one of the most attractive cities in New Zealand, a city of many gardens and of wonderful views of the Tasman Bay. The whole of the town reflects the nautical flavour of the name: many of the streets are named after the battles that Nelson fought and the ships that brought pioneer settlers to the region. The *pakeha* name is perhaps better than the Maori name of Wakatu, which can be translated as 'the place where you dump broken canoes'.

Abel Tasman, the Dutch explorer, arrived off the coast on 13 December 1642. Six days later the members of his crew got into an altercation with the local Maori, and four of the crew were killed. Tasman then made the decision to leave the coast 'as no friendship could be made with these people, nor water nor refreshments could be obtained'. He named the place 'Murderers Bay'.

Next, whalers came to the Marlborough Sounds, followed, in 1839, by Colonel William Gibbon Wakefield of the New Zealand Company. He desired rich settlers but got 'too few gentlemen with too little money'. In 1844 the New Zealand Company was declared bankrupt, which left Nelson in parlous straits. Help arrived in the form of a group of German immigrants, who had earlier been solicited by the New Zealand Company, and they were critically important in pulling the area through its problems.

When you look at Nelson and the surrounding area these days, it is very difficult to imagine what those problems might have been. The city enjoys fertile land, with a backdrop of green hills, and a coastline of beaches and tidal estuaries fed by fresh, clear rivers. The population is just under 50,000, which is a manageable size – large enough to be interesting but small enough to be intimate. And, as an added bonus, Nelson has more than 2,500 hours of sunshine a year, which makes it either the sunniest spot in New Zealand or joint equal with neighbouring Blenheim.

Nelson can also claim to be the birthplace of the great scientist, Lord Rutherford of Nelson, who can rightly be called the father of nuclear physics. Nelson's most important building is its **Cathedral**

**Arts and crafts**

Nelson has a lively arts scene. Meet the artists and commission your own piece. Check out **Craft Habitat** *Richmond.*

(*open daily 0800–1900*), which stands, stern and grey and somewhat Gothic, at the top of Trafalgar Street, the town's main thoroughfare. Building of the cathedral started in 1925, on the site of earlier churches dating back to 1850. Construction continued for many years amid arguments about whether it should be completed (because it was not earthquake-proof, especially as far as the proposed Gothic tower was concerned). A new modified design was tried in the 1960s, and the cathedral was eventually finished in 1967, being consecrated in 1972. Another pioneer building houses the **Bishops School** (*Nile St East; tel: (03) 548 4794*), which was in operation from 1840 until the 1930s. **Suter Art Gallery** (*Bridge St, next to Queen's Gardens; tel: (03) 548 4699; www.thesuter.org.nz; open daily 1030–1630*) houses the region's public art collection and was founded in 1889 by Andrew Suter, Bishop of Nelson.

**Founders Park** (*open daily 1000–1630*) is 2km outside the city and has a collection of old Nelson buildings showing the history of the town. The exhibits include a working newspaper office, bakery, and even an organic brewery. The **Nelson Provincial Museum** (*Cnr Hardy and Trafalgar Sts; tel: (03) 548 9588; open weekdays 1000–1700, weekends 1000–1630*) in the heart of the city is one of the best provincial museums in the country. It has what is claimed to be the largest photographic collection in New Zealand. In Isel Park just outside town is **Isel House** (*open Tue–Sun 1400–1600*), a stone mansion built before the turn of the 19th century, with collections of china and hand-carved furniture. The lovely grounds, full of trees from around the world, are open all week.

**Broadgreen** (*276 Nayland Road, Stoke; open daily 1030–1630*) was based on a farmhouse in Devon and was built about 1855. It has now been restored and gives a good idea of New Zealand life in Victorian days.

South of the city, the **World of Wearable Art and Collectable Cars** (*95 Quarantine Rd, Annesbrook; tel: (03) 547 4573; www.wowcars.co.nz;*

## First among equals

Once Nelson had got over its early problems it galloped ahead. It can claim many firsts, including the first 8-hour working day in the world (which came in 1842), the first commercial brewery in New Zealand (which opened in the same year and, yes, there may be a connection), the first recognised racecourse (in 1845), the first commercial thoroughbred horse breeding (in 1852), and the first railway (the Dun Mountain Railway, which opened in 1862 – though, in truth, this was originally a horse-drawn tramway and Christchurch claims the first railway with a steam engine). Perhaps most important of all, Nelson Rugby Club was the first rugby club in New Zealand, founded on 14 May, 1870 (yet again this claim is challenged by Christchurch – but Nelson was playing rugby in 1870, while Christchurch Football Club was playing football and did not adopt rugby until five years after Nelson).

**Above**
Isel House

open daily 1000–1700) showcases the historic Wearable Art Garment collection (now an iconic aspect of the region). There is a fully scripted show that uses mannequins with all the usual elements of sound and lighting. The second gallery has an impressive collection of classic cars formerly on view in the town centre.

Nelson has many splendid beaches, of which the best is **Tahunanui**, located some 5km from the centre of the town. Further out, 25km northwest of the city centre, is **Rabbit Island**, with some 13km of beach. Almost all the normal outdoor adventure sports are available at Nelson, with the exception of bungee jumping – for which relief, much thanks.

## Accommodation and food in Nelson

**Accents on the Park $$** *335 Trafalgar Sq; tel: (03) 548 4335; www. trafalgaraccommodation.co.nz.* A beautifully renovated Victorian villa with plenty of class. Excellent rooms and also has a lovingly constructed basement lounge bar, with open fire and plenty of character.

**Admirals Motor Inn $$** *26 Waimea Rd; tel: 0800 745 755; www.admiralsmotorinn.co.nz.* Near the city centre.

**The Boatshed $$** *Wakefield Quay; tel: (03) 546 9783.* Licensed. Book well ahead, especially if you want a table outside – pure magic in summer. Seafood cooked and presented with flair.

**Lambrettas Café Bar $$** *204 Hardy St; tel: (03) 545 8555; open 0900–late.* Good-value café specialising in all things Italian, including scooters.

**Wheelhouse Inn $$** *41 Whitby Rd; tel: (03) 546 8391; www.wheelhouse.nelson.co.nz.* Plenty of character and good value.

**Victorian Rose Pub and Café $$** *281 Trafalgar St; tel: (03) 548 7631.* Licensed restaurant.

# PICTON

 **Picton Visitor
Information
Centre** *The Foreshore;
tel: (03) 520 3113; fax:
(03) 573 5021; email:
picton@i-site.org; www.
destinationmarlborough.com*
**Department of
Conservation Office,**
*Port Marlborough Building,
14 Auckland Street;
tel: (03) 520 3002;
fax: (03) 520 3003;
www.doc.govt.nz/*

As the ferry comes in from Wellington it arrives at Picton. This is a marvellous preview of what awaits you on the South Island of New Zealand. For Picton is a beautiful town in itself, and it is surrounded by the Marlborough Sounds, a series of fiord-like drowned river valleys which, you could happily argue, make Picton one of the most beautiful places on Earth. The town has something over 4,500 people, is 30km north of Blenheim and 145km east of Nelson.

Originally the town site was called Newton but the name was changed in 1859 to honour one of the generals at the Battle of Waterloo – Sir Thomas Picton, who fell leading his men in a charge. Initially the town was the capital of the province of Marlborough, but this was transferred to Blenheim in 1865.

Picton was, for a while, a whaling station. Now it handles the ferries and also provides a mooring for the yachts of wealthy wine estate owners. In the harbour, the old sailing vessel ***Edwin Fox*** has been restored. This was built in 1853 using Burma teak and, as a fully rigged clipper, carried convicts from Britain to Australia and migrants to New Zealand. When steam arrived, the ship was converted into a coal hulk and then used as a breakwater. The remains were purchased by the Restoration Society for 10 cents and the ship is now being rebuilt. The visitor centre has displays on the history of the ship.

**Picton Community Museum** is also on the quay, and is far better than most small community museums in New Zealand. It has a collection focused on the whaling trade, which was carried on locally

**Below**
The Picton waterfront

**Dolphin Watch Eco-Tours** (*tel: (03) 573 8040*) offers twice-daily guided ecotours of the Moutara Island bird sanctuary. **Endeavour Express** (*tel: (03) 573 5456; www.boatrides.co.nz*) is a major cruise company. **Marlborough Sounds Adventure Company** (*tel: (03) 573 6078*) has guided one-day and multi-day sea kayak trips. Try **Sea Kayaking Adventure Tours** (*tel: (03) 574 2765*), based at Queen Charlotte Sound, for day or multi-day guided tours.

for over a century. You can see everything from harpoons to the tools used for catching and cutting down the whales.

Next door to the *Edwin Fox* is **Eco-World Aquarium** (*tel: (03) 573 6030; open daily 0900–1700*). As one of the few aquariums in the country it is perhaps worth a look, housing all the usual suspects including an octopus called Larry, some seahorses, of course, rays, and yes, the obligatory sharks.

The only way to appreciate the Marlborough Sounds fully is to go out by boat. There are many self-drive hire boats available from sites on the waterfront, and several tour ships. Alternatively you can follow the **Queen Charlotte Track**, which can be walked in short sections or as a serious four-day hike. Local boat services can take you there and back and it is a peaceful walk with stunning views. The track is suitable for all levels of fitness and there are many accommodation options available. Contact the Picton Department of Conservation office (*see opposite*).

## Accommodation and food in Picton

**Aldan Lodge Motel $** *86 Wellington St; tel: (03) 573 6833 or 0800 277 278; fax: (03) 573 6091; www.aldanlodge.co.nz*

**Bell Bird Motel $** *96 Waikawa Rd; tel/fax: (03) 573 6912.*

**Harbour View Motel $** *30 Waikawa Rd; tel: (03) 573 6259; fax: (03) 573 6982; email: harbourviewpicton@callplus.net.nz; www.harbourviewpicton.co.nz*

**Le Café $** *33 London Quay; tel: (03) 573 5588.* Asian and European food served by friendly staff; *open daily 0800–2200 (closed Mon and Tue Jun–Aug).*

**Yacht Club Hotel $$** *25 Waikawa Rd; tel: (03) 573 7002; www.theyachtclub.co.nz*

# Suggested tour

**Total distance:** 360km.

**Time:** 6 hours' driving (excluding sightseeing).

**Links:** Christchurch (*see page 202*) can be reached by driving down the coast from Blenheim.

Start at **PICTON ❶**, for that is where the ferry comes in from Wellington and it is a logical place to begin. Take the scenic route to **HAVELOCK ❷**, which is well signposted. From Havelock, the SH6 runs inland and west through Canvastown, Pelorus Bridge,

**ℹ Travel and Information Centre** *Domestic Terminal, Christchurch Airport; tel: (03) 353 7774; fax: (03) 353 7754.*

**Department of Conservation Office,** *195 Hereford St; tel: (03) 341 9102; fax: (03) 365 1388.*

Canterbury Pilgrims referred to these original settlers as the 'Pre-Adamites'. A certain snob value still attaches to being descended from the settlers who arrived in the First Four Ships (note the capitalisation in every reference to them).

Now, there are something like 350,000 people, plus one live wizard, living in the city. And, yes, there is a style to the city which plainly has its roots in England and the Anglican Church. Christchurch is also very much a city of learning – appropriate, as it was named after a university college – as well as of parks. The University of Canterbury was founded in 1873 and nearby Lincoln University was founded in 1878, as Canterbury Agricultural College.

## Topography

Christchurch is now the second-largest city in New Zealand. Up until World War II, the prosperity of Christchurch depended upon the rich agricultural land that surrounded it. After 1945 the position of the city, its adequate supplies of water and inexpensive hydroelectric power made it New Zealand's second most important industrial

**Above**
Christchurch Botanic Gardens

Christchurch has a very lively theatre scene, and many excellent art galleries. This strength of culture partly comes from the local Canterbury University, which is well regarded internationally for its high academic standards. The magnificent Arts Centre is a focal point for New Zealand arts, crafts and the performing arts, and is housed in Gothic-revival buildings previously occupied by the University of Canterbury before its needs outgrew the size of the site. Now it is home to theatres, cinemas, galleries, shops, cafés, bars and restaurants and it could well keep you occupied for the better part of a day.

Worth an excursion, only 90 minutes north of Christchurch, is Hanmer Springs. This is an alpine village in, strange to relate, an active thermal area. There is a river snaking through the valley backed by peaks that are normally snowcapped. This has always been a popular spot for the people of Christchurch but, more and more, it is being discovered by international tourists. It has a wide range of activities, from the thermal pools complex, with its adjacent health and fitness centre, to a canyon with jet boating and, within easy distance, skiing at the Amuri and Mount Lyford ski fields.

centre. Its transport needs are well catered for with an international airport and a splendid port in Lyttelton, a natural deepwater anchorage 11km southeast of the city.

Because Christchurch is so flat it is an ideal place to explore by bicycle. Or, because it is such a compact city, you can walk. It is unlikely you will ever get lost for very long. This is because Christchurch is defined by the Avon River, which meanders through the city. The Avon, by the way, was not named after the river of Stratford-upon-Avon, as is generally thought, but after the Scottish birthplace of the Dean brothers, who were early settlers in the area.

The city is laid out in a neat grid pattern – though the Avon River does intrude and push things around a bit – and the city centre is a maze of one-way streets, with its centre of focus at Cathedral Square, from which all streets radiate. This was once a busy bus terminus, but sanity has prevailed and it is now a splendid pedestrian area.

Over 12 per cent of the city area is devoted to parks, public gardens and other recreational areas. That is why Christchurch is known as the 'Garden City of the Plains'. No one ever actually calls it by that singularly naff name, you understand, but the town council and the business association trot it out every now and again.

The two best-known parks are Hagley Park and the Botanic Gardens. **Hagley Park** has English lawns and woodland, plus a wide variety of native and exotic trees and plants, and it lies within a loop of the Avon River. The **Botanic Gardens** probably have the finest collection of exotic and indigenous plants to be found anywhere in New Zealand (*tel: (03) 941 8999; open daily 0700–1 hour before sunset; conservatories within the park open 1015–1600*).

The Avon arrives at the city at the point where it merges with the Heathcote River. Going for a punt on the Avon is very popular with both residents and tourists. Indeed, it is one of the few places in the southern hemisphere where it is possible to go punting as well as the normal canoeing and rowing. The place to go to hire a canoe or arrange a punting trip on the river is the **Antigua Boat Sheds**, near the hospital at 2 Cambridge Terrace (*tel: (03) 366 5885*).

# Sights

### Christchurch Cathedral and civic buildings

The **Anglican Cathedral** is at the centre of the city and dominates Cathedral Square with its tall copper-covered spire. The foundation stone was laid in 1864 – just 14 years after the arrival of the first organised settlers. For a small sum, and a lot of energy, you can climb the 133 steps of the Bell Tower (*open Mon–Sat 0900–1700; Sun 0730–1700*) and get tremendous views over the city, the surrounding plains and the distant Southern Alps. Sadly, the authorities seem to be hellbent on destroying the original charm of the cathedral. First they

**Gothic revival**

Wandering around Christchurch, you'll see many examples of the Gothic-revival architecture that gives the city such an English look and feel. Whether you think that Gothic revival was one of the more unfortunate happenings in architecture is another matter. A person of the cloth in this city voiced the opinion that 'Gothic revival hit us very hard.' There are about 30 distinguished buildings within the city and the Historic Places Trust publishes free leaflets, available at the visitor information centre.

**Little River Stores**

On the way to Akaroa is the minute town of Little River, home to the Little River Stores and Art Gallery, as well as a café, craft shop and information centre located in the old railway station. The Stores sell almost everything and the café offers a good range of excellent food and healthy snacks. The gallery promotes the work of New Zealand artists, and holds monthly exhibitions. Also in the area is the Birdlands Sanctuary (*admission free*), where you can admire the birdlife in the aviaries and picnic under the trees.

### Antarctic Centre

One of the great exhibitions of Christchurch is the Antarctic Centre, on the way to the airport, about 15 minutes from the city centre (*tel: (03) 353 7798, 0508 736 4846; www.iceberg.co.nz*). This has amazing exhibits all connected with Antarctic exploration. Despite the fact that Captain Scott looks remarkably clean-shaven and well-groomed for a man who is stormbound in a hut in the Antarctic winter, the exhibition is intelligent and shows the role of Christchurch as the base for the Antarctic exploration programmes of many nations, including those from New Zealand, the United States and Italy. Given all the emphasis on ice, it would perhaps be rude not to have penguins in there somewhere and this is the most recent addition to the display repertoire. However, it features native (and rehabilitated) little blue penguins, which are more at home in the warm waters of Australasia than down in 'the fridge'.

## Accommodation and food in Christchurch

**The Oxford on Avon $–$$** *794 Colombo St; tel: (03) 379 7148.* Something of a Christchurch institution offering set-price, no-nonsense buffet breakfasts, lunches and dinners, from 0700.

**Stonehurst $–$$** *241 Gloucester St, Latimer Sq; tel: (03) 379 4620 or 0508 786 633; www.stonehurst.co.nz.* Centrally located with a wide range of options including powered sites for camper vans.

**Alcala Motor Lodge $$** *100 Sherborne St; tel: (03) 365 8180; fax: (03) 365 8378; email: alcala@ihug.co.nz; www.alcala.co.nz*

**Dux De Lux Restaurant $$** *Arts Centre, Cnr Hereford and Montreal Sts; tel: (03) 366 6919; www.thedux.co.nz.* In the Christchurch Arts Centre, with

**Below left**
Oxford Terrace – known as
the 'Restaurant Row' of
Christchurch

Gothic Victorian architecture, large shady trees and garden bars. Serves fresh fish and vegetarian food; on-site brewery and great wine list.

**Il Felice Italian Restaurant and Bar $$** *Tel: (03) 366 7535; fax: (03) 379 4205.*

**Sherborne Motor Lodge $$** *94 Sherborne St; tel: (03) 377 8050; fax: (03) 377 0696; email: sherborne@clear.net.nz; www.sherbornemotorlodge.co.nz*

**Tap Room Bar and Restaurant $$** *124 Oxford Terrace; tel: (03) 365 0547.* Combine atmosphere with quality bar food at this, one of the city's most popular venues.

**Tramway Restaurant $$** *Tel: (03) 366 7511; www.tram.co.nz.* A unique dining option on board a heritage tram, adding a very pleasant convivial edge to the usual sightseeing trip.

## Three remarkable New Zealanders

Canterbury University has produced many famous scholars, but the great star was Ernest Rutherford (1871–1937), who was born near Nelson. He went on to take three degrees at Canterbury and from there he went to Britain and Canada to further his theories about the structure of the atom. The theoretical analyses of Ernest Rutherford led the way to the discovery of atomic energy and the splitting of the atom. You can view the basement room where he started his research, newly reburbished, in an exhibition at the Arts Centre in Worcester Street, which was the original university.

Dame Edith Ngaio Marsh was born in Christchurch just before the turn of the 20th century and died aged 87. She had two separate careers, both of which brought her fame and respect. Outside New Zealand she was known for meticulously constructed detective stories, mainly starring Inspector Roderick Alleyn of Scotland Yard. Even to this day they read well. Less well known is the fact that she was also a Shakespearean actor and an even more successful theatrical producer in New Zealand.

Charles Upham is the only fighting soldier ever to be awarded the Victoria Cross twice. He was born in Christchurch in 1908 and earned his first Victoria Cross in Crete in May 1941. The second was awarded at Ruweisat Ridge, Egypt, in July 1942, where he was severely wounded. Captured by the Germans, he ended the war in Colditz Castle. When he returned from the war he went back to being a sheep farmer at Hundalee, North Canterbury. He refused all honours, all glory, all limelight. He just went back to farming, as a quiet, unassuming New Zealander.

# AKAROA

**Akaroa Information Centre** *80 Rue Lavaud; tel/fax: (03) 304 8600; email: info@akaroa.com; www.akaroa.com*

One of the great delights of Christchurch is often skipped over by tourists. That is the town of Akaroa, on the shore of French Bay, on the Banks Peninsula. Akaroa is steeped in New Zealand colonial history or, to be more precise, in failed French–New Zealand colonial history. At one point it was thought possible that New Zealand could become a French dominion. Certainly the British government was worried at the possibility.

**Akaroa Cottages**
$$ SH75;
tel: (03) 304 7195;
www.akaroacottages.co.nz

**L'Hotel Motel** $$ 75
Beach Rd; tel: (03) 304
7559; fax: (03) 304 7455.

**Akaroa Criterion
Motel** $$$ 73 Rue Jolie;
tel: 0800 252 762, (03)
304 7775; fax: (03) 304
7850; email:
akaroacriterion@
paradise.net.nz; www.
holidayakaroa.co.nz

Captain Jean Langlois, a French whaler, negotiated the purchase of 12,150ha of the Banks Peninsula from a group of Maori in 1838. Having done that, he returned to France to form the Nanto-Bordelaise Company. He also tried to get the support of the government of France to colonise the whole of New Zealand. Captain Langlois and 80 colonists arrived in a ship called the *Comte de Paris* on 17 August 1840, ready to establish, as it were, a beachhead for the *tricolor* and the glory of France.

The best-laid plans of mice and men gang aft agley for, in the meantime, Governor William Hobson had, on behalf of Queen Victoria, declared British sovereignty. New Zealand was now part of the British Empire. When the governor heard of the potential French arrival he did exactly what British Victorian politicians were supposed to do in those days. He damned the French for their impudence and sent a gunboat. In fact he sent HMS *Britomart*, under Captain Stanley, with two magistrates aboard. They arrived in Akaroa on 10 August 1840 and hoisted the Union Flag.

Thus, when the main body of the French colonists arrived, the British were already there, and the dreams of French dominion over the whole of New Zealand evaporated. But that did not mean that the French colony disappeared. Despite a long-drawn-out dispute with the Maori over the title to the land, the French managed to establish a settlement which existed quite peaceably, and in accord with the other settlements in the area – but it was a French settlement under the British flag.

Today there are just a few reminders of the town's French origins, though the local tourist industry plays the French card for all it is worth and you will find all the roads are called 'rue' on the street signs. It may sound somewhat over the top but in fact it is utterly charming.

All of Akaroa is stunningly attractive but the jewel in the crown is the **Langlois-Eteveneaux House and Museum**. This is the oldest house in Canterbury, supposed to have been built between 1841 and 1845. It was probably designed along French colonial lines and it is possible the building was prefabricated and shipped to New Zealand for its original owner, Aimable Langlois, a former officer of the French whaler *Nancy*, who settled in Akaroa. In 1959 the property was declared a National Historic Reserve. The museum faithfully depicts a home of the 1840s during the height of the French influence. On display, among a wealth of other treasures, is a French imperial provincial-style bed made for the wedding of Monsieur and Madame Le Lièvre.

But Akaroa has more to offer than just the museum. It has in its harbour an amazing range of wildlife, including Hector's dolphins, the world's smallest dolphin, which are found only on the New Zealand coast. Several cruises will take you out to see the dolphins in the right season, November to April. Try **Black Cat Cruises** (*tel: (03) 304 7641; www.blackcat.co.nz*) or **Dolphin Experience** (*61 Beach Rd; tel: (03) 304 7726*).

**Right**
The Banks Peninsula

# South Canterbury

| | |
|---|---|
| Scenery | ●●●●● |
| Outdoor activities | ●●●● |
| Ski resorts | ●●●● |
| Wildlife | ●●●● |
| Dining | ●●○○○ |
| Watersports | ●●○○○ |
| Heritage | ●●○○○ |
| Children | ●○○○○ |

This is sheep country and, perhaps more importantly, Mackenzie country. It has a special place in the hearts of all New Zealanders. Although, as far as is known, James Mackenzie only committed the one crime of sheep rustling, he has become, in a sense, New Zealand's Ned Kelly. He survived in a harsh landscape and he escaped from the law on at least three occasions. In fact, it is probable that he was an excellent sheepherder who simply fell to temptation when offered twenty quid to move some stolen sheep.

This is a tough area. Along the coast there were literally scores of shipwrecks. Inland farming was difficult, at times impossible. The winters can be severe and the summers very warm. And yet the area has a tremendous style and charm all of its own. People who visit here never forget the place or its legends.

## FAIRLIE

**ⓘ** **Visitor Information Centre** *The Resource Centre, 64 Main St; tel: (03) 685 8496; open 0900–1700.*

Fairlie is a small, secure island in the centre of the harsh wilderness of the Mackenzie country. This small town is on the crossroads of the SH79 and the SH8, which are called Allendale Road and Main Street in the town. This last becomes Mount Cook Road as it leaves the town.

The countryside around is mainly made up of major sheep runs, including Clayton, which covers 15,390ha and lies some 22km east of Fairlie. The town has always serviced the area and once had a railway service to Timaru, called the *Fairlie Flyer*. This was closed in 1868 but the town has continued to prosper. As well as serving the surrounding district, Fairlie acts as a dormitory for skiing on **Mount Dobson** located 26km away. This is a quiet ski field, excellent for families, with no long queues at the lift. The population of the town is normally about 600, but it booms in the skiing season.

It is probable the name of the town (originally called Fairlie Creek) comes from James Fairlie, who lived in a hut just outside the town

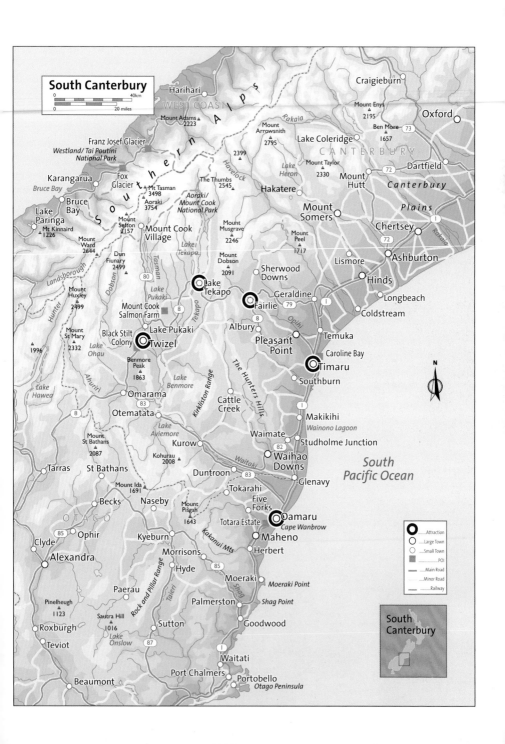

South Canterbury
0        40km
0        20 miles

Craigieburn

Harihari

WEST COAST

Mount Adams ▲
2223

Mount Enys
▲ 2195

Oxford

Mount
Arrowsnith
2795

Rakaia

Ben More — 73

Lake Coleridge
1657

CANTERBURY

Franz Josef Glacier
Westland/ Tai Poutini
National Park

2399
▲

Lake
Heron

Mount Taylor
▲ 2330

72

Dartfield

Karangarua
Bruce Bay

Fox
Glacier

▲ Mt Tasman
3498

Havelock

The Thumbs
2545 ▲

Mount
Hutt

Canterbury

Bruce
Bay

Aoraki ▲
3754

Aoraki/
Mount Cook
National Park

Hakatere

Mount
Somers

Plains

Lake
Paringa

Mt Kinnaird
▲ 1226

Mount
Sefton
3157

Mount Cook
Village

Mount
Musgrave
▲

Mount
Peel
1717

Chertsey

72

Rakaia

Mount
Ward
2644

Dun
Fiunary
2499

Lake
Tekapo

Mount
Dobson
▲ 2091

Mount
Dobson
2246

Lismore

Ashburton

Landsborough

80

Sherwood
Downs

Hinds

Mount
Huxley
▲ 2499

Dobson

Lake
Pukaki

Lake
Tekapo

Geraldine

79

Longbeach

Tasman

Mount Cook
Salmon Farm

8

Fairlie

Coldstream

Hunter

Mount
St Mary
▲ 1996

Black Stilt
Colony ▲
2332

Lake
Ohau

Lake Pukaki

Twizel

8

Albury

Opihi

Pleasant
Point

Temuka

Caroline Bay

Benmore
Peak
▲ 1863

Lake
Benmore

Kirkliston Range

The Hunters Hills

Timaru

Southburn

N

Lake
Hawea

Ahuriri

Omarama

83

Cattle
Creek

Otematata

Lake
Aviemore

Waimate

Makikihi

Wainono Lagoon

8

Mount
St Bathans
▲ 2087

Kurow

Kohurau ▲
2008

82

Studholme Junction

Waitaki

Tarras

St Bathans

Duntroon

83

Waihao
Downs

South
Pacific Ocean

Mount Ida ▲
1691

Tokarahi

Glenavy

Becks

Naseby

Mount
Pisgah
▲ 1643

Five
Forks

OTAGO

85

Ophir

Totara Estate

Oamaru

Clyde

Kyeburn

Kakanui Mts

Cape Wanbrow

Alexandra

Morrisons

Hyde

85

Herbert

Maheno

Rock and Pillar Range

Moeraki

Moeraki Point

Paerau

Talen

Palmerston

Shag Point

Pinelheugh
1123

Sautra Hill
1016

Shag

Sutton

Goodwood

Roxburgh

Lake
Onslow

87

Teviot

Waitati

Beaumont

Port Chalmers

Portobello
Otago Peninsula

○ Attraction
○ Large Town
○ Small Town
■ POI
— Main Road
— Minor Road
— Railway

South
Canterbury

centre. The town has a Scottish tradition and hosts the Mackenzie Highland Show on Easter Monday.

You can get a fairly good idea of the harshness of early life in Mackenzie country by going to the **museum** on Mount Cook Road, with its collection of veteran transportation and, of course, farm machinery. The old railway station has been moved here, as has the century-old Mabel Binney Cottage, originally inhabited by the blacksmith and now furnished in the style of the period.

A **walkway** runs for 3km, starting below the Allendale Road Bridge and running along the shaded banks of the Opihi River.

## Accommodation and food in Fairlie

**Old Library Café $** *6 Allendale Rd. Open 0800–very late.* All meals, including Thai curries which may not be authentic Thai, but are very inexpensive and filling.

**Mackenzie Motel $$** *12 School Rd; tel: (03) 685 8452 or 0800 685 001; www.mackenziemotel.co.nz*

**Mount Dobson Motel $$** *SH8 6km west of town; tel: (03) 685 8819; www.mtdobsonmotel.co.nz.* Quiet and yet near to the ski fields.

**Rimuwhare Motels and Restaurant $$** *53 Mount Cook Rd; tel: (03) 685 8058; open daily for lunch and dinner.* An amazing find for such a small town: great style and excellent food. Licensed, and also has accommodation.

**Below**
Wildflowers on the shores of Lake Tekapo

# LAKE TEKAPO

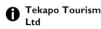

**Tekapo Tourism Ltd**
www.tekapotourism.co.nz

Lake Tekapo Village makes an impact totally out of proportion to its size. Consisting of little more than two lines of buildings, with a population of around 400, Lake Tekapo Village is pretty much just a way-station on the lake. But arrive there in the late afternoon or the early evening and drive along the lake and you will enjoy, as the sun is setting, as superb a view as any you will get in the southern hemisphere. Even the local townspeople come to the shore to look across the water.

There is magic in the atmosphere here, for this is supposed to be the clearest air in the southern hemisphere. The colours, especially at dawn and dusk, are vibrant and vivid. This is a photographer's paradise. The lake itself is a turquoise colour, which comes from suspended rock particles. Do not even think of swimming in the water, for it is freezing cold most of the year.

The lake is now part of a major hydroelectric scheme, and is fed by the Godley and Cass rivers. It is at an elevation of 700m and covers 83sq km. The exit flow is by way of a dam, which is under the road bridge, into the Tekapo River, from where it runs across the Mackenzie basin and joins the Pukaki and Ohau rivers.

On the lake shore, the **Church of the Good Shepherd** is one of the prettier churches of New Zealand. It was built in 1935 as a memorial to the pioneers of the Mackenzie country. At the back wall, a window frames the lake and the hills and mountains beyond, so that the scenery becomes the altar. See it as the sun is setting for a truly religious experience.

About 50m further along the waterfront, there is a monument to the **sheepdog**, erected by the sheep farmers of the Mackenzie country in 1966. The sculpture was created by the wife of one of the farmers. Without the aid of these dogs it would be totally impossible to farm the rough Mackenzie country. (It is part of the Mackenzie myth that this statue was of Friday, the fabulous dog of the sheep rustler, James Mackenzie. It is not. It is a tribute to all working sheepdogs.)

Lake Tekapo Village is a good place to use as a base for walks in the area. For a start there is an excellent 10km walk to **Mount John Lookout**, beginning at the end of Lakeside Drive. Head towards the lake, following the road from the village centre on the river side of the Alpine Inn. As you enter the Domain you'll see a walkway map. The walk goes through the Domain, past the motor camp to the foot of Mount John. There is another map near the entrance to the ice-skating rink. You then climb through the larch forest to a loop track that circles the summit of the mountain. There are splendid views of the Mackenzie basin, the lake and the Southern Alps as you walk around the loop. The whole walk takes about three hours.

The name of Mount John comes from John Hay, a farmer who set up here in 1857. Other than the superb views from its summit, the

mount also boasts an internationally significant observatory, which is well worth a visit. **Earth and Sky** (*tel: (03) 680 6960; www.earthandsky. co.nz; observatory tours 1100–1500; stargazing summer 2200, winter 2000; café open 0900–1700*) offers daytime guided tours of Mt John Observatory, as well as night-time stargazing tours at both Mt John and Mt Cook National Park. Provided weather allows, the stargazing tour, which lasts about two hours, is fascinating. Even if you cannot stay for the evening, the daytime observatory tour is well worth it, as are the memorable views on offer from the in-house Astro Café.

### Accommodation and food around Lake Tekapo

**Astro Café $** *Mt John Observatory (follow signs west end of the village); open daily 0900–1700.* Excellent venue atop Mt John for good coffee and light meals.

**The Chalet $$** *14 Pioneer Drive; tel: (03) 680 6774; email: info@thechalet.co.nz; www.thechalet.co.nz.* Six self-contained units and staggering views of the lake.

**Godley Resort $$** *Tekapo River Bridge; tel: (03) 680 6848; www.tekapo. co.nz.* Contains shops and restaurants and a range of rooms at different prices.

**Jade Palace Chinese Restaurant $$** *SH8; tel: (03) 680 6828.* Licensed.

# OAMARU

**ⓘ Oamaru Visitor Centre** *Thames St; tel: (03) 434 1656; fax: (03) 434 1657; www.visitoamaru.co.nz*

Oamaru is the principal town and port of North Otago. It is 115km northeast of Dunedin and 85km southwest of Timaru, on the highway between Christchurch and Dunedin. Its name comes from a Maori term meaning 'place of sheltered fire'. The town is quite lovely because of the widespread use of limestone, which is quarried in the area and is called Oamaru Stone. You will find it on many of the major buildings throughout the country.

The first settler was a runholder – someone who farmed sheep on a sheep run. That was Hugh Robinson, who arrived in 1853. Only five years later they were laying out the town and eight years after that it became a borough. The town is a service centre for a farming area which is diversifying into other types of produce but is still very much sheep country. Just 8km out of town is **Totara Estate** which produced the stock that made up the first shipment of refrigerated meat to Britain on board the *Dunedin* in 1882. You can visit the estate, which is in an excellent state of preservation. This is the place of origin of the Corriedale sheep, and it was the site where, in 1852, Walter B D Mantell discovered the remains of the moa, the now-extinct giant flightless bird.

**Above**
Limestone building in Oamaru

To see the town at its best, go to **Lookout Point** at the end of Tamar Street early in the morning as the sun is rising. The town, the beaches and the harbour positively glisten. There are some wonderful buildings in the town and an excellent place to start is the **Harbour-Tyne Historic Precinct** which has been redeveloped and refurbished with style and delicacy.

One of the great attractions is the **Oamaru Blue Penguin Colony** (*Waterfront Rd; tel: (03) 433 1195; www.penguins.co.nz*) where you can see the world's smallest penguin returning home at dusk, or about half-an-hour afterwards. You may also see penguins when you take the **Graves Walkway**, a coastal track running for 2km from Waterfront Road. There is a hide from which you can watch the penguins, with your best bet to see them being late in the afternoon.

### Accommodation and food in Oamaru

**AAA Thames Court Motel \$\$** *252 Thames St; tel: (03) 434 6963; email: stay@aaathamescourt.co.nz*. Very close to the centre of the town and the blue penguins viewing station.

**Colonial Lodge Motel \$\$** *509 Thames Highway; tel: (03) 437 0999; email: stay@coloniallodgemotel.co.nz*. Close to the blue penguins.

**Star and Garter \$\$** *9 Itchen St; tel: (03) 434 5246; open daily 1030–very late*. A sort of music hall revival restaurant which provides excellent fun and solid food.

# TIMARU

**Below**
The Canterbury Plains

The name probably comes from a 'place of shelter', used by Maoris travelling by canoe along this fairly exposed coastline. Around 1838 it was briefly settled as a whaling station, and the first European resident was a whaler called Samuel Williams. There is still a massive pot, once used for rendering down whale fat, on the beach at Caroline Bay. The real developers of the area were George and Robert Rhodes, brothers who came from Yorkshire, in England. They owned the area's first sheep run and also the 50ha of land on which Timaru was eventually built. The town had a very small population until 1859 when the

# TIMARU

**Visitor Information Centre** *Lower George St; tel: (03) 688 6163; fax: (03) 684 0202; email: timaruinfo@southisland.org; www.southisland.org*

The name probably comes from a 'place of shelter', used by Maoris travelling by canoe along this fairly exposed coastline. Around 1838 it was briefly settled as a whaling station, and the first European resident was a whaler called Samuel Williams. There is still a massive pot, once used for rendering down whale fat, on the beach at Caroline Bay. The real developers of the area were George and Robert Rhodes, brothers who came from Yorkshire, in England. They owned the area's first sheep run and also the 50ha of land on which Timaru was eventually built. The town had a very small population until 1859 when the

**Below**
The Canterbury Plains

English ship *Strathallan* arrived with 120 migrants. Originally there were two towns but these were incorporated as a borough in 1868. An artificial harbour was begun in 1877 and this started to fill the rocky beach to the north – Caroline Bay – with sand, converting it into a popular summer resort. The first steam train came to Timaru in 1876. Timaru is now the largest town and port in South Canterbury, and it looks over the green hills that mark the end of the rich Canterbury Plains. The town is built on lava flow, which came from the nearby Mount Horrible.

The **South Canterbury Museum** (*tel: (03) 687 7212; open Tue–Fri 1000–1630, Sat and Sun 1300–1630*) is in Perth Street. Hanging from the ceiling, in the elegant octagonal building, is a replica of the first aircraft built by Richard Pearse (*see feature, page 220*). He even built the engine, which uses horizontally opposed cylinders, as seen on modern BMW motorcycles. The museum also has some interesting exhibits on the local area but it is even better for its archives on the history of South Canterbury.

The third-largest public art collection in the South Island is at the **Aigantighe Art Gallery** (*49 Wai-Iti Road; tel: (03) 688 4424; open Tue–Fri 1000–1600, weekends 1200–1600*). You pronounce the odd name 'egg and tie' and it is Gaelic for 'At Home' or 'Welcome'. The sculptures in the garden are quite remarkable and the gallery normally has a touring exhibition.

The area is full of gardens, of which the best known are the **Botanic Gardens** (*Queen St; open daily 0800–dusk*) near the public hospital. These splendid gardens include a very large collection of native plants, displays of threatened species and a herb and rose garden.

Perhaps the greatest attraction of the town is **Caroline Bay**, a good sandy beach, considered one of the safest in New Zealand, and with plenty of shady trees.

## Accommodation in Timaru

**Anchor Motel $$** *42 Evans St; tel: (03) 684 5067; www.anchormotel.co.nz*

**Panorama Motor Lodge $$** *52 The Bay Hill; tel: (03) 688 0097 or 0800 103 310; www.panoramic.net.nz*

**Parklands Motor Lodge $$** *65 Evans St; tel: (03) 688 4108; fax: (03) 688 4107; email: parklands@timaru.com*

## The amazing Timaru trio

The town has three famous characters. The first is Phar Lap, the greatest racehorse the world has ever known, born in October 1926 at Seadown, which is close enough for you to make a pilgrimage to see his statue in the paddock where he was born. Failing that, you can go to the local raceway, which is just to the north of the city and is named after the great red galloper, who was one of the biggest racehorses of all time.

An Australian, Hugh Telford, bought Phar Lap for 160 guineas in June 1928. Phar Lap won 37 out of 51 races during three years in Australia, despite the fact that, at the end, he was carrying penalty weights that should have made his legs buckle. The horse died shortly after winning in the United States, which put an immense strain on international relations for some time, although it would be wrong to suggest there was any direct threat of war. Australians love to think of Phar Lap as being their own. He was not: he was born in New Zealand, raced in Australia and was (possibly) murdered in the United States.

The Richard Pearse Airport services Timaru and is named after a pioneer aviator – probably the first aviator in the world. A replica of his aircraft hangs in the museum where the curators keep a very open mind on possible claims that Richard Pearse flew before the Wright brothers. They will only admit that it is possible – the wimps.

Even though Richard Pearse lived until 1953, it is difficult, at this stage, to prove who was the first to fly. There is considerable evidence, however, to suggest that Richard Pearse was the first to manage powered flight. He was certainly airborne very early in 1903, nine months before the Wright Brothers. That is now accepted by the definitive work on aviation, *Jane's All the World's Aircraft*. Richard Pearse plainly had kangaroos loose in his top paddock – the locals used to throw potatoes at him and he ended his life in a psychiatric hospital in Christchurch. But he was an honest and decent man and he considered a flight should be recognised only if it was a full circular trip. So he let the honours go to the Wright brothers.

Although Robert Fitzsimmons was born in 1862 in Cornwall, England, he came to New Zealand with his family in 1871 to live in Timaru. He became a blacksmith in his father's shop and, in his spare time, a boxer. He first beat everyone in New Zealand, then went to Australia and did the same there. Finally he moved to San Francisco where he won the world middleweight championship in 1891, at the age of 28, by beating Jack Dempsey.

That was one title. In 1897 he became the world heavyweight champion when, in Carson City, Nevada, he knocked out 'Gentleman' Jim Corbett in the 14th round. In 1903, at the age of 41, he also won the world light-heavyweight title on points against George Gardner.

Fitzsimmons revisited New Zealand in 1908 and Timaru went mad welcoming the local hero. A statue to this amazing man stands in the courtyard beside the ANZ bank in the centre of the town.

**Right**
Farmers use unconventional
vehicles in this part of the
world

# TWIZEL

Visitor Information
Centre *N entrance,*
*Twizel Events Centre; tel:*
*(03) 435 3124 for all*
*bookings and tour*
*information; www.twizel.com*
**Department of**
**Conservation Office**
*Wairepo Rd; tel: (03) 435*
*0802.*

Twizel is one of the newest towns in New Zealand and, it is fair to warn you, is some considerable way away from being the loveliest. It came about in 1966 as part of the power development scheme in the upper Waitaki. It was basically built for construction workers, and at one time there were nearly 6,000 people living here. When the job was finished the government gave the town to Mackenzie County. With its style of Scandinavian design, the town was at odds with its surroundings. Bit by bit, nature has softened the edges, grown back trees and added greenery. Now the town, with its artificial Mackenzie Hydro Lakes, is being slowly transformed into a recreation area. So successful has this been that, in the peak Christmas period, it is nigh on impossible to get a room. The town is also the centre for several adventure activities including mountaineering, ski touring, hot-air ballooning and wilderness fishing.

Many people come here on their way to Mount Cook. Others come to see the **Black Stilt Colony**, located 3km out of town on the SH8. These birds have been brought back from the edge of extinction. At one time there were probably fewer than 40 pairs. Now that number has doubled, but there is no certainty that they will survive. You can view the stilts from a hide, with binoculars provided (*open Aug–Apr daily 0930–1400; tel: (03) 435 0802 in season to make a booking*).

Also worth seeing is the **Mount Cook Salmon Farm** (*15-min drive out of town on the Tekapo Canal; tel: (03) 435 0085*), which makes use of the immense amount of fresh water available for the breeding of salmon that were introduced into the river nearly a hundred years ago from Canada. The wild colony was threatened by the hydroelectric development and this farm is part of a plan to protect the fish and grow them commercially.

## Accommodation and food in Twizel

Hunters Café Bar $ *2 Market Place; tel: (03) 435 0303; open from 1100.*

Colonial Motel $$ *36 Mackenzie Dr; tel: (03) 435 0100 or 0800 355 722; fax: (03) 435 0499.* Near town centre.

Mountain Chalets Motel $$ *Wairepo Rd; tel: (03) 435 0785; email: mt.chalets@xtra.co.nz; www.mountain/chalets.co.nz.* Mountain views.

## The legend of James Mackenzie

The Mackenzie myth is one of New Zealand's most important stories. It is one of those stories that defines the way that New Zealanders regard themselves. James Mackenzie's date of birth is not known, but it is believed he was born in Inverness, Scotland, some time in the 1820s, emigrating to Australia during the 1840s. He then came to New Zealand with the object of taking up land for a sheep run, although no one has ever been able to trace any application in his name. It is important to understand that his first language was Gaelic and that he spoke English only when necessary, and then not well.

In 1855 about 1,000 sheep went missing from Levels Station, at Timaru. The sheep were tracked by the Levels overseer, James H C Sidebottom, and two Maori assistants. The tracks led into the backcountry and over the Mackenzie Pass into what is now known as Mackenzie Country. This is brutally tough country to traverse and for one man to move a mob of 1,000 sheep, even helped by the best sheepdog in the world, would be well-nigh a total impossibility. Either you believe the myth that Mackenzie was some sort of other-world figure or he had outside help.

Late in the afternoon of 4 March 1855 the tracking trio found James Mackenzie with the sheep and overpowered him. They removed his boots and tied him up. During the night he escaped and in his bare feet found his way over broken and rough country to Lyttelton, where he went into hiding. Sergeant Edward Seager eventually found him hiding in an attic. He was tried and convicted of theft and was also accused of 'standing mute with malice'. He was sentenced to five years in gaol.

He escaped from prison twice and, after 18 months, was pardoned by the Provincial Superintendent, who accepted that James Mackenzie's silence when cross-examined in court came from his almost total lack of comprehension of the English language. Later, James Mackenzie claimed to have been helping a James Mossman to drive the sheep. Before running away, Mossman admitted to Mackenzie that the sheep were stolen but asked Mackenzie to stay with them as he, Mackenzie, was innocent. It is perhaps relevant to realise that the word Mossman is similar to a Gaelic phrase for 'thief'. And also that Mackenzie had on him £21 when captured, most of which he said was a sheep-droving fee. That would be a phenomenal amount to pay for a legal piece of droving in those days. But it would not be out of order to pay an accomplice that much for rustling sheep. After he was pardoned, Mackenzie is thought to have left New Zealand for Australia. According to other reports, he was not deported.

This much is the truth about James Mackenzie, but many other legends have attached to him, mostly total balderdash. He did not, for example, discover the pass through the mountain that bears his name. It had appeared on maps years before and was well known to the local Maori. His dog Friday did not rush into the court and identify him, or have its tongue slit to keep it silent, and it was not shot or hanged at the direction of the court. All of these stories seem to have come from the fertile imagination of Sergeant Edward Seager. It is not widely known that Seager was the grandfather of the crime writer, Ngaio Marsh. It could be said that perhaps she inherited her story-telling talents from Sergeant Seager.

**Above**
The Moeraki Boulders

# Suggested tour

**Total distance:** 300km.

**Time:** 5 hours' driving (excluding sightseeing).

**Links:** From Oamaru, Queenstown (*see page 245*) is 120km west.

From **TIMARU ❶**, drive inland on the SH8 through Pleasant Point to **FAIRLIE ❷** and then to **LAKE TEKAPO VILLAGE ❸** on the edge of the lake. The road then runs down past Lake Pukaki to **TWIZEL ❹** and from there to **Omarama ❺**, all of this on the SH8. From there you take the SH83 to the coast and then the SH1 to **OAMARU ❻** and back up the coast to Timaru along the SH1.

As a detour from Oamaru, you can drive along the coast road towards Dunedin where you will come across the **MOERAKI BOULDERS ❼**, scattered along the beach at Moeraki. There are about 50 of these boulders and they are up to 4m in circumference, with the largest estimated at 7 tonnes. The Maori version of how they got there is that they were spilled from the ancestral canoe, *Araiteuru*, that was wrecked nearby. If you look at the rocks with an unsuspicious eye it is true that the very nearly perfectly circular stones each have the appearance of a woven net holding a gourd.

Technically the rocks are classified as septarian concretions. They were probably formed some 60 million years or so ago. In soft mud on the sea floor lime minerals adhered to an object – a fossil shell, bone fragment or piece of wood – and gradually grew in size. They were not, in fact, shaped by erosion by the sea, as seems the logical explanation, but rather by the chemical action of minerals within their core pushing their way out.

**Right**
Mount Cook

## Also worth exploring

You simply must make a detour to see **Mount Cook** (Aoraki) from the Mount Cook National Park. You will be able to see it from the coast, as well, but it is one of those mountains where one view is never enough. From Twizel take the SH80, which runs along with Lake Pukaki on your right and the Ben Ohau Range on your left. At the head of the lake where it is fed by a glacier (it looks more like a large and ugly mud and rock plain at this point) you arrive at Mount Cook Village, which is in Mount Cook National Park. You can see Mount Cook very clearly in front of you and it may occur to you that it might make a pleasant half-hour stroll. This would be a mistake. The mountain is 3,754m high and perpetually capped by snow. Mount Cook is suited to experienced climbers only, preferably with a guide. It is also some 35km from where you are standing. The mountain was not climbed until 1894 and it is still considered a formidable peak.

The Mount Cook National Park Visitor Centre (*1 Larch Grove; tel: (03) 435 1186; email: mtcookvc@doc.govt.nz*) will advise you of walks you can take. Several can be undertaken in a matter of a few hours and require no special equipment. Near the visitor centre is **The Hermitage** (*tel: (03) 435 1809; www.mount-cook.com*), which has remarkable views and is the most famous hotel in New Zealand. The first hotel was built here in 1884 but was destroyed by flood in 1913. The replacement was burned down in 1957 so this is the third attempt – a great place to relax and wallow in the views.

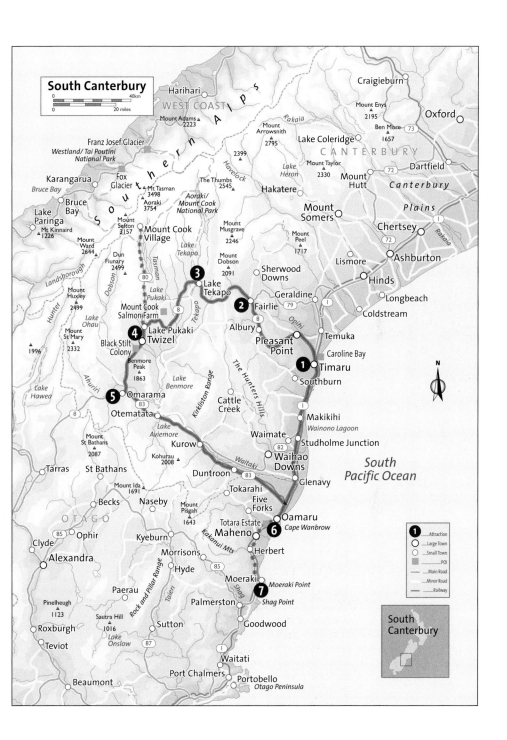

## South Canterbury

0 ———— 40km
0 ———— 20 miles

Harihari
WEST COAST
Mount Adams ▲
2223

Franz Josef Glacier
Westland/ Tai Poutini
National Park

Karangarua
Bruce Bay
Fox
Glacier
Bruce
Bay
Lake
Paringa
Mt Kinnaird
▲ 1226
Mount
Ward
2644 ▲

Mount
Sefton
3157

Mount Cook
Village

Mt Tasman
3498
Aoraki
3754
Aoraki/
Mount Cook
National Park

The Thumbs
2545 ▲

Hakatere

Dun
Fiunary
2499 ▲

Mount
Huxley
2499 ▲

Landsborough

Mount
St Mary
▲ 2332

▲
1996

Lake
Hawea

Hunter

Ahuriri

Dobson

Lake
Pukaki

Mount Cook
Salmon Farm

Lake
Ohau

Black Stilt
Colony

Benmore
Peak
1863

80

Lake
Tekapo

8

Lake
Benmore

Tasman

Tekapo

Mount
Dobson
▲ 2091

Sherwood
Downs

Geraldine

Fairlie

Albury

Pleasant
Point

Southburn

79

8

Opihi

Temuka

Caroline Bay

Timaru

Kirkliston Range

The Hunters Hills

Cattle
Creek

Waimate

82

Studholme Junction

Waihao
Downs

Makikihi
Wainono Lagoon

**South
Pacific Ocean**

Tarras
St Bathans
Mount
St Bathans
2087

Kohurau
2008 ▲

Kurow

Waitaki

Duntroon

83

Glenavy

Tokarahi

Five
Forks

Oamaru
Cape Wanbrow

Totara Estate
Maheno

Herbert

Moeraki
Moeraki Point

Palmerston
Shag Point

Goodwood

Sutton

87

Waitati

Port Chalmers
Portobello
Otago Peninsula

Beaumont

Roxburgh
Teviot

Lake
Onslow

Sautra Hill
1016

Pinelheugh
1123

Paerau

Rock and Pillar Range

Taieri

Hyde

Morrisons

Kakanui Mts

85

Becks
Naseby
Mount
Pisgah
1643

Mount Ida ▲
1691

St Bathans

Clyde
Ophir
Kyeburn
85
Alexandra

OTAGO

Craigieburn
Mount Enys
▲
2195

Oxford

Rakaia

Mount
Arrowsmith
▲ 2795

Ben More
1657

73

Lake Coleridge
CANTERBURY

2399 ▲

Lake
Heron

Mount Taylor
▲ 2330

72

Dartfield

Mount
Hutt
Canterbury

Mount
Somers

Plains

Chertsey

72

Rakaia

1

Mount
Musgrave
▲ 2246

Mount
Peel
▲ 1717

Lismore

Ashburton

Hinds

Longbeach

Coldstream

N

South
Canterbury

1 ..... Attraction
O ..... Large Town
○ ..... Small Town
▦ ..... POI
—— ..... Main Road
—— ..... Minor Road
—— ..... Railway

# Southland

## Ratings

| | |
|---|---|
| Scenery | ●●●●○ |
| Museums | ●●●○○ |
| Railways | ●●●○○ |
| Outdoor activities | ●●●○○ |
| Heritage | ●●○○○ |
| Children | ●●○○○ |
| Dining | ●●○○○ |
| Watersports | ●○○○○ |

The southernmost region of New Zealand is called, with precise logic, Southland. It covers the land south of Balclutha in the east and Te Anau in the west. In all, this amounts to 32,000sq km of highly productive agricultural land, with sheep farming predominant. Southland has a population of around 100,000 – many of whom are direct descendants of the original Scottish pioneers, and a distinctive rolling of the 'r' is a dead giveaway for spotting a true Southlander. The region has about three people to the square kilometre so it is by no means overcrowded. And, indeed, it is not overcrowded with tourists except for its stellar attraction of Fiordland (*see pages 254–63*). Tourists tend to go directly to the better-known destinations, such as Queenstown, and leave out the rest of Southland. This is a mistake, for all of this is beautiful countryside, with a magic and appeal all its own.

## BALCLUTHA

**Clutha Information Centre** *4 Clyde St; tel: (03) 418 0388; fax: (03) 418 1877; www.cluthacountry.co.nz*

Balclutha is 85km to the southwest of Dunedin and has a population of just over 4,000 people. It straddles the banks of the Clutha River and is a service town for a sheep-farming region. Balclutha is Gaelic, and means 'town on the Clyde'. The Clutha (Gaelic for the Clyde) is New Zealand's largest river, for although it is some 16km shorter than the Waikato it discharges double the volume. The river drains about 2.2 million hectares of land. In Maori mythology the River Clutha, as it runs through the town, is personified as two people who were journeying to the sea from Lake Wanaka. They had a fight at the place which is now Balclutha, and went their separate ways.

**Right**
The Clutha River

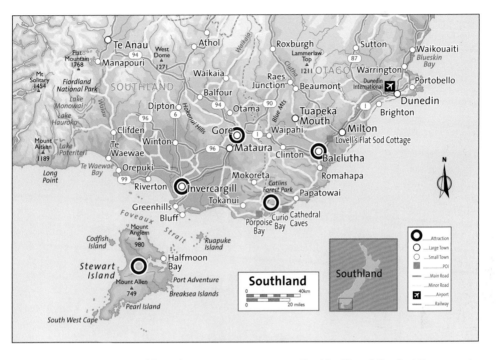

There is some argument as to the identity of the first European to settle in the area. One claimant is Thomas Redpath, who is said to have settled there in 1849. In 1852 James McNeil built a hut which became the first house. He started a ferry service, around which a town grew up when gold was discovered. The river itself was a rich source of gold, and over 100 dredgers worked the river at the end of the 19th century.

The first road bridge appeared in 1868, but lasted only ten years. It was washed away, as was the town and much of the surrounding countryside, in a series of devastating floods in 1878. In 1935 a ferroconcrete bridge was erected which now dominates the town. Large flood banks have also been raised.

There are several walks in the area, of which two are most suitable for day visitors. The first is the **Blair Athol** walkway, which takes about two hours there and back. It starts at Naish Park in Charlotte Street and follows the bank of the Clutha River to the Blair Athol farm. The other is the **Awakiki Bush** walkway, which also takes about two hours. It starts on the Awakiki Road, off the SH92, just by Telford. The bush here is a fine example of podocarp forest, with some 300-year-old totara trees.

On the SH1, some 12km to the north, is the **Lovell's Flat sod cottage**, which has been restored and finished in period style to provide an example of a classic single-room colonial home of the early pioneering era.

## Accommodation and food in Balclutha

**Helensborough Motor Inn $$** *Main North Rd; tel: (03) 418 1948; www. helensboroughmotorinn.co.nz*

**Picasso's $$** *Rosebank Lodge, 265 Clyde St; tel: (03) 419 0021; www. rosebanklodge.co.nz*

**Below**
Dunedin Railway Station

**Rosebank Lodge $$** *265 Clyde St; tel: (03) 419 0021; www. rosebanklodge.co.nz*

# CATLINS

**Catlins Information Centre and Museum** *10 Campbell St; tel: (03) 415 8323; www.catlins-nz-com; open Mon–Fri 0930–1630, Sat–Sun 1000–1600.* The main town of the area is Owaka, which is some 38km from Balclutha and has a population of around 200.

**Fill up your tank** Note that in the Catlins the petrol stations tend to be few and far between, and you should always fill up when you have a chance.

The Catlins stretch from Waipapa Point, in Southland, to Nugget Point in Otago and are a complex mixture of rivers, bush and forest. This is where the Maori once came to hunt the giant moa, which they did with such success that this gentle and defenceless giant of a bird disappeared some 500 years ago, and the Maori left the area for other hunting grounds.

The name is a misspelling. The area was named after Edward Cattlin, who, in 1840, surveyed the Clutha River. It is not known how the spelling mistake crept in.

The **Catlins Forest Park** lies between Invercargill and Dunedin and is very popular with day visitors from Dunedin. This wooded area was once heavily cropped, with the result that it had some 30 sawmills, supported by thriving towns, and its port, Huahine, was kept busy shipping out the lumber. Logging ended partly because the resource ran out, but also partly due to intense political activism by the green movement, which wanted, and has pretty much succeeded in obtaining, an end to all logging in New Zealand, except in plantations and replaceable forests.

The eastern edge of the park is defined by a rugged coastline and this has always been a refuge for marine life, including many species that are endangered. There are, for example, hooker sea lions, Hector's dolphins (the world's smallest dolphins) and the hoiho, which has just been dragged back from the very real threat of extinction. Also in the Catlins are the **Cathedral Caves** which have some passing resemblance to a cathedral and in which you can see quite clearly the imprint of fossilised trees and shells. The whole area is a wonderland of blowholes, lakes and forest paths.

One coastal feature not to be missed is **Nugget Point**, a headland complete with rocky outcrops and a lighthouse that has become one of the country's most recognised scenic icons. There is also a site from which you can view the comings and goings of the rare yellow-eyed penguins.

# GORE

**Gore Information Centre** *Cnr Hokonui and Norfolk Sts; tel: (03) 208 9288; fax: (03) 203 9286; email: goreinfo@goredc.govt.nz*

Gore is Southland's second town, with a population (being generous) just over 13,000. More importantly, it boasts of being the Brown Trout Capital of the World (there are more than 40 streams in the area and there is no way you can miss making a catch); and it lays claim to being New Zealand's Country Music Capital – a sort of antipodean Nashville writ small. Every June, Gore plays host to the Golden Guitar festival. You should plan your visit to avoid this time unless you particularly like country-and-western music.

The town was named after Sir Thomas Gore Browne, an early Governor of New Zealand. In 1855, when settlers arrived to start sheep farming, the area was known as Longford, after a long ford across the Mataura River. In 1862 the town was surveyed and subdivided and in 1885 became a borough. Another settlement on the other side of the river, called Gordon, joined Gore in 1890 and became East Gore.

## Accommodation and food in Gore

**Gore Motor Camp $** *35 Broughton St; tel: (03) 208 4919.* Camping sites and small cabins.

**Howl at the Moon $$** *2 Main St; tel: (03) 208 3851.* No werewolves and a reasonable blackboard menu.

**Riverlea Motel $$** *46–48 Hokonui Dr; tel: (03) 208 3130; www.riverleamotel.co.nz.* A short walk from town; 10 ground-floor units.

**Scenic Circle Croydon Hotel $$** *Queenstown Highway; tel: (03) 208 9029; www.scenic-circle.co.nz.* Licensed restaurant.

# INVERCARGILL

**ⓘ Invercargill Visitor Information Centre** *Queens Pk, 108 Gala St; tel: (03) 211 0895; fax: (03) 218 4418; email: invercargill@i-site.org; www.southlandnz.com*

**Department of Conservation Office** *Don St; tel: (03) 214 4589.*

This is the southernmost city in New Zealand and it lies 187km south of Queenstown, and about 175km southwest of Dunedin. The city served as the capital of the former Otago province from 1861 to 1930. In 1853 the New Zealand Company bought the surrounding area from the Maoris and two years later the first settlers arrived at the site. It was originally known as Kelly's Point. Its name was changed in 1857 to honour Captain William Cargill, Dunedin's co-founder. It was surveyed in 1859, by which time the population had reached 1,000, and proclaimed a town in 1861. When the population had soared to nearly 2,000 in 1871 it was declared a borough and became a city in 1930. Most of the early settlers were Scots and there is still something of the Scottish burr in the way in which the locals speak.

There is a sort of feeling in New Zealand that Invercargill – being on the south coast of the South Island and the southernmost city of the country – is somehow the end of the line; that, in some way, it is a little behind the times; perhaps a little rustic. And there may be some truth in this, but Invercargill is nevertheless one of the most pleasant cities that you will ever visit. The locals are a gentler breed of people, full of the pleasant courtesies of life – not unduly stressed. When a motel proprietor saw a large nail in the tyre of the car the author had hired, he went and got a jack and changed the wheel.

Some of the sites in Invercargill are very special. For example, the **Southland Museum and Art Gallery** *(tel: (03) 219 9069; www.southlandmuseum.com; on Gala St)* is a most splendid building architecturally, and is home to the tuatara, which is a lineal descendant of the dinosaur. This lizard-like reptile is very small, and you have to be very sharp-eyed to spot it; even when someone points out that the small stick-coloured creature resting on a stick against a background of sticks is a tuatara, it is difficult to work out what is the tuatara and what is stick.

This magnificent museum was originally a small collection exhibited by Alexander McKenzie from 1871 in his Invercargill barber's shop. In 1915 it was taken over by a newly formed Southland Museum Board and transferred to the Invercargill Technical College building. The present building, at the entrance to the city's Queens Park, was built to commemorate Southland's centenary, and opened in 1942. The two art galleries have been added since, among a number of additions to the original structure.

The emphasis in the museum's Maori gallery is the reconstruction of everyday aspects of pre-European life in Southland. The growing permanent art collection of predominantly southern New Zealand paintings, sculptures and weaving is shown between exhibitions, while a collection of ceramics is on permanent display.

Near the city centre is **Queens Park** which has an amazing display of rhododendrons, a rose garden and a wildlife sanctuary.

The port for Invercargill is **Bluff**, located 27km to the south. In the season, which runs from March through August, it can give you a

**Below**
The fishing fleet at Bluff

royal feast of oysters. The oysters are a deep-water breed and have a sweet and succulent flavour. Bluff is an all-weather mechanised port, but it also has a fishing fleet to harvest Bluff oysters from Foveaux Strait. As a port it lacks the charm of tourist destinations, and it is very much a working town.

Just outside is Bluff Hill which, at 265m, gives a tremendous view of the harbour, the Foveaux Strait and Stewart Island in the distance. Sterling Point–Ocean Beach Walk runs for 7km and offers panoramic views over the islands and surrounding coastline. When you get to Sterling Point you have reached the end of the road as far as the South Island is concerned, and this point is reinforced by a signpost showing the distance to various major cities around the world. It is rare to see it without a smiling tourist standing underneath to be photographed.

## Accommodation and food in Invercargill

**Invercargill Top 10 Holiday Park** $–$$ *77 McIvor Rd (northern edge of town off SH6); tel: (03) 215 9032; www.invercargilltop10.co.nz.* Small and very friendly.

**Zookeepers Café** $–$$ *50 Tay St; tel: (03) 218 3373.* Local favourite.

**Balmoral Lodge** $$ *265 Tay St; tel: (03) 219 9050; www.balmoralmotel.co.nz.* Scottish theme.

**Cabbage Tree** $$ *379 Dunns Rd, Otatara; tel: (03) 213 1443.*

**HMS King's Restaurant** $$ *80 Tay St; tel: (03) 218 3443; lunch and dinner weekdays. Dinner only Sat and Sun.* Right over the top nautical décor. Amateur but friendly service. Superb seafood.

**Surrey Court Motels** $$ *400 Tay St; tel: (03) 217 6102 or 0800 188 333; www.surreycourt.co.nz.* Close to the centre of town and the aquatic centre.

## Bankrupt province

Southland became a province in 1861 by achieving its independence from Otago Province, which had been established in 1853. In hindsight, this was a mistake. The new province had based its spending levels on the flow of money from the northern goldfields. When this source of revenue dried up, Southland went bankrupt. As a result it was forced to rejoin Otago Province in 1870. Now Southland is technically a local government region, although it is known as a province by the inhabitants, and it is considered slightly vulgar to bring up the unfortunate fact of the bankruptcy.

# STEWART ISLAND

**ℹ Stewart Island Visitor Centre**
*Elgin St; tel: (03) 219 1400; www.stewartisland.co.nz*

**Department of Conservation Information** *tel: (03) 219 0009; www.doc.govt.nz*

**☕ Bay Motel $$** *9 Dundee St, Halfmoon Bay; tel: (03) 219 1119; www.baymotel.co.nz. Views across the bay and just a short walk to all amenities.*

**South Sea Hotel $$**
*Main Rd, Oban; tel: (03) 219 1059; www.stewart-island.co.nz. Traditional hotel rooms and self-contained motel units on an adjacent property. Obviously there is an in-house bar and a restaurant where you can sample the local delicacy – muttonbird.*

New Zealand is not just the two major islands. There are others. The Foveaux Strait, which is 30km wide, separates Stewart Island from the south coast of the South Island. You can get there by catamaran from Bluff, which is an hour's trip, or you can fly there. You will note that there is a strong wind and that the water is generally cold, so it is worth recording that, in January 1963, John Van Leeuwan, of the Oreti Surf Life-Saving Club, swam across from the South Island in 13 hours and 40 minutes.

Stewart Island could be considered Captain Cook's other mistake. When he saw it in 1770 he thought it was a peninsula attached to the mainland and marked it so on his charts. It was not until 1804 that an American, Captain Owen F Smith, in his ship the *Favourite*, corrected the mistake. There was an attempt to call it Favourite's Strait but the authorities would have none of that damned Yankee nonsense and it was renamed Foveaux Strait after the Lieutenant-Governor of New South Wales, Major Joseph Foveaux. The island itself is named after Captain William Stewart, who first charted it in 1809. It was bought from the Southland Maori by the New Zealand government in 1864, for £6,000. Its Maori name is Rakiura, which means 'glowing skies', perhaps a reference to the *aurora australis* which can often be seen.

The island is about 1,746sq km in extent and the main industry is fishing. The population is 360 and declining – because life on the island is fairly harsh and primitive. The climate is also something less than enticing. The tourist brochure says: 'Sunshine hours are lower than the national average and whilst it may be true that it rains on a higher number of days in a year, our annual rainfall is less than Auckland.' There is one general store on the island and two cafés, which are also takeaways. These are in Halfmoon Bay. Having said all that, this is a paradise for nature lovers, especially twitchers, and in the summer holidays it can be difficult getting accommodation.

## Suggested tour

**Total distance:** 360km.

**Time:** 6 hours' driving (excluding sightseeing).

**Links:** Invercargill is also the start point for exploring Fiordland (*see page 254*).

From **INVERCARGILL ❶**, head down McQuarrie Street to take the southern scenic route along the coast to **BALCLUTHA ❷**. The narrow and winding road goes past **TOKANUI ❸** and **CURIO BAY ❹** in the Catlins, which has dolphins and a swimming beach, plus **CATHEDRAL CAVES ❺**, which are accessible at low tide, and the spectacular **NUGGET POINT ❻**.

Balclutha is a little inland from the coast. At this point you rejoin the SH1 and continue to **MILTON** ❼ . From here you can detour to Dunedin, where you can make a side trip along the Otago Peninsula (see *page 244*).

From Milton, take the SH8 as if you were travelling to Cromwell, then take the turning back to **GORE** ❾ at **RAES JUNCTION** ❽ , which will bring you back on the SH1 and return you to Invercargill.

## Also worth exploring

To the west of Invercargill along the **Southern Scenic Route** is the small and pleasant fishing town of **Riverton** – or Aparima, to use its former Maori name. It is one of the oldest settlements in the country and the oldest permanent European settlement in Southland. Set on the banks of the estuary formed by the Aparima and Purakino rivers, it was formerly a safe haven for whalers and sealers and was first established as early as the 1830s. Now having gradually developed into a popular coastal holiday resort, Riverton is a fine place to stop for lunch, a short walk on the beach, or even to consider as a quieter alternative base to Invercargill, now only 42km to the east.

**Left**
Invercargill

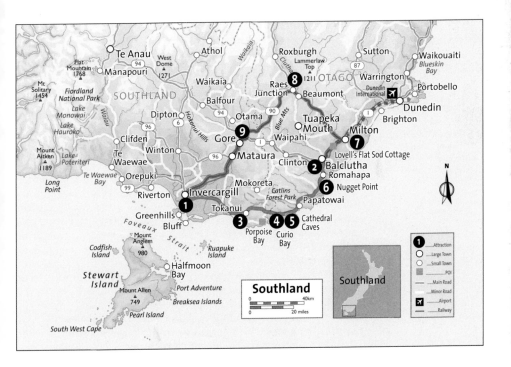

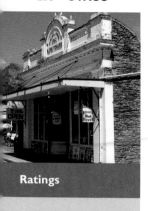

# Otago

## Ratings

| | |
|---|---|
| Scenery | ●●●● |
| Outdoor activities | ●●●● |
| Watersports | ●●●● |
| Heritage | ●●●● |
| Railways | ●●●● |
| Children | ●●● |
| Dining | ●●● |
| Ski resorts | ●●● |

The rest of New Zealand has ambivalent feelings about Queenstown and the surrounding area. North Islanders will tell you that the whole area is ruined by tourist development – that it is not what it was in the old days. Enquire gently when they last went there and you will probably find that they have never been to the Queenstown area, and they have probably never been to the South Island. It is, as it were, criticism by folklore. Do not listen to it. Queenstown, Arrowtown, Wanaka and Cromwell, and all the attractions in between, are utterly charming and fascinating. In this area you can go skiing, sail on several different lakes, ride on a steam train, eat at some of New Zealand's better restaurants, go fishing, climb a mountain or dance the night away. It is an area that has almost everything that you would ever require on holiday, except for a beach and a seaside.

## ARROWTOWN

 **Visitor Information, Lakes District Centennial Museum**
*Buckingham St; tel: (03) 442 1824.*

Arrowtown is on the western bank of the Arrow River, 21km northeast of Queenstown. The town – we are being polite here, for it is but a village with pretension – was founded on gold. The discovery was made by Maori Jack-Tewa in 1862, although an American prospector, William Fox, claimed that he was the first and ran the diggings like something out of the old West. Though Fox managed to keep the finds secret for some months, the news eventually leaked out and gold miners flooded to the region, creating mayhem. Problems with claim jumpers led to some gun play, and the area was not brought under control for some years.

The small town that grew up to cater for this dubious trade consisted more of taverns than anything else. Of these early taverns, the **Royal Oak** still exists. To get the style of the place, you should know that, in 1864, the proprietor ran a raffle with a golden nugget as a prize. The winner, who in the end had to prove his claim in court, was Albert Eichardt, a German who was making a living selling ginger

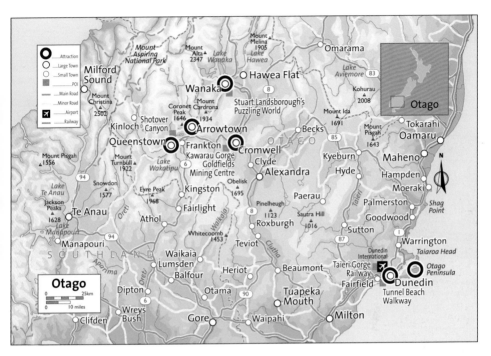

beer. He sold the nugget and used the proceeds to buy Eichardt's pub, in Queenstown, which exists to this day (*see page 246*).

Arrowtown is still pretty much as it was at the turn of the 20th century. Over 50 of the town's buildings are listed as Historic Places by the New Zealand Historic Places Trust. At one end of the town is the **Lakes District Centennial Museum**, a small but extremely interesting and intelligently designed museum with a good section on gold mining (*Buckingham St; tel: (03) 442 1824; email: museum@queenstown.co.nz, open daily 0900–1700*) and a portrait of the notorious pub landlord, Bully Hayes (*see feature, page 238*).

At the western end of town is the **Chinese settlement**. The Chinese came in the 1860s from the Victoria goldfields at the invitation of the Otago Provincial Council, who hoped they would revive the goldfield when it was going into decline. The Chinese miners were ostracised and so created their own settlement. Their stone and mud-brick dwellings have now been excavated and restored, as has Ah Lumb's store, which was built around 1880. Ah Lumb continued to run the store, and operated as a translator and leader of what was left of the Chinese community, until his death in the 1920s. The store sold opium, which was legal in New Zealand until 1901. Outside the store is Ah Wak's lavatory, also listed as a Historic Place and thought to be the only outdoor lavatory in New Zealand to be accorded this honour.

**Above**
Picturesque Arrowtown

## Bully Hayes

Arrowtown threw up its share of colourful adventurers – but none more colourful than Bully Hayes. In his time, Hayes was accused of murder, rape, piracy, cheating at cards and bigamy. He was not a nice man. Burly of build and very strong, he kept his long hair crimped with a lady's curling iron to disguise the fact that one ear had been cut off for cheating at cards. Contemporary accounts suggest he looked like a defrocked bishop.

The *Sydney Morning Herald* of 6 January 1860 denounced him as a thief, a liar and a scoundrel. In the next day's issue it announced he was to be charged with the sexual assault of a 15-year-old girl. That day Bully Hayes left Australia and escaped to Arrowtown. There he worked as a gold miner and set up a pub called the United States Hotel. This was not a pub as we know it today – just a tented roof over sod walls.

A pub run by the Buckingham family started up in competition, and was a far superior establishment. Bully Hayes retaliated by seducing and bigamously marrying Rosa Buckingham, the daughter of the house. He took her with him to Nelson and there, in 1864, she and their child drowned in a boating accident. Hayes managed to swim to safety. In scathing editorials the *Nelson Colonist* openly accused Hayes of murdering his family.

He immediately left New Zealand and sailed for Vanuatu and the island of Pentecost. There he became fascinated by the rituals of the natives who leapt from trees with vines attached to their ankles. In later years he would boast how he had been brave enough to try this and had been told by the locals that he was the first white man to do so. Which makes him, disreputable character that he was, the first New Zealand bungee jumper. A few years later, at Apia, in Western Samoa, a cook hit Hayes over the head with a tiller and pitched him into the sea, where he drowned. No attempt was made to charge his murderer.

## Accommodation and food in Arrowtown

**Arrowtown Born of Gold Holiday Park $–$$** *Centennial Ave; tel: (03) 442 1876; www.arrowtownholidaypark.co.nz.* Cabins, camping and caravan sites.

**Café Mondo $$** *Ballarat Arcade, Buckingham St; tel: (03) 442 0227; open Mon 1000–1730, Tue and Wed 0800–1730, Thu–Sun 0800–late.* Traditional café-style meals and occasional live music.

**Mace Motel $$** *Main St; tel: (03) 442 1825; fax: (03) 442 1855; email: macemotels@xtra.co.nz; www.macemotel.co.nz*

**The Stables $$** *28 Buckingham St; tel: (03) 442 1818; closed Mon.* Beautiful food in a stylish old stone building.

**Viking Lodge Motel $$** *21 Inverness Cres; tel: (03) 442 1765; www.vikinglodge.co.nz.* Self-contained A-frame units.

# CROMWELL

**ⓘ Cromwell and District Information Centre and Museum** *47 The Mall; tel: (03) 445 0212; fax: (03) 445 1319; email: cromwell@i-site.org; www.cromwell.org.nz*

Cromwell, 63km east of Queenstown and 57km south of Wanaka, is a town that was, in a sense, partly drowned. The town was redeveloped in the 1980s for the building of the Clyde dam and it was here that the construction workers were housed. The dam was finished in 1989 and Lake Dunstan was created as the waters rose. At the same time, sadly, they flooded some of the lower and older streets in the town. There is no doubt that the dam has completely changed the character of the Clutha River and there has been some local opposition. In the original scheme there were going to be five power stations, but it now seems unlikely that there will be any further development.

The lake now offers a splendid range of watersports, from fishing to water-skiing and jet boating. If you want to spend time on the lake you can get more information from the visitor centre or contact Trout Fishing Services (*tel: (03) 445 1745*).

The lake the dam created also swamped some 1,400ha of fertile and productive land. You can see the total story of how it happened, and the history of Cromwell when it was a gold mining town, in displays at the **Information Centre and Museum**. This is in the Mall at the centre of town, which has now been made into a pedestrian precinct.

Several historic buildings were salvaged before the waters rose and rebuilt and refurbished to form **Old Cromwell Town** (*tel: (03) 445 1746*) on the lake shore next to the Victoria Arms Hotel.

The **Kawarau Gorge Goldfields Mining Centre** (*8km west of the town on the SH6; tel: (03) 445 1038; www.goldfieldsmining.co.nz; open daily 0900–1730, with working demonstrations at 1200 and 1500*) is remarkably authentic. The 25ha reserve covers an area once known as Gees Flat. It has been mined on and off for nearly a century. Visitors can pan for gold and will very probably find traces of the metal, which will get you excited even if they are worth nothing. The centre shows in an intelligent and interesting way how gold was recovered in different ways, using a stamper battery and water races. The marks left by the gold mining operations of the 1860s are still visible, as are the rock shelters of some of the early Chinese gold miners.

On the SH8 is a footpath that starts from the Bruce Jackson Memorial Lookout and goes to an old reservoir dating from 1875 and built when an outbreak of typhoid fever was blamed on Cromwell's existing water supply. The reservoir was enlarged and faced with stone in 1882. From there you can continue along Brewery Creek and down to the highway to complete your round trip.

## Accommodation and food in Cromwell

**Cromwell Top 10 Holiday Park $** *Alpha St; tel: (03) 445 0164; www.cromwellholidaypark.co.nz.* Has cabins, camping and caravan sites.

**Grain and Seed Café $–$$** *Melmore Tce; tel: (03) 445 1077.* One of a number of reconstructed historic buildings of 'Old Cromwell'.

**Anderson Park Motel $$** *9 Gair Ave; tel: (03) 445 0321; fax: (03) 445 1523; email: andersonparkmotel@xtra.co.nz*

**Bannockburn Hotel $$** *420 Bannockburn Rd; tel: (03) 445 0615.* Located 8km from Cromwell. Excellent lunch option in pleasant setting. Extensive wine list.

**Golden Gate Lodge $$$** *Barry Ave; tel: (03) 445 1777; fax: (03) 445 1776; email: stay@goldengate.co.nz; www.goldengate.co.nz*

### Colourful characters

Cromwell was originally called The Junction, as it stands at the confluence of the Clutha and Kawarau rivers, at the northern end of the Cromwell Gorge. Gold was discovered in 1862, and the town grew to service the miners. In 1864, a toll bridge was built over the Clutha by an Australian – one Henry Hill. In true Australian convict style he later absconded to South America with money he had filched from the government.

Hill was not the only colourful Australian to be associated with the town. Cromwell's first mayor was Captain Jackson Barry. He is reputed to have been, variously, a drover in New South Wales, a trader in Malaysia, a whaler in the Pacific, a miner in California and a coach driver in Victoria in Australia. He arrived in Cromwell in 1863 and started the Victoria and Sydney Butchery, offering cut-price meat. As mayor, he once thumped a councillor who moved a motion against him. Charged with assault, he said in his own defence, 'I still think I took the proper course, if a forceful one, of putting my councillors straight.'

# DUNEDIN

**Dunedin Visitor Centre** 48 The Octagon; tel: (03) 474 3300; fax: (03) 474 3311; email: dunedin@i-site.org; www.dunedinnz.com

Dunedin is the old Gaelic name for Edinburgh, and many of the city's streets bear the same names as those of the Scottish capital. Indeed, the street layout was based on Edinburgh's and the city looks as if it ought to be in Scotland.

Dunedin was founded in 1848 by the New Zealand Company, and a dozen years later it expanded rapidly due to the discovery of gold in central Otago. Although the goldfields were over 100km inland, this was the nearest port and the money flowed in. Between 1861 and 1865 the population grew five-fold and Dunedin became one of New Zealand's wealthiest cities. During this time many of the buildings which now decorate the city were erected, including New Zealand's first university. Dunedin had the first cable tramway outside the United States although, sadly, this was closed in 1957.

Dunedin's prosperity may now have faded, but the city is kept alive and pulsing by an estimated population of 18,000 students attending its four tertiary educational institutions. This has led to a very powerful entertainment, café and music scene – the Dunedin Sound is internationally recognised, with several successful bands based here.

The heart of Dunedin is the **Octagon**. It is here you will find the Robert Burns statue with 'his back to the kirk and his face to the pub'. And that splendid saying is correct, for his back is towards **St Paul's Cathedral**, a fine twin-spired church that is an example of Gothic

**Below**
Dunedin Botanical Gardens

Revival at its very best. The interior has a great vaulted ceiling, but with some modern additions that are something less than architecturally impressive. On the north side of the eight-sided square are the municipal chambers.

The **Dunedin Public Art Gallery** (*tel: (03) 477 4000; www. dunedin.art.museum.co.nz; open daily 1000–1700*) has one of the best collections in the country, possibly second only to that of Auckland. Certainly its collection of contemporary New Zealand works must be one of the best in the world.

The **railway station** at Dunedin was designed by architect George Troup who seemed to work on the basis that nothing succeeds like excess. His designs earned him the nickname of Gingerbread George. This station claims to be one of the most photographed railway buildings in the world and, indeed, in that respect it competes on equal terms with the one in Kuala Lumpur.

The **Otago Settlers Museum** is a short distance from the railway station (*31 Queens Gardens; tel: (03) 474 2728; www. otago.settlers.museum.co.nz; open Mon–Fri 1000–1700, weekends 1300–1700*). It tells in a very intelligent and interesting way the story of Otago, including the early Maori settlers and the European and Chinese gold diggers. This museum has been expanded by taking over the bus station next door, which was originally part of the railway station. The Art Deco booking hall, which is gorgeous, now houses a permanent exhibition of the history of transport in Otago. Guided city walks are also available.

Next door to the Settlers Museum is the new **Dunedin Chinese Garden** (*tel: (03) 479 0368; email: chinesegarden@dcc.govt.nz; open daily 1000–1700, Wed also 1900–2100*). Completed in 2008, it is a fine example of a Chinese garden and a great place to escape the buzz of the city.

Further along on Great King Street is the **Otago Museum** (*tel: (03) 474 7474; www.otagomuseum.govt.nz; open daily 1000–1700*), which has an outstanding collection of Maori and Pacific Island culture. The latest addition to the permanent exhibits is Discovery World Tropical Forest – Live Butterfly Experience, featuring around 1,000 imported tropical butterflies (additional charge). It is a great place to go on a cold, rainy day!

At 42 Royal Terrace you can see how a prosperous Edwardian family lived. The Jacobean-style house **Olveston**, originally built in 1906, has been kept in a perfect state of preservation since 1933. There are guided tours daily starting at 0930 (*for bookings tel: (03) 477 3320; www.olveston.co.nz*).

In the *Guinness World Records* book Dunedin is listed as having the world's steepest street. This is **Baldwin Street**, which climbs at a gradient of 1:2.7 although some suggest it is, in truth, only a wimpish 1:2.9. There are 270 steps to the top. As you climb up, consider that the current record for running all the way to the top and down again

**Above**
Dunedin's Otago University

is just about two minutes. This is a dead-end road and trying to drive a car up the street is truly not a very good idea, as many visiting car drivers have found to their great expense.

Dunedin is a splendid city for walking, with several excellent waymarked walks. Perhaps the easiest and the most scenic is the **Tunnel Beach Walkway** which takes only an hour for the return walk. It is off Blackhead Road, some 7km south of the city. There is a stairway tunnel, which gives direct access to the beach. It was dug in the 1870s by a farming family, the Cargills. This tunnel is on private property and is closed during the lambing season, in September and October.

If you are an anorak (as is the author of this book) you mustn't miss the train journey through the **Taieri Gorge** (*www.taieri.co.nz; for bookings tel: (03) 477 4449*). This amazing journey takes you over Victorian bridges and through tunnels, following the Taieri River, from which gold was once extracted. The railway track runs for 77km into the high country, and it ranks in excitement with the journey to Los Mochis, along the Copper Canyon, in Mexico. Your best bet is the return run to Pukerangi (*departs 0930 Fri, Sun & holidays, 1430 Oct–Apr Mon–Fri, 1230 May–Sep Mon–Fri*).

## Accommodation and food in Dunedin

**Larnach Lodge $** *Camp Rd; Otago Peninsula; tel: (03) 476 1616; email: larnach@larnachcastle.co.nz.* Stay in the converted stables and coach house of the Hon William James Mudie Larnach (*see feature, page 244*).

**97 Motel $$** *97 Moray Pl: tel: (03) 477 2050; www.97motel.co.nz.* Centrally located with parking.

**Beach Lodge Motel $$** *38 Victoria Rd, St Kilda; tel: (03) 455 5043.* Handy for the beach but only a few minutes from the city centre.

**Etrusco at the Savoy $$** *8a Moray Pl (1st floor); tel: (03) 477 3737; open daily from 1730.* Fine Italian choice that is good value, despite the plush surroundings.

**High Tide Restaurant $$** *29 Kitchener St; tel: (03) 477 9784.* Set in a garden with harbour views. Bistro style with blackboard menu. BYO and licensed. Good value.

**Scotia Restaurant and Whiskey Bar $$** *Dunedin Railway Station; tel: (03) 477 7704; www.scotiadunedin.co.nz.* Fine Scottish flavours in a historic setting.

# OTAGO PENINSULA

One of the principal reasons for visiting **Dunedin** is to drive along the **Otago Peninsula**, which stretches east along the southern edge of Dunedin's harbour. This has several internationally known wildlife reserves and some of the world's rarest birds can be seen here in their natural habitat. All along the peninsula you will see lots of examples of the common cormorant or shag (which, despite the rhyme, does not lay eggs inside a paper bag), and herds of sea lions – who will probably regard you with amused condescension. Incidentally, these are not fat, funny, furry animals that you can pet. Keep your distance as they can get quite angry with tourists who take liberties.

## Larnach Castle

Obsession can take many forms. In the case of banker William James Mudie Larnach, it took the form of building the perfect house on the Otago Peninsula, a stately pleasure dome in a New Zealand setting. The cost of the house, when finished, was estimated to be £125,000. It took 200 workmen three years to complete the shell and the interior was not finished for another 12 years. In current terms the total cost would be something approaching US$8 million, which would make it possibly the most expensive house in the southern hemisphere.

After Larnach's third wife ran off with his eldest son, and he suffered financial misfortune, he made his last magnificent gesture. One day in 1898 the Hon William James Mudie Larnach dressed himself in all his glory, with silk topper, tail coat and two gold fob watches – contemporary accounts stress the *two* watches as a sign of wealth – and went to a committee room in Wellington's Parliament House. There he blew his brains out. You can see Larnach's folly on your way out to the albatross colony on the Otago Peninsula (see *opposite*).

**Above**
The Otago Peninsula is famed for its albatross colony

The crowning glory, at the very tip of the Peninsula – about 30 minutes' drive from Dunedin – is the world's only mainland colony of royal albatross (*Diomedea epomophora*) at **Taiaroa Head**. There is a well-equipped visitor centre, open every day, with lots of audiovisual information. You can walk out to a special viewing bunker on the headland and, if you're lucky, see the birds coming and going. From February to September albatross chicks can often be seen in the nests. Windy days are best, because the birds need a breeze to take off and land successfully. The main viewing area is closed during the breeding season (mid-September–late November) and on Tuesday mornings. Tour bookings can be made with the Taiaroa Visitor Centre (*tel: (03) 478 0499; www.albatross.org.nz*).

It is much easier to see the penguins at the **Yellow Eye Penguin Conservation Reserve**, close to the albatross centre. This has a hide for viewing and is open from October to March for three to four hours before sunset (*tel: (03) 478 0286; www.penguinplace.co.nz*).

# QUEENSTOWN

Queenstown is a most remarkable place. This is not a singular opinion. The Condé Nast *Leisure and Travel* magazine ranked it third as a world destination and it topped the world in the categories of fun, friendliness and environment. A survey of first-class passengers flying around the world – serious travellers who are seriously rich – made Queenstown their favourite destination, ahead of Kenya and Sydney.

**Above**
Downtown Queenstown

**ℹ Queenstown Visitor Centre**
*Clocktower Bldg, Cnr Shotover and Camp Sts; tel: (03) 442 4100; fax: (03) 442 8907; email: info@qvc.co.nz; www.queenstown-vacation.com.* Note that there are three offices facing each other on these corners, all claiming, correctly, to be visitor information centres. The one to go for has the green triangle, which confirms that it is a member of the Visitor Information Network. This is not of vital importance as, in truth, the other two will hand out the same leaflets, although basically they are there to sell tours.

Is Queenstown a city? It certainly acts like one although, in truth, it is a small town with a population just nudging over 10,000. What makes it so special? Perhaps partly its history. Queenstown is a place of myth and stories. Consider the story of the first two serious European settlers. One was said to be the godson of the Tsar of all the Russias. His name was Paul Nicholai Balthasar von Tunzelman and, along with William Gilbert Rees – how inadequate he must have felt with just three names – he explored the area around Lake Wakatipu in 1859.

The two explorers drew lots as to who should own each side of the lake. Rees took Queenstown and Tunzelman took the other side of the lake. For two years they farmed there undisturbed until gold was found in the Arrow River. This resulted in the largest gold rush in New Zealand and William Rees, Welsh and a very decent chap, supplied the miners with provisions and with a ferry across the lake. His place became known as The Camp and his woolshed was transmogrified into the Queen's Arms Hotel. That hotel remains to this day under the name of **Eichardt's**. In the great flood of 1879, when the floodwaters rose to within 8cm of the top of the bar, Eichardt's kept serving beer to customers seated up to their waists in water.

Partly, then, it is the history and partly the setting that has something to do with it. Queenstown is surrounded by high peaks that are wonderful with snow in winter, and are inviting, rather than forbidding, in summer. The stunning view is always of Lake Wakatipu and across to the exceptional scenery of the serrated Remarkable Mountains.

There is a wealth of things to do all year round, from the idiocy of bungee jumping to jet boating and rafting. The following list of activities is in no particular order.

Sail across Lake Wakatipu in the **TSS *Earnslaw*** (*tel: 0800 656 503; www.realjourneys.co.nz*) to Walter Peak Station. The *Earnslaw* is a 1912 vintage twin-decker with coal-fired boilers and is, as far as is known, the last coal-fired steamer operating in the southern hemisphere. It sails to sheep stations around the lake, such as the Walter Peak sheep station, founded by the McKenzies in 1860, running along the rugged peaks and only accessible by steamer across the lake. Walter Peak is so taxing that the steepness of the terrain actually wears out sheepdogs; after three years at Walter Peak they have to be moved to a lowland farm for the rest of their working lives.

Slide down **Coronet Peak** on a tin tray – not the correct technical term, but it will do. On Coronet Peak they have built a 600m-long metal Cresta Run, rather like giant guttering. You sit on a tin tray

**Below**
Queenstown sunset

equipped with a brake and then come screaming, literally or not, down the mountain. Serious riders hit 65kph, which, that close to the ground, seems like breaking the sound barrier.

Take a mountain bike to the top of Coronet Peak and then ride down. This is not for the faint-hearted, nor yet the thin of skin. Mountain bikes are widely available for hire in Queenstown and the ski lift to the top of Coronet Peak runs through the summer.

Shoot the **Shotover Canyon** in a Johnson-powered jet boat (*Shotover Jet; tel: (03) 442 8570; www.shotoverjet.com*). In this case, because you are strapped in, the feeling that you are going to crash at full speed into the rock walls of the canyon is tempered by the sure knowledge that the driver and the rest of the passengers will go with you.

Fly tandem over some of the world's most magnificent scenery in a hang-glider made for two or on a two-person manoeuvrable parachute. This last is called parapenting and is, in truth, one of life's more amazing pastimes. As William Congreve almost wrote, 'Thus grief still treads upon the heels of pleasure; Take off in haste, parapente at leisure.'

Curse you, Red Baron. **Actionflite** (*tel: (03) 442 9708; www. actionflite.co.nz*) will dress you up like an early aviator, sit you in the front seat of a Tiger Moth and then take you on a trip that includes barrel rolls, looping the loop and other adrenalin-stimulating aerobatics. Perhaps best done before lunch.

Ride on the **gondola** (*tel: (03) 441 0101; www.skyline.co.nz*) some 446m to the top of Bob's Peak and wallow in the view over the town, lake and mountains.

## Skiing

Skiing in New Zealand is not quite like skiing in other countries. There are one or two exceptions, but you can take it as a general rule that all the ski fields are away from the accommodation. That is, you cannot ski-in/ski-out to and from your accommodation. You have to get to the ski field first, either by car or by bus. This has advantages and disadvantages. The advantage is that, in the evening when you go out to dinner or for a drink, you do not have to shuffle through a lot of slush. And on those days when you do not feel like skiing – many skiers can only handle two or three days before having a break – then going sightseeing or exploring is very easy. The downside is that on the days when you do ski you have to get up very early in the morning. That is because the drive to the ski field is going to take you at least half an hour, and it is as well to work on the basis that it will be a full hour.

Queenstown offers a staggering range of skiing, from the beginner's slopes of The Remarkables and the runs of Coronet Peak to heli-skiing in remote areas such as Harris Mountain, for the serious skier who wants to sample untouched powder snow. There are also three major and internationally rated ski fields – Treble Cone, Cardrona and Waiorau Nordic – within an hour's drive of Wanaka. For ski information, visit *www.snow.co.nz*

Even if the closest you want to come to bungee jumping is the elastic in your own underwear then you can still derive terrific entertainment from simply spectating. The best place to do that is at the original bungee site at the Kawarau Suspension Bridge, run by the ubiquitous AJ Hackett Bungy Company (*tel: (03) 442 4007 or 0800 286 495; email: bungycentre@bungy.co.nz*). The multi-million-dollar centre is testament to the commercial success of the concept in the last 20 years.

Is there any downside to this seeming paradise on Earth? Yes. In winter it attracts a young push of ski and snowboard bums who spend the days on the slopes and then go on the town in the evening. The adrenalin is still pumping and they tend to be boisterous, noisy and obtrusive, but harmless. The worst thing they do is body surf on the bonnets of parked cars. Fine if it's not your car. If you're looking for a totally quiet life, Queenstown is not for you. You will probably find Wanaka, which has much the same attractions on a quieter scale, more your speed (*see next page*).

**Below**
Shotover Canyon jet boat

## Accommodation and food in Queenstown

In Queenstown more than anywhere else in New Zealand there is an ever-changing scene. At any given time there are 30-plus restaurants and they go in and out of style as the seasons change. You can check what is current in *Queenstown Today and Tonight,* a free publication available at all information centres.

**McNeill's Brewery $** *Church Street; tel: (03) 442 9688.* Boutique beers and a good atmosphere.

**Queenstown Lakeview Motor Park $** *Main St; tel: (03) 442 7252; fax: (03) 442 7253; email: reception@holidaypark.net.nz; www.holidaypark. net.nz.* Short walk from town. Has cabins, camping and caravan sites with excellent facilities.

**Roaring Meg's $** *57 Shotover St; tel: (03) 442 9676; open for dinner only.* Old miners' cottage.

**Boardwalk Seafood Restaurant $$** *Steamer Wharf Village; tel: (03) 442 5630.*

**The Cow $$** *Cow Lane; tel: (03) 442 8588; open daily 1200–2300.* Excellent pizza and pasta.

**Lakeside Motel $$** *18 Lake Esplanade; tel: (03) 442 8976; fax: (03) 442 8930; www.queenstownaccommodation.co.nz*

**Queenstown Lodge $$** *Sainsbury Rd; tel: (03) 442 7107; fax: (03) 442 6498; email: stay@queenstownlodge.co.nz; www.queenstownlodge.co.nz*

**Rydges Lakeland Resort $$** *38–54 Lake Esplanade; tel: 0800 446 187 in NZ, or (02) 9261 4929; email: reservations@rydges.com*

# WANAKA

**❶ Wanaka Visitor Information Centre** *Ardmore St; tel: (03) 443 1233; fax: (03) 443 1290; email: lakewanaka@i-site.org; www.lakewanaka.co.nz*

Wanaka is some 120km to the north of Queenstown. It is based on Lake Wanaka, which extends into the Mount Aspiring National Park and has a most beautiful view of the surrounding alps. Get there on the right day and you can see these mountains reflected in the lake. The headquarters of Mount Aspiring National Park is in the town and Wanaka is an ideal base for exploring the park. There is excellent fishing in the lake, which is New Zealand's fourth largest. Its depths actually plunge to below sea level. In the winter, this is the centre for skiing at Cardrona and Treble Cone, and during the skiing season the town is very lively, with an active nightlife. And, quite importantly, it is generally cheaper than Queenstown.

There are different explanations as to where the name Wanaka came from. One suggestion is that it should properly be Wananga, which means 'sacred knowledge'. Another is that it is called after a chief

**Above**
Fishtail Falls, in Mount Aspiring National Park

whose name was Oanaka, pronounced Wanaka, who once came here to fish. In fact, until 1940, the town was simply called Pembroke.

The first European to see the area was probably Nathaniel Chalmers, who was 23 years of age when he came here in 1853. He did not stay. The first European settler was John Turnbull Thomson, who arrived in 1857. He was quickly followed by farmers who set up sheep runs. Then came the gold rush in Central Otago, and trees were cut and floated down the Clutha River to supply the gold miners. Nearby gold mines had splendid names, including Homeward Bound, The Pirate, and Gin and Raspberries.

One of the great attractions of the area is the **Mount Aspiring National Park**. There are walks throughout the park, but it is important that you start with the Department of Conservation visitor centre in Wanaka before you set off on anything serious, as some of the walks can be dangerous. If one in particular is to be highly recommended, it is the Rob Roy Glacier Walk (4 hours return).

🅽 **Mt Aspiring National Park**
**Visitor Centre** *Ardmore St, Wanaka; tel: (03) 443 7660; email: wanakavc@doc.govt.nz*

By contrast, **Stuart Landsborough's Puzzling World** (*2km out of Wanaka; tel: (03) 443 7489; www.puzzlingworld.com*) is an eccentric three-dimensional maze which is equally challenging for children and adults. The aim is to visit the four corners of the maze in order and this will take you an hour, at the very least. If you get totally lost and fed up, there are emergency exits throughout the maze.

Wanaka is also famous for its **War Birds Over Wanaka** air show, which happens every other year on even-numbered years and lasts for four days. It will probably be difficult to time your visits to coincide with that event, but the **New Zealand Fighter Pilots Museum** (*tel: (03) 443 7010; www.nzfpm.co.nz*) at the airport has some tremendous exhibits, including a wide range of historic aircraft. If you have unlimited financial resources, you can pay to go up in one of the exciting aircraft, including a Tiger Moth, a Pitts Aerobatic or a Mustang designed in the 1940s.

Next door is the **Wanaka Transport and Toy Museum** (*tel: (03) 443 8765; open daily 0830–1700*). The vehicles are in a superb state of preservation. This may have to do with the fact that New Zealanders keep their vehicles running on the roads much longer than any other country, and because the air at Wanaka is generally dry this helps to prevent rust.

### Accommodation and food in Wanaka

**Panorama Court $** *29–33 Lakeside Rd; tel: (03) 443 9299; email: jen.bruce@xtra.co.nz; www.panoramacourt.co.nz*

**Wanaka Lakeview Holiday Park $** *212 Brownston St; tel: (03) 443 7883; www.wanaka lakeview.co.nz*. Has tourist flats, cabins, camping and caravan sites.

**Brook Vale Manor $$** *35 Brownston St; tel: (03) 443 8333; fax: (03) 443 9040; email: info@brookvale.co.nz; www.brookvale.co.nz*

**Kai Whakapai $$** *Cnr Helwick and Ardmore Sts; tel: (03) 443 7795.* Good blackboard fare and a great spot to watch the world go by.

**Te Wanaka Lodge $$** *23 Brownston St; tel: (03) 443 9224; fax: (03) 443 9246; email: info@tewanaka.co.nz.* Modern design. Excellent buffet breakfast.

## Suggested tour

**Total distance:** 14km.

**Time:** 45 minutes.

Rather than a car ride, the best tour you can do in the Queenstown area is to take a ride on the *Kingston Flyer* (*tel: (03) 248 8848; email:*

*info@kingstonflyer.co.nz; the return trip takes 45 minutes and the service typically runs from October through to April, but it may run in other months).* KINGSTON ➊ is a 45-minute drive from Queenstown, turning south at Frankton and then following the shore of Lake Wakatipu on the SH6. The steam train runs for 14km on what is left of the much longer Lumsden to Kingston line. Sadly the train now runs only from FAIRLIGHT ➋ to Lake Wakatipu, but even this is a rapturous journey back in time.

The original wooden line was built in 1863. The present track was completed in 1878, when a wharf was built at Kingston so that a lake steamer could connect with the trains. Originally the *Kingston Flyer* ran between the Kingston Wharf and the main trunk line at Gore. The name *Flyer* was given in recognition of the speed of the train, which used to reach 80kph – a frightening pace in the 19th century.

Now Pacific locomotives pull restored carriages in late 19th-century railway green. There are two New Zealand-built Pacific Class AB steam locomotives and each of the trains has run nearly 2.5 million kilometres in its working life, all of which has been spent on the South Island of New Zealand. The present-day train was restored by the government's Railways Department and started running in 1971 as a reminder of what train travel was like in the 1920s. All the carriages are genuine antiques, having been lovingly restored. In the dining car they serve authentic railway tea in thick cups.

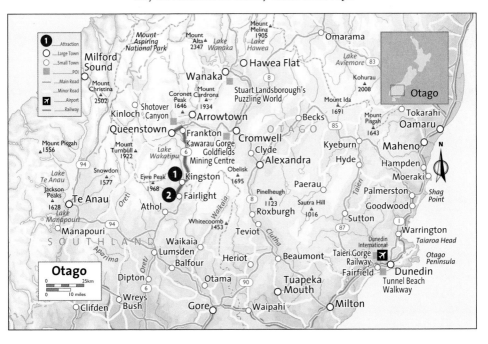

# Fiordland

**Ratings**

| | |
|---|---|
| Scenery | ●●●●● |
| Outdoor activities | ●●●●○ |
| Watersports | ●●●●◔ |
| Waterfalls | ●●●●○ |
| Cruises | ●●●○○ |
| Children | ●●○○○ |
| Heritage | ●○○○○ |
| Dining | ●○○○○ |

Of all the many glories of New Zealand, Fiordland is surely the most magnificent. It is the largest national park in the country and at 1,251,924ha is one of the largest in the world. It covers much of the southwestern portion of the South Island. The whole Fiordland region is now a World Heritage Park in recognition of the fact that it is one of the key ecological areas in the world. The park authorities are very conscious of the fact that this is not only one of the most naturally beautiful and fascinating spots on Earth – but that it should also remain so. Thus the access to the park is intelligently but not intrusively controlled and there are some parts of the park, with rare and significant plants and wildlife, where entry is limited through a permit system.

## MILFORD SOUND

Milford Sound is the most instantly impressive part of the park, and the most visited. All those visitors are right, for it would be a terrible mistake to visit New Zealand and not, at the very least, take a **cruise on the Sound** – and the very best time to visit is when it is raining. Many visitors find this hard to comprehend, but the staggering beauty of the area really is enhanced by rain. The absolutely ideal way of seeing the Sound is to be there during a heavy rain storm – the heavier the better – and then to have the sun break through while you are travelling the Sound. Then, like magic, the fiord is suddenly full of rainbows. This happens more times than you would think. The odds are in your favour, as it rains on average 200 days of the year. This area normally gets 6m of rain a year though it can reach a phenomenal 7m.

If your luck holds, the clouds will then part and you will see Mitre Peak rising like a dramatic statement from the Sound. Mitre Peak

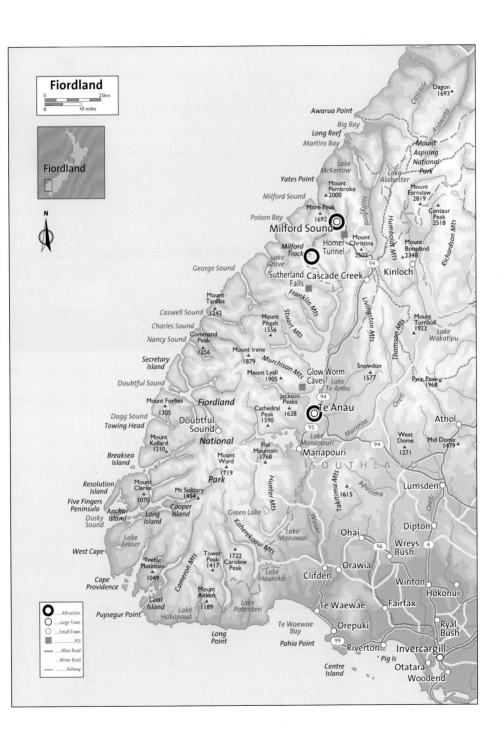

## Fiordland

0 _____ 25km
0 _____ 10 miles

Fiordland

N

Cascade
Dagon
1693 ▲

Arawata

Awarua Point
Big Bay
Long Reef
Martins Bay

Mount
Aspiring
National
Park

Lake
McKerrow

Lake
Alabaster

Yates Point

Mount
Pembroke
▲ 2000

Mount
Earnslaw
▲ 2819

Milford Sound

Holyford

Centaur
Peak
2518 ▲

Richardson Mts

Mitre Peak
▲
1692

Poison Bay

◎

**Milford Sound**

Homer
Tunnel

Mount
Christina
2502 ▲

Humboldt Mts

Mount
Bonpland
▲2348

Milford
Track

◎

Lake
Grave

94

Kinloch

George Sound

Sutherland Cascade Creek
Falls

Franklin Mts

Livingston Mts

Mount
Tanilba

Mount
Turnbull
1922

Caswell Sound 1242

Mount
Pisgah
1556 ▲

Stuart Mts

Lake
Wakatipu

Charles Sound

Command
Peak

Nancy Sound

▲
1256

Mount Irene
▲1879

Murchison Mts

Thomson Mts

Secretary
Island

Mount Lyall
1905 ▲

Glow Worm
Caves

Snowdon
▲1577

Doubtful Sound

Lake
Te Anau

Eyre Peak
1968

Mount Forbes
▲
1305

Jackson
Peaks

**Fiordland**

94

Te Anau

Oreti

Dagg Sound

Cathedral
Peak
1590

▲
Peak

◎ Te Anau

Athol

Towing Head

**Doubtful
Sound**

1628
▲

95

West
Dome

Mid Dome
1479 ▲

Mount
Kellard
1210▲

**National**

Lake
Manapouri

Mararoa

94

1271

Breaksea
Island

Flat
Mountain
1768

**Manapouri**

SOUTHLAND

Mount
Ward
▲
1719

Resolution
Island

Mount
Clerke
▲
1070

Mt Solitary
1454 ▲

**Park**

Hunter Mts

Takitimu Mts

Aparima

Lumsden

Oreti

Five Fingers
Peninsula

Anchor
Island

Cooper
Island

▲1615

Dusky
Sound

Long
Island

Green Lake

Waiau

Dipton

Lake
Fraser

Kaherekoaui Mts

Lake
Monowai

Ohai

Wreys
Bush

6

West Cape

Treble
Mountain
1049

Cameron Mts

Tower
Peak
1417

1722
Caroline
Peak

Lake
Hauroko

Clifden

Orawia

Winton

96

Cape
Providence

Mount
Aitken
▲1189

Lake
Poteriteri

Hokonui

Coal
Island

Lake
Hakapoua

Te Waewae

Fairfax

Puysegur Point

Te Waewae
Bay

Orepuki

Ryal
Bush

Long
Point

Pahia Point

99

Riverton

Invercargill

Centre
Island

Pig Is

Otatara

Woodend

◎ ......Attraction
◉ ......Large Town
○ ......Small Town
■ ......POI
━━━ ......Main Road
——— ......Minor Road
------- ......Railway

**Above**
Mitre Peak, Milford Sound

reaches 1,692m and was named in 1851 by the survey ship HMS *Acheron*. From the south, it looks like a bishop's mitre, though from any other angle you can see it is a line of five peaks rather than just one. The Maori name for Milford Sound is Piopiotahi, which means 'place of the singing thrush', a native bird which is now extinct.

Almost certainly you will drive to Milford Sound from Te Anau (*see pages 261–2*), which is a journey of 119km and, no matter what the weather is like, it will take longer than you think. Along the way you will pass **Cascade Creek**, which is home to the long-tail bat, New Zealand's only native land mammal. The road into the park from Te Anau passes along the gorge-like Upper Hollyford Valley and then through the Homer Tunnel. The granite hills and mountains on either side have no dense cover of soil or vegetation. When it rains there is nothing to hold or soak up the water and the result is a series of literally hundreds of episodic waterfalls and cascades.

One cascade follows another, each in turn more spectacular than the last in height and volume. In some places, the rock wall is a solid sheet of water; in others, permanent waterfalls spill out in foaming torrents of tumbling, crashing water. The river by the side of the road changes into a mad thing and smashes and crashes its way over the rocks on its desperate and hurried way to the Sound.

When you get to the **Homer Tunnel** you need to be prepared. The unlined tunnel carries a road steeply downhill from the Hollyford

Valley through to the Cleddau Valley – one of the rare Welsh names in New Zealand – and then on to Milford Sound. The tunnel was named after Henry Homer, the man who discovered the saddle through which the tunnel runs. He suggested the tunnel in 1889 but work did not start until 1935. The driving of the tunnel was completed in 1940 but work was abandoned because of the war. Work started again in 1951 and was completed in 1953.

The tunnel is very small and unlit. It is hewn out of the mountainside, the inside is bare rock and there are no lights – none. It is just over 1km long and once you are inside it you cannot see the far end. No other tunnel appears so graphically to let you know that you are in the heart of a mountain.

If you are driving a hire car it is important that before you enter the tunnel you know exactly where the headlight switch is placed and check that it is working. Once you are in there is no turning back and the darkness is absolute. The tunnel is single track, with what are optimistically called passing places. If you are going this way to catch a specified tour of the Sound you will be in luck because all the other traffic in the tunnel will probably be going your way.

Understand, it is not that the tunnel is hazardous. It is just that it would give the most experienced driver pause, for you feel it will

## Doubtful Sound

Unusually, the Doubtful Sound area has many Spanish place names. They recall the Spanish explorer, Malaspina, who led a five-year expedition from 1789. The expedition mapped part of Doubtful Sound while trying to test the force of gravity in the southern hemisphere. The two sailing ships, technically corvettes, the *Descubiepita* and *Atrevida*, arrived off the sound on 25 February 1793. The hydrographer Felipe Bauza took a party inside in a ship's boat. His chart includes the Nec Islets at the entrance – named after Luis Nec, botanist on the *Atrevida* – Malaspina Reach, Bauza Island and Marcaciones Point, where he took the gravity measurements.

The English name of Doubtful Sound came from our hero, Captain James Cook, who was there in 1770 and thought it 'a very snug harbour'. He was doubtful how long he would be held there waiting for the right wind and decided not to sail into the sound, which he marked 'Doubtful' on his chart.

The name Milford Sound was probably given in 1823 by a Welsh sealer named John Grono, who is said to have named the sound after the Welsh harbour of Milford Haven. Despite this possible Welsh connection all of the early settlers in the area were of Scottish descent. The most remarkable of these was the Scottish eccentric Donald Sutherland who settled here after a brief visit as a whaler and for two years met not a single other human being. Eventually he built the John O'Groats Hotel in what is now Milford and tourists came to see the falls named after him, which were for a long time thought to be the tallest in the world, at 580m.

to Pompolona, over the pass to Quintin, and then out to Milford Sound. The first *pakeha* to take this route was almost certainly Quintin Mackinnon who made the crossing from the east in 1888. Tourists started walking almost immediately afterwards and within a year there was a series of huts. Now 10,000 people make the walk annually (the numbers are carefully controlled by the Department of Conservation).

**Below**
Sailing boat cruising through the Fiordland National Park

# TE ANAU

**ⓘ Fiordland Visitor Information Centre** *Cnr Town Centre and Lake Front Drive; tel: (03) 249 8900; fax: (03) 249 7022; email: fiordland@i-site.org; www.destinationfiordland.org.nz.* Opposite the visitor centre is an underground trout observatory where you can feed the fish so that you can have a close-up view. **Fiordland National Park Visitor Centre** *Lakefront; tel: (03) 249 7924; email: greatwalksbooking@doc.govt.nz*

**ⓠ Tawaki Dive** *Tel: (03) 249 9006 or 0800 829 254; www.tawakidive.co.nz,* arranges skin diving in the area. **Fiordland Ecology Holidays** *5 Waiau St, Manapouri; tel: (03) 249 6600.* Natural history cruises for 3–10 days aboard *Breaksea Girl*, a 7-year-old 20m motor sailing yacht. Maximum of 12 passengers. Sails Doubtful, Dusky and Milford Sounds. **Fiordland Wilderness Experiences** *tel: (03) 249 7700; www.fiordlandseakayak.co.nz*

Although this is a pleasant enough place, it mainly exists as a service town for people who are visiting Fiordland and, more specifically, the Milford Sound. Te Anau is 167km southwest of Queenstown and on the second-largest lake – 342sq km in area – in New Zealand. One of its many claims to fame is that on the western side of the lake is a colony of what was once considered to be an extinct species of bird – the takahe. This colony was discovered by a doctor from Invercargill in 1948. At the time it was thought that the takahe had been extinct for at least 50 years. So that the birds are not disturbed, a portion of the national park has been closed off to visitors and there are strong hopes that a full breeding colony will be established – there are now some 160 birds. However, the depredations of stoats have made their protection a difficult task for the Department of Conservation. Safe (ie stoat-free) breeding areas have been set up on various islands and it does appear that the future of the takahe is now relatively assured.

If you want to see a takahe, visit the **Te Anau Wildlife Park** on the road out towards Manapouri. The birds are bred there using eggs taken from the conservation area. It has been found that the takahe will only raise one chick, even though the female may lay a whole clutch of eggs, so the surplus eggs are brought here and hatched and the takahe are raised in conditions approaching those experienced in the wild.

A wide range of trips is available on the lake, with the most interesting being the two-hour excursion to the **Te Ana-Au Caves** where the glow-worm grotto can be entered only by boat. As well as boat trips there is a wide range of (relatively expensive) scenic flights across Milford Sound and the Sutherland Falls. One operator specialising in flights over the Milford Sound is Air Fiordland (*tel: (03) 249 6720*). Wings and Water (*tel: (03) 249 7405*) uses floatplanes, which adds a new dimension to the experience.

## Protecting Fiordland National Park

Some areas are retained as wilderness by the simple expedient of allowing access by foot only. If you are not dedicated enough to walk, you are not going to see them. Areas classified as 'natural environment' will remain pretty much as nature fashioned them, but with some additions by the park authorities, such as huts, bridges and tracks to make access slightly less arduous. Finally, some places are classified as 'facilities areas' where controlled development is allowed.

The best example of this is the part that most tourists will see for certain. That is the cruise-ship terminal in Milford Sound. This has been laid out so that it is accessible, speedy and not overly intrusive. There is no snack bar, no particularly vulgar development – just a clean and well-designed building which can move thousands of visitors a day on to boats to take them on a tour of the Sound and out again with the minimum impact.

### Accommodation and food in Te Anau

**Fiordland National Park Lodge $** *Milford Sound Highway; tel: (03) 249 7811; fax: (03) 249 7753; www.teanau-milfordsound.co.nz*

**Te Anau Great Lakes Holiday Park $** *Cnr Luxmore Drive and Milford Rd; tel: (03) 249 8538; fax: (03) 249 8539; email: info@greatlakes.co.nz*

**Keplers Restaurant $$** *Town Centre; tel: (03) 249 7909.*

**Lakefront Lodge $$** *Lakefront Drive; tel: (03) 249 7728; fax: (03) 249 7124; email: stay@lakefrontlodgeteanau.com; www.lakefrontlodgeteanau.com*

**Redcliff Restaurant and Bar $$** *12 Mokonui St; tel: (03) 249 7431.*

## Suggested tour

**Total distance:** 320km.

**Time:** 5 hours' driving (excluding sightseeing).

**Links:** Southland (*see page 226*) lies immediately to the southeast.

Head north out of **TE ANAU** ❶ along the bank of Lake Te Anau until you reach **PLEASANT BAY** ❷, where a regenerating beech forest borders the lake. From there the road passes by the sheltered harbour of Te Anau Downs, which is also the starting point for the walkers who are going to tackle the **MILFORD TRACK** ❸. Shortly after, on the left of the road, 58km after leaving Te Anau you come to Mirror Lakes, which have wonderful reflections of the mountains in calm weather.

You then pass the Avenue of the Disappearing Mountain, which gets its name because it bobs in and out of sight. Then, at 75km from Te Anau, you come to Lake Gunn, which was named after an early explorer in the area, George Gunn. There is a pleasant 30-minute stroll, well signposted, which takes you by way of a loop track to the shores of the lake.

Just 10km down the road is The Divide which is the lowest east–west pass in the Southern Alps, at 534m. It marks the start of the Routeburn Track, a three-day walk over a 1,277m-high alpine pass to Lake Wakatipu.

The road then goes straight down to the Homer Tunnel which is 101km from Te Anau and which runs 1,219m with a gradient of 1 in 11 (*see Milford Sound, page 256*). From the tunnel the road continues to the Chasm, which is where the Cleddau River drops in a series of spectacular falls down a rocky gorge. There are walkways which will take you there on a 15-minute round trip. Note: it is dangerous to step outside the safety barriers.

From the Chasm it is just over 10km to **MILFORD SOUND** ❹. Return along the same route to Te Anau.

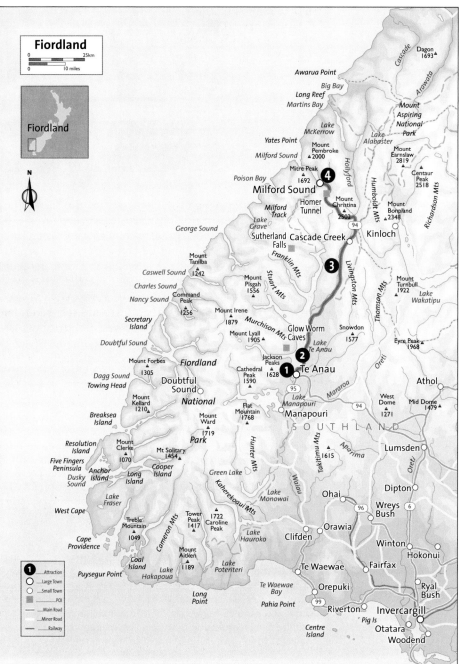

## Fiordland

0                     25km

0            10 miles

Fiordland

N

Cascade

Dagon
1693 ▲

Arawata

Awarua Point

Big Bay

Long Reef

Martins Bay

Mount
Aspiring
National
Park

Lake
McKerrow

Lake
Alabaster

Yates Point

Mount
Pembroke
▲ 2000

Mount
Earnslaw
2819 ▲

Milford Sound

Hollyford

Mitre Peak
▲
1692

Centaur
Peak
2518 ▲

Poison Bay

❹

Milford Sound

Milford
Track

Homer
Tunnel

Mount
Christina
2502 ▲

Humboldt Mts

Mount
Bonpland
▲ 2348

Richardson Mts

Lake
Grave

94

Kinloch

George Sound

Sutherland
Falls

Cascade Creek

Mount
Tanilba

Franklin Mts

❸

Livingston Mts

Caswell Sound

Mount
1242

Mount
Pisgah
1556

Stuart Mts

Mount
Turnbull
1922

Charles Sound

Command
Peak
▲
1256

Thomson Mts

Lake
Wakatipu

Nancy Sound

Mount Irene
▲
1879

Murchison Mts

Secretary
Island

Mount Lyall
1905 ▲

Glow Worm
Caves

Snowdon
▲
1577

Mount
Turnbull

Eyre Peak ▲
1968

Doubtful Sound

Lake
Te Anau

Oreti

Mount Forbes
1305

Fiordland

Jackson
Peaks

❷

Dagg Sound

Cathedral
Peak
1590

1628 ▲

❶  Te Anau

Athol

Towing Head

Doubtful
Sound

95

Lake
Manapouri

Mararoa

West
Dome

Mid Dome
1479 ▲

Mount
Kellard
1210 ▲

National

Flat
Mountain
1768

Manapouri

94

1271

Breaksea
Island

Mount
Ward
▲
1719

S O U T H L A N D

Resolution
Island

Mount
Clerke
▲
1070

Park

Mt Solitary
▲
1454

Takitimu Mts

1615

Aparima

Lumsden

Oreti

Five Fingers
Peninsula

Cooper
Island

Hunter Mts

Dusky
Sound

Anchor
Island

Long
Island

Green Lake

Waiau

Dipton

Lake
Fraser

Kaherekoaui Mts

Lake
Monowai

Ohai

Wreys
Bush

6

West Cape

Treble
Mountain
▲
1049

Cameron Mts

Tower
Peak
1417

1722
Caroline
Peak

Lake
Hauroko

Clifden

Orawia

96

Winton

Cape
Providence

Coal
Island

Mount
Aitken
▲
1189

Lake
Poteriteri

Te Waewae

Fairfax

Hokonui

Puysegur Point

Lake
Hakapoua

Te Waewae
Bay

Orepuki

Ryal
Bush

Long
Point

Pahia Point

99

Riverton

Invercargill

Centre
Island

Pig Is

Otatara
Woodend

❶ .......Attraction

○ ....Large Town

○ ....Small Town

▪ ....POI

— ....Main Road

..... ....Minor Road

— ....Railway

# West Coast

## Ratings

| | |
|---|---|
| Scenery | ●●●● |
| Children | ●●●● |
| Glaciers | ●●●● |
| Gorges | ●●●● |
| Outdoor activities | ●●● |
| Watersports | ●● |
| Heritage | ●● |
| Dining | ●● |

Westland runs down the west coast of the South Island, from just north of Greymouth southwards to Awarua Bay, before running back inland to the central division of the Southern Alps. The area could be classified as the forgotten region. It was isolated from the beginning, and for many years it was undeveloped. Coal mining came to the rescue, but in recent years the area has again been hammered economically. The coal mines have mostly closed, although there are still some open-cast mines. The area now has the lowest population of any provincial region in New Zealand. Despite all this, the region has some exceptional attractions, including two glaciers, a dramatic gorge, waterfalls and industrial remains now made romantic by the passage of time.

## Fox Glacier

**ⓘ Department of Conservation Visitor Centre** *Main Rd, Franz Josef; tel: (03) 752 0796; www.doc.govt.nz*

The Fox Glacier is stunning, both visually and in its statistics. For this is a river of ice slowly making its way from a snowfield below two peaks – the Douglas Peak, at 3,085m, and the Glacier Peak, at 3,007m. The glacier starts at 2,750m above sea level and eases its way down an incline dropping about 200m per kilometre until it grinds and melts and disappears when it gets to 245m above sea level.

Fox is at the western foot of the Victoria Range. The town that services the glacier was not opened until 1927, when the bridging of the Waiho River started to bring in significant numbers of tourists. The town is 25km south of Franz Josef Glacier (*see page 267*) on the SH6. Fox is a larger glacier than Franz Josef – 13km long compared to 10km – and is not moving as rapidly (this is a comparative term) in its descent. The Fox Glacier also has some features that are not to be seen on the Franz Josef – for example the **deep-blue kettle lakes**, which are formed by the slow melting of dead ice left by the retreating glacier.

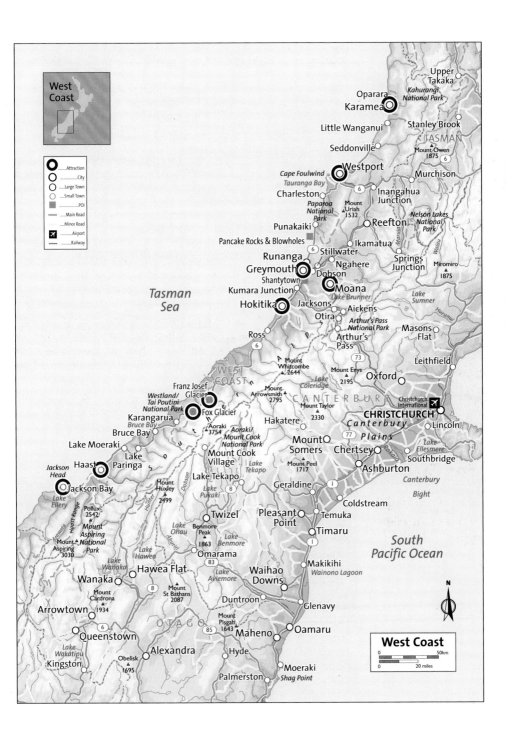

West Coast

West Coast
0 _____ 50km
0 _____ 20 miles

This is also kea country, and these splendid alpine parrots take great delight in attacking the windscreen wipers and windscreen sealing of parked cars.

There is a track from the car park, which is about 8km from town. From there it is a half-hour walk to the glacier. Perhaps even better is the River Walk, which is along the Glacier Road before you get to the car park and runs for 2km, taking about half an hour.

Near to Fox is Lake Matheson, 6km away by road, which has become a major tourist attraction in its own right. When the weather is clear the reflections of Mount Tasman and Mount Cook create a magnificent sight in the still waters of the lake. The view is often used for postcards from New Zealand.

## Accommodation and food in Fox Glacier

**Café Neve $** *SH6, in centre of Fox Glacier township; tel: (03) 751 0110.* Wholefood.

**Fox Glacier Holiday Park $$** *Lake Matheson Rd; tel: (03) 751 0821; fax: (03) 751 0813; www.fghp.co.nz*

**High Peaks Hotel $$** *167 Cook Flat Rd; tel: (03) 751 0131; www.highpeakshotel.co.nz*

**The Plateau $$** *Sullivan Rd; tel: (03) 751 0058; open daily 0900–late (seasonal).* Good reputation and open fire.

### So what is a glacier?

One way of regarding it is as a series of giant blocks of snow crystals that have been made over thousands of years through great pressure. They move slowly and majestically to their eventual doom but are continually renewed at the source.

### Growth and decline

When Julius von Haast first saw the glacier, it was 3km nearer the main highway than it is today. Its surface was up to 300m higher. So for some decades the glacier has been shrinking. Then, in 1980, the process started to reverse and the glacier pushed forward nearly a kilometre. It is not known what will happen with the effects of global warming.

**Right**
Franz Josef Glacier

# FRANZ JOSEF GLACIER

**Franz Josef Glacier Visitor Centre** *Main Rd; tel: (03) 752 0796; fax: (03) 752 0797; email: franzjosefvc@doc.govt.nz.* **Department of Conservation Visitors Information Centre** *Westland National Park, SH6; tel: (03) 751 0807; www.glaciercountry.co.nz*

The Franz Josef Glacier is served by the town sharing its name. Franz Josef town is on the east bank of the Waiho River, which runs from the end of the Franz Josef Glacier. The town is 150km southwest of Hokitika and is on the northern boundary of Westland National Park in South Westland. It has a tourist hotel and many other resort facilities.

This is one of the most accessible glaciers in New Zealand. To view it on foot, drive to the car park 5km south of the village and walk to the face of the glacier following one of several easy routes mapped out by the Department of Conservation. You will see the glacier better and understand it more clearly if you have a skilled guide who will explain what has happened and why. You can also fly up by helicopter or light aircraft and actually land on the glacier. As an investment there is little in this life that could be considered to offer such amazing value for money. When you land, normally above the clouds, you see a view that is totally numbing in its beauty and awesome majesty.

Europeans have been aware of the Franz Josef Glacier for a very long time. Abel Tasman saw it in 1642 and James Cook again in 1770. Why the odd name? The pioneering geologist who did so much to map the South Island was called Julius von Haast. He shared a first name with the reigning Austro-Hungarian emperor, Julius Franz Josef, and so the glacier was named in the emperor's honour.

## Accommodation and food in Franz Josef Glacier

**Blue Ice Café $$** *SH6; tel: (03) 752 0707.* Good in-house pizza and light snacks. Licensed.

**Château Franz $$** *8 Cron St; tel/fax: (03) 752 0738 or 0800 728 372; www.kiwi-backpackers.co.nz.* Backpackers.

**Rainforest Retreat $$** *Cron St; tel: 0800 873 346 or (03) 752 0220; www.rainforestretreat.co.nz.* Eco-based log cabins in a quiet bush setting. Also has camper-van facilities and tent pitches, with modern facilities including a camp kitchen. Spa and internet access.

## Glacier township

When writing about the Franz Josef and Fox Glaciers, it is difficult not to comment on the tourist development that has been allowed to build up around these two great manifestations of nature. Franz Josef, the one-street town that services two of the great glaciers of the world, is intended to show how tourism development can work alongside conservation. In this it does not succeed. It is vulgar, tawdry, ill-designed and generally very nasty. No place in New Zealand so cries out for the intervention of the Department of Conservation to hammer through some severe limitations on signage and to lay down some basic design standards.

## The amazing Thomas Brunner

Thomas Brunner, who lived from 1821 to 1874, was an explorer, as tough as old boots, who went through a series of amazing adventures and appears to have regarded them as just part of another day's work.

He came to New Zealand as a survey assistant with the New Zealand Company in 1841. First he made two journeys of exploration – one with William Fox and Charles Heaphy, and the second with Heaphy. In December 1846 he set out with two Maori guides and their wives to find the source of what is now called the Buller River. The party ran out of food and Thomas Brunner cooked his dog for rations until the party reached a Maori settlement at Arahura. Thomas Brunner wintered there living on fern root and walking barefoot.

He arrived back near Nelson on 15 June 1848, 560 days after his departure and long after he had been presumed dead. He had traced the Grey and Buller rivers from source to mouth, and the Inangahua from its source to its junction with the Buller. During the last few weeks of his journey, he lost the use of one leg almost entirely.

After a period of unemployment, Brunner settled down to become a government surveyor, then Chief Surveyor for Nelson Province, and later Nelson's Commissioner of Public Works.

# GREYMOUTH

**Greymouth Information Centre** Cnr Herbert and Mackay Sts;
tel: (03) 768 5101;
fax: (03) 768 0317; email: greymouth@i-site.org;
www.greydistrict.co.nz

Greymouth was originally established in 1863 as a government depot at the mouth of the Grey River. The town went through several name changes. It was first known as Crescent City. Later it became Blaketown. Then, in 1846, it was named, as was the habit of the times, after the then Governor of New Zealand, Sir George Grey. It was declared a town in 1864.

Greymouth's first impetus in life came, as was the case with so many towns in New Zealand, with the discovery of gold. The gold, as is its wont, soon ran out and was replaced with coal, which had been discovered in 1848. Now coal as an industry has declined almost to extinction and the area is suffering economically, although some of the slack has been taken up by timber, cattle raising and, to a very minor extent, tourism.

For over a century the people of the town have been concerned about flooding from the river and in 1988 there were two massive floods which devastated the town. The result is the **Great Wall** that protects the town from flooding. As an added bonus, it has also become a very attractive walk. You can walk from the centre of the town on top of the wall, past the Fisherman's Wharf to the breakwater. This takes about 90 minutes. From the breakwater there are spectacular views and on a clear day you can see Mount Cook.

This is also a good place to see how difficult the area has been for shipping. From the breakwater you can see where the Grey River meets the Tasman Sea, forming a notorious bar. The floodwall was tested in 1994 when the rains came and the wall held back the waters. The Grey River, now that it is no longer a threat to the town, has become one of its main attractions, offering fishing and rafting.

The breakwater provides one view. Another is the walk from Mount Street, past the railway station, up the hill that runs through the King Domain to **The Gap** which is the best viewing spot in the town. One major attempt to provide a tourist attraction is **Shantytown** (*tel: (03) 762 6634*), a replica of a west coast gold-mining town of the 1860s. It is 8km to the south of Greymouth, some 3km off the main highway, in a native bush setting. In Shantytown you can pan for gold, but your chances of making a major find are, frankly, not great. The town also has a Chinese den, gaol, livery stables with gigs and horses, printing works, carpenter's shop, general store and a gold-buying trading bank, a 166-year-old church, tea rooms and the Golden Nugget Hotel.

One of the great attractions of Greymouth is greenstone (*pounama* in Maori) or, technically, nephrite jade. This has always been a traditional centre for this stone and the range available is amazing. The definitive place to visit is **Jade Country** (*tel/fax: (03) 768 0700; email: info@jadeboulder.com; www.jadeboulder.co.nz; open daily*) in Guinness Street. This has a splendid display of the stones in their natural setting, a sort of jade walk, where you can see what they look like before they are carved, polished and set. There is an extensive range of jade artefacts for sale.

**Below**
Panning for gold in Shantytown

## The TranzAlpine Express

One of the great train journeys of the world, the TranzAlpine Express travels daily from Christchurch to Greymouth. The journey takes 4¹/₂ hours and leaves Christchurch at 0900 every day (for bookings, tel: 0800 872 467; www.tranzscenic.co.nz). It has an observation car, serves snacks and morning tea and, if you are very unlucky, you will get the Irish conductor who feels that some of the most magnificent scenery in the world needs a non-stop commentary. The train starts off crossing the agricultural wealth of the Canterbury Plains – note the way the trees are planted as windbreaks – and starts its climb after Springfield. On the 231km journey the train goes through 19 tunnels. At the Arthur's Pass Station there is normally a change of engines and then you go through the 8.5km-long Otira tunnel. The train then descends down past Lake Brunner to Greymouth – a magical journey.

Wild West Adventures (8 Whall St; tel: 0508 286877 or (03) 768 6649; www.fun-nz.com) is a major activity operator in the region, offering a range of trips including an exhilarating half-day blackwater rafting experience in the Taniwha Cave system, or a Jungle Boat Rainforest Cruise on board an imaginative range of traditional Maori craft and more conventional rafts. The three-hour trips are certainly different and offer a fine opportunity to learn more about the rich Maori culture and traditions of the west coast.

## Accommodation and food in Greymouth

The Smelting House Café $ 102 MacKay St; tel: (03) 768 0012. Breakfasts, lunches and afternoon snacks only. Specialises in home-made food with 90 per cent being made on the premises.

Jade Boulder Café $–$$ 1 Guinness St; tel: (03) 768 0700. Good, licensed, daytime option.

Ashley $$ 74 Tasman St; tel: (03) 768 5135. A la carte restaurant.

Charles Court Motel $$ 350 Main South Rd; tel: 0800 800 619; email: charlescourtmotel@xtra.co.nz

Greymouth Seaside Top 10 Holiday Park $$ Chesterfield St; tel: (03) 768 6618 or 0800 867 104; email: info@top10greymouth.co.nz

Hotel Ashley $$ 74 Tasman St; tel: (03) 768 5135; email: ashley.grey@xtra.co.nz; www.hotelashley.co.nz. Heated pool, spa and sauna.

**Right**
Shantytown

**Opposite**
The TranzAlpine Express crosses Arthur's Pass

# HAAST

**ℹ Haast Visitor Centre** *Jnc SH6 and Jackson Bay Rd; tel: (03) 750 0809; fax: (03) 750 0832; email: haastvc@doc.govt.nz*

The town of Haast is, in all fairness, not very much. But the Haast Pass, which runs through the Mount Aspiring National Park, is something totally different. It is what first made a crossing of the Southern Alps possible at the southernmost end. It connects Central Otago to Westland beside the Haast River. The complete circuit was only finished in 1965, when Lake Paringa was linked down the West Coast to Haast. The pass, at 565m, is the lowest of the major routes across the main divide. The other passes are Arthur's Pass, at 921m, and the Lewis Pass, at 863m. The Maori originally used the pass when they were collecting greenstone. They called it Tiori-patea, which can be translated as 'the way ahead is clear'. Julius von Haast, the geologist, crossed it in 1863 starting from Wanaka, though he was not

### The parks of the coast

The west coast is home to a number of national parks, namely Mount Aspiring, Westland and Paparoa. Each has its subtle differences. For example, Mount Aspiring National Park is an alpine wilderness with spectacle on a grand scale. Westland National Park combines both the west coast – a rugged place – and the mountains of the Southern Alps. Mainly it is covered by dense rainforest. Paparoa National Park was established in 1987 and covers 27,818ha, It lies on the West Coast between Westport and Greymouth and runs inland of SH6. This rugged coastal area includes the Pancake Rocks, at the mouth of the Punakaiki River, 40km north of Greymouth. These are a series of eroded limestone rocks that look like giant stacks of pancakes.

the first European to use this route. J H Baker, a surveyor, discovered it in 1861 and a gold prospector called Charles Cameron was probably the first to cross the pass. Gold miners then started to use it as a pack track, an alternative to sailing around Southland.

The road takes you through some remarkable scenery, past lakes, forests and waterfalls. The most dramatic section is the 15km run from Pleasant Flat to Haast Pass where you have a climb of about 450m in less than 3km, passing through the gorge, with its towering walls, called the **Gates of Haast**. Despite the difficulty of constructing the road – bridges were swept away in 1957 and 1961 – it is now an easy drive, and there are plenty of places where you can pull off the road and view the river smashing its way down across the boulders. If it has been raining there is an amazing 28m-high waterfall just off the main road at **Thunder Creek Falls**, about 2km out of Pleasant Flat.

When you get to Haast itself you must first cross the Haast Bridge. This, at 737m, is the longest bridge on the West Coast. Until the bridge was opened the river proved a formidable obstacle. The explorer Charles Douglas wrote that in the early days: 'The Haast River was navigated in a baker's dough trough, sluice boxes, tin pumps and other impossible looking contrivances.' Now the bridge offers views of the Alpine Gap as it cuts through towards Milford Sound.

Haast itself is very small. It has a superb information centre, a petrol station and the Haast Hotel. There is a police station 3km up the road and another petrol station, store and post office 4km south of the bridge at what is called Haast Beach. The beach itself forms a great wild sweep covered with driftwood and often assailed by stormy waters.

## Accommodation in Haast

**World Heritage Hotel $$** *junction of SH6 and Jackson Bay Rd; tel: (03) 750 0828 or 0800 502 444; email: info@world-heritage-hotel.com; www.world-heritage-hotel.com.* A bit of a barracks but a perfectly adequate motel with restaurant attached. The open fire is an attraction in itself.

# HOKITIKA

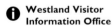
ℹ **Westland Visitor Information Office**
*The Carnegie Bldg, 7 Tanered St; tel: (03) 755 6166; fax: (03) 755 5011; email: hokitika@i-site.org*

Hokitika is 40km south of Greymouth on the SH6. The town has a population of less than 4,000 people. Located at the mouth of the Hokitika River, it was once the provincial capital partly thanks to the gold rush, but also because its river port was considered marginally superior to the one at Greymouth.

The first Europeans here were Thomas Brunner and Charles Heaphy, who came in 1847 as they made their way down the west coast of the South Island. It was to be nearly another 20 years before the first

**Above**
Haast Gorge

European settlers were to arrive. In 1865 John Hudson and James Price set up a store on the river bank for the miners seeking gold in the interior. By the following year there were probably more than 6,000 people in the town, digging for gold along the river banks or working for the gold mining industry, which was using dredges in the river.

Now, as well as gold, the miners extract greenstone, the rock that was used by the Maori to make their weapons and ornaments. Within the town itself there are many greenstone shops. The biggest store is Mountain Jade, at 41 Weld Street, which gives cutting demonstrations. The **West Coast Historical Museum** in Tancred Street contains an interesting collection of greenstone, as well as historic gold mining memorabilia. **Ross Goldfields** (*23km from Hokitika*) has the largest working alluvial gold mine in the Southern Hemisphere.

### Accommodation and food in Hokitika

**Beachfront Hotel $$** *111 Revell St; tel: (03) 755 8344; www. beachfronthotel.co.nz.* Well-established and beach-side. Also has a good restaurant.

**Café de Paris $$** *19 Tancred St; tel: (03) 755 8933; open 1930 until late.* Good food, brilliant atmosphere. Licensed and BYO.

**Shining Star Log Chalets and Motor Camp $$** *11 Richards Dr; tel: (03) 755 8921 or 0800 744 646; www.shiningstar.co.nz.* Motel-cum-motor park with tidy self-contained lodges close to the beach. Also takes camper vans.

**Stumpers $$** *2 Weld St; tel: (03) 755 6154; fax: (03) 755 6137; email: enquiries@stumpers.co.nz.* Budget accommodation, restaurant and bar.

# JACKSON BAY

Jackson Bay is just 50km down the road from Haast, where the road comes to a dead end, first passing through a podocarp forest, which resembles a prehistoric landscape. The town consists of a huddle of houses with a small pier. This is the southernmost community on the west coast of the South Island and, at one time, it was intended that it would be a major metropolis.

The first Europeans to come here were probably sealers who started in the 1790s and did not stop until they had annihilated the southern fur seal. A small whaling station followed in the early 1800s.

Then in 1875 someone conceived a grand plan to open this up as a major town – a special settlement that would rival Greymouth. The planner in fact never visited the area and buildings, streets, development blocks and public buildings were all planned for laying out on totally unsuitable swampy soil. A grave omission on the planner's part was the lack of any wharf. So the settlers never came, and all that remains is a grandiose map.

The wharf was finally built in 1876 and provides a fair harbour. One of the attractions of the area is on **Jackson Head**, which has one of the world's largest colonies of Fiordland crested penguins. As you drive to Jackson Bay you will see several signs warning: 'Please watch out for penguins crossing the road.'

**Above**
Early summer brings carpets of wild lupins to the West Coast

# KARAMEA

**Karamea
Information and
Resource Centre** *Tel:
(03) 782 6652;
www.karameainfo.co.nz*

Karamea is the terminal of what is called the Heritage Highway and the gateway to the Kahurangi National Park. You get there by way of Little Wanganui and across the Karamea River. The town is on the estuary of the Karamea River and is 100km northeast of Westport. The Nelson Provincial Government established it as a special farm settlement in 1874, but the soil was dense and infertile and hundreds of the assisted migrants walked off their properties. In 1929 the town was badly damaged in the Murchison earthquake. Now it has, arcing away to the north, the huge expanse of the **Kahurangi National Park**, with long stretches of beaches which run along the Tasman Sea.

The main reason for coming here is to get to the start of the **Heaphy Track**, which begins along the beachfront and eventually winds up at Collingwood. Even though you may not intend to walk the whole of the track, the start of it out of Karamea is truly scenic and you can choose your pace and distance. The **Nikau Loop Walk**, 15km north of Karamea on the Kohaihai River, takes about 40 minutes and has well-graded paths. Scotts Beach takes you up and over the hill with magnificent views; allow an hour and a half for the return trip.

To the north of Karamea and inland is one of the South Island's best kept secrets. The **Oparara Basin** is a magical place that offers some of the most interesting concentration of karst (limestone) topography in the country. Although the karst features, including a huge river arch, will keep you spellbound, the thick veil of ancient rainforest that covers them also creates a wonderful atmosphere all of its own. Some amazing animals have been found here. Ancient moa bones have been discovered in the caves, and today you may still stumble across the huge carnivorous snail *Powelliphanta* or the wonderfully named Gradungula spider, the largest in New Zealand. But, even if the prospect of such creatures leaves you cold, the Oparara Basin is still a 'must see'. Note the road in is unsealed.

## Accommodation and food in Karamea

**Karamea Village Hotel Restaurant $** *Tel: (03) 782 6800.* Modern units and restaurant.

**Bridge Farm Motels $$** *Tel: (03) 782 6955; email: info@ karameamotels.co.nz.* Free continental breakfast.

**The Last Resort $$** *71 Waverley St; tel: (03) 782 6617 or 0800 505 042; email: info@lastresort.co.nz.* Has a good licensed restaurant.

# MOANA

Moana is a small township on the shores of Lake Brunner, 42km from Greymouth. It has some of the best trout fishing in the South Island and anglers are practically guaranteed a catch all year round. The best time for fly-fishing and spinning is from October to April. The town is also the centre for some splendid sightseeing. Cross the Arnold River footbridge near the town and you have access to kilometres of lake shore and a forest full of birdlife. **Lake Brunner** also has swimming and hire boats. To get there drive inland first on the SH17 to Stillwater and then take the turning to Moana. Instead of returning the same way you can continue to Te Kinga, also on the lake, then to Rotamanu and Inchbonnie and over to the lower half of the Arthur's Pass Road. Then drive down to Kumara Junction on the SH73, along the Taramakai River to Kumara Junction and then back up the SH6 to Greymouth.

# WESTPORT

**Westport Visitor and Information Centre** / *Brougham St; tel: (03) 789 6658; fax: (03) 789 6668; email: westport@i-site.org; www.westport.org.nz*

**Department of Conservation Office** *72 Russel St; tel: (03) 788 8008.*

**Paparoa National Park Visitor Information** *Jnc Main Rd and SH6, Punakaiki: tel: (03) 731 1895; fax: (03) 731 1896; email: paparoavc@doc.govt.nz*

Westport, 105km northeast of Greymouth, near the mouth of the Buller River, is the commercial centre and port for the Buller region. Coal and gold were discovered in the region in 1859 by a Nelson surveyor, John Rochfort. Two years later a settlement had been established using the port at the mouth of the river. Gold mining lasted for some years and was then overtaken by coal which, in its turn, has been overtaken by other power sources.

The mines around Westport remain one of New Zealand's principal sources of bituminous coal. You can follow the history of coal mining in the area at **Coaltown** (*Queen Street, tel: (03) 789 8204; open daily 0900–1630*) which shows, with some considerable style, the way the Buller coal field was mined. It is also the nearest town to **Westland National Park**, which was established in 1960 and covers 117,600ha of rugged mountains and dense forest in south Westland. It contains the greatest diversity of vegetation and wildlife in the New Zealand national parks system.

The town is worth coming to as an entrance to Cape Foulwind, which has a major seal colony. Captain Cook named the cape for reasons that are not difficult to guess. It is 12km west of the town, and has a walkway going for 4km, with superb views. You get eventually to the **Tauranga Bay Seal Colony** where viewing platforms overlook the seal colonies. The seals are there mainly from October to January, but can also be seen at other times of the year.

## Accommodation and food in Westport

**Ascot Motor Lodge $$** *74 Romilly St; tel: (03) 789 7832 or 0800 657 007; email: ascotmotorlodge@paradise.net.* Away from traffic and train noise.

**Bay House Café $$** *Tauranga Bay; tel: (03) 789 7133.* Licensed and BYO. B&B accommodation available and also has a gallery featuring local arts and crafts.

**Above**
Franz Josef Glacier

**Seal Colony Top 10 Holiday Park $$** *Marine Parade, Carters Beach; tel:*
*(03) 789 8002; fax: (03) 789 6732; www.top10westport.co.nz.* Closest
accommodation to the seal colony.

**Serengetis Restaurant $$** *Westport Motor Hotel, Palmerston St; tel: (03)*
*789 7889; open daily from 1800.* Good option, especially for its Sunday-
evening smorgasbord.

## Suggested tour

**Total distance:** 865km.

**Time:** 15 hours' driving (excluding sightseeing).

**Links:** Wanaka (*see page 250*) links to the Otago region (*see page
236*).

This is a one-way journey, as backtracking is difficult and the Southern
Alps are crossed in only three places. The SH6 starts from **WANAKA** ①
and runs through the amazing **GATES OF HAAST** ② down to the
coast and the minute settlement of **HAAST** ③. There is a worthwhile
detour from there to Jackson Bay.

The road proceeds from Haast along the coast to **LAKE MOERAKI** ④
and then moves inland to pass **LAKE PARINGA** ⑤ before coming
back to the coast at **BRUCE BAY** ⑥. From there go inland to
Karangarua to see first the **FOX GLACIER** ⑦ and then the **FRANZ
JOSEF GLACIER** ⑧. After that the road dodges around the estuaries to
the sea until it gets to Ross and **HOKITIKA** ⑨.

From Hokitika the road runs along the coast to **GREYMOUTH** ⑩ where
there is a way over the mountains to Christchurch by way of **ARTHUR'S
PASS** ⑪ along SH73 (*see Also worth exploring, page 278*). The SH6

continues with the Paparoa Range on the right and the sea on the left through **PUNAKAIKI** ⓬, with its pancake rocks, and Charleston, to reach **WESTPORT** ⓭.

There the main road runs off to the right and heads towards Nelson (*see pages 195–7*) and Blenheim (*see pages 186–91*), but the extension of the west coast road goes on through Little Wanganui to **KARAMEA** ⓮. Just beyond lies the end of the drivable road. If you want to get from there to Collingwood in Golden Bay by the most direct route then you will need to walk along the **HEAPHY TRAIL** ⓯.

## Also worth exploring

The **Grey Valley**, which runs inland from Greymouth, is, in fact, very green. The area has a high rainfall and consists mainly of forest, interspersed with small towns. The region was once full of gold seekers and you can still see abandoned equipment, houses and, indeed, whole settlements. Start by driving up the Grey Valley on the SH7 through Dobson, Stillwater, Ngahere, Ikamatua and Reefton. Continue on to Inangahua Junction, where you can still see the scars on the hillside of the great earthquake of 1968. The road now goes through the Lower Buller Gorge to Westport, then along the Heritage Highway past Charleston, which was the site of one of New Zealand's great gold rushes, and then back to Greymouth. The drive covers 253km and offers a wide mix of terrain with a final coastal stretch.

Arthur's Pass is the main pass across the Southern Alps connecting the two coasts. It is a miracle of road engineering. The pass is named after Arthur Dobson who was told about it by the local Maori who had been using it for centuries. Dobson immediately surveyed the pass and thus achieved a form of immortality. By 1864 teams of horses were making use of the pass, and by 1923 the railway had been built.

You can, of course, drive straight across either to or from Christchurch, but there is a drive from Greymouth with very little backtracking that will take you to the summit of the pass and, if you like, a little further to the other side.

You leave Greymouth on the SH6 through South Beach and Gladstone until you come to Kumara Junction. Turn left on the SH73, which goes up and up into the mountains until you reach Jacksons, Aickens, Otira and, eventually, Arthur's Pass itself, with its railroad station.

You can backtrack from there to Jacksons and then, shortly afterwards, take the right turn to Inchbonnie. Note that you are now following the railway, in its journey back to Greymouth. The road goes through Rotamau, Te Kinga and Moana, passing Lake Brunner, and then to Stillwater, where you turn left towards the coast for the short run down to Greymouth. Leave a day for this drive. It is never difficult, never dangerous, but it is totally wonderful scenery all the way.

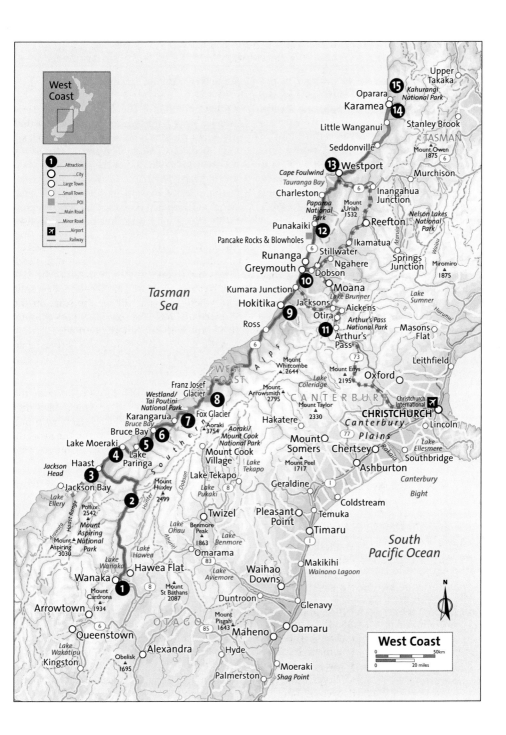

West Coast

- ⓵ ....Attraction
- ◯ ....City
- ◯ ....Large Town
- ◯ ....Small Town
- ▣ ....POI
- ─── ....Main Road
- ─── ....Minor Road
- ✈ ....Airport
- ━━━ ....Railway

Upper Takaka
Oparara ⑮ Kahurangi National Park
Karamea ⑭
Little Wanganui    Stanley Brook
Seddonville    TASMAN
⑬ Westport    Mount Owen 1875 ⑥
Cape Foulwind    Murchison
Tauranga Bay
Charleston    ⑥ Inangahua Junction
Paparoa National Park    Mount Uriah 1532
Punakaiki ⑫    Reefton    Nelson Lakes National Park
Pancake Rocks & Blowholes
⑥ Ikamatua
Runanga    Stillwater
Greymouth    Ngahere    Springs Junction    Miromiro 1875
Dobson ⑩
Kumara Junction    Moana
Hokitika    Lake Brunner    Lake Sumner
Jacksons ⑨    Aickens
Ross    Otira    Arthur's Pass National Park    Masons Flat
⑪    Arthur's Pass
⑥
Mount Whitcombe 2644    Mount Errys 2195    Leithfield
Lake Coleridge
Franz Josef Glacier ⑧    Mount Arrowsmith 2795    Oxford    73
Westland/ Tai Poutini National Park
Karangarua ⑦    Fox Glacier    Mount Taylor 2330    Christchurch International ✈
Bruce Bay    Aoraki 3754    Aoraki/ Mount Cook National Park    CHRISTCHURCH
Bruce Bay ⑥    Hakatere    Canterbury    Lincoln
Lake Moeraki ⑤    Mount Cook Village    Mount Somers    Chertsey ⑦    Lake Ellesmere
⑷    Lake Paringa    Mount Peel 1717    Southbridge
Jackson Head    Haast    Lake Tekapo    Ashburton
⑶    Mount Huxley 2499    Lake Pukaki    Geraldine    Canterbury Bight
Jackson Bay
Lake Ellery    Pollux 2542    Coldstream
⑵    Twizel    Pleasant Point    Temuka
Mount Aspiring National Park    Lake Ohau    Benmore Peak 1863    Lake Benmore    Timaru
Mount Aspiring 3030    Lake Hawea    Omarama    83
Lake Wanaka    Hawea Flat    Lake Aviemore    Waihao Downs    Makikihi    Wainono Lagoon
Wanaka ⑴    ⑧    Mount St Bathans 2087    Duntroon    Glenavy
Arrowtown    1934    Mount Pisgah 1643    85    Maheno    Oamaru
Queenstown    Alexandra    Hyde
Lake Wakatipu    Obelisk 1695    Moeraki
Kingston    Palmerston    Shag Point

Tasman Sea

South Pacific Ocean

N

West Coast
0    50km
0    20 miles

# Language

The New Zealand accent is stronger in the South Island than in the North. Indeed, the further south you go the stronger the accent. The most famous characteristic of New Zealand pronunciation is the substitution of 'U' for 'I', as in 'fush and chups'. That is how it sounds and, until you get used to it, it is quite amusing. Other words change as well. The proprietors of a motel introduce themselves as 'It and Junny'. It takes you a little while to work out that Jenny is married to Ed.

New Zealanders swear much less than the Australians (in truth, probably everybody swears less than Australians). And when they do swear, it is very mild. Thus the proprietor of a motel in Invercargill, finding a puncture on a car, exclaimed, 'Blimey, you've got a flattie'. The use of the diminutive (as in flattie, tinnie, barbie) is not as widespread as it is in Australia, but it is a widely found characteristic of antipodean speech.

There are two distinct streams of New Zealand slang. A lot of Maori words have entered the language, enriching it tremendously. Thus *pakeha* is the widely used term for non-Maori (it is interesting to know that, apart from meaning 'foreigner', this word also means 'flea' or 'pest' – though it is not used as a pejorative term by the Maori or Europeans, who use it extensively). *Hapu* is a sub-tribal Maori unit, and several of them make up an *iwi*. This latter word is sometimes used by *pakeha* to refer to a group of people. *Puku* is the Maori word for stomach, but it is also often used as a term of endearment for someone who is of a rotund persuasion.

Also widely used by *pakeha* is the name Aotearoa for New Zealand (literally 'land of the long white cloud'). Many believe that this will one day become the official name for New Zealand. The same cannot be said for Godzone, which is also widely used, and is an abbreviation of 'God's own country' (normally, but not always, used satirically).

## Some New Zealand vocabulary

**ANZAC:** stands for the Australian and New Zealand Army Corps, which is a very serious and important subject. Every town in New Zealand has a memorial to those men and women of the ANZAC who fell in one or the other of the two World Wars. The name is also used in Anzac biscuit, made from wholemeal flour, rolled oats, syrup and shredded coconut. This was invented by the troops and has become the national dish. No visitor to New Zealand should miss sampling this culinary treat.

**Bach:** is a holiday home. It is suggested that the word derives from 'bachelor pad', although this is open to debate. Now it means a country or seaside retreat, and can range from a literal shack to a large and palatial mansion.

**BYO:** an unlicensed restaurant at which diners may drink their own wine etc.

**Chilly bin:** an essential part of New Zealand life, being an insulated case for carrying picnic supplies (and, more importantly, beer) to the beach and sporting events.

**Chunder:** the result of an excessive intake of beer (also referred to as 'talking to God on the big white telephone').

**Gorse in your pocket:** means someone slow for their shout (where 'shout' means buying a round). Similar to the Australian 'death adder in your pocket'.

**Greasies:** splendidly descriptive New Zealand word for takeaway food.

**Judder bars:** the New Zealand name for speed humps.

**Skull:** to knock back your drink very quickly – probably derived from the Scandinavian *skol*.

**Ute:** a car-sized pick-up truck (possibly from 'utility').

# Index

# Acknowledgements

**Project management:** Cambridge Publishing Management Limited
**Project editor:** Karen Beaulah
**Series design:** Fox Design
**Cover design:** Liz Lyons Design
**Layout:** Cambridge Publishing Management Limited
**Mapwork:** PCGraphics (UK) Ltd
**Repro and image setting:** PDQ Digital Media Solutions Ltd and
   Cambridge Publishing Management Limited
**Printed and bound in India by:** Ajanta Offset & Packaging Ltd

We would like to thank Larry Dunmire for the photographs used in this book, to whom the copyright in the photographs belongs, with the exception of the following:

**Darroch Donald** (pages 18, 31, 34, 35, 42, 45, 80, 86, 92, 128, 168 and 193).

**Dreamstime** (pages 27 (Joe Gough), 31 (Bjlongmore) and 50 (Lex Schmidt)).

**Eastwoodhill Arboretum** (page 105).

**Gladstone Vineyard/AMP** (page 162).

**Chris Metcalf** (pages 1A, 6, 100, 107, 124, 129, 131, 132, 133, 135, 156, 159, 214, 221, 224, 226 (both), 271, 273, 274 and 277).

**New Zealand Rugby Museum** (page 152).

**Greg O'Beirne** (page 211).

**Pictures Colour Library** (page 219).

**Tourism New Zealand** (pages 78 and 218 (Peter Morath), 106 and 109 (Tourism Eastland Inc), 122 (Fay Looney), 148 (David Wall), 155 (Gareth Eyres), 160 (Fri Gilbert) and 171 (Ian Trafford)).

**World Pictures/Photoshot** (page 102).

# Feedback form

We're committed to providing the very best up-to-date information in our travel guides and constantly strive to make them as useful as they can be. You can help us to improve future editions by letting us have your feedback. Just take a few minutes to complete and return this form to us.

**When did you buy this book?** ........................................................................................
........................................................................................................................................

**Where did you buy it? (Please give town/city and, if possible, name of retailer)**
........................................................................................................................................
........................................................................................................................................

**When did you/do you intend to travel in New Zealand?** .............................................
........................................................................................................................................

**For how long (approx)?** .................................................................................................

**How many people in your party?** ................................................................................

**Which cities, national parks and other locations did you/do you intend mainly to visit?**
........................................................................................................................................
........................................................................................................................................
........................................................................................................................................
........................................................................................................................................

**Did you/will you:**
❏ Make all your travel arrangements independently?
❏ Travel on a fly-drive package?
Please give brief details: ...........................................................................................
........................................................................................................................................

**Did you/do you intend to use this book:**
❏ For planning your trip?            ❏ Both?
❏ During the trip itself?

**Did you/do you intend also to purchase any of the following travel publications for your trip?**
Thomas Cook *traveller guides New Zealand* ...........................................................
A road map/atlas (please specify) .............................................................................
Other guidebooks (please specify) ...........................................................................

**Have you used any other Thomas Cook guidebooks in the past? If so, which?**

..................................................................................................................................

..................................................................................................................................

Please rate the following features of *driving guides New Zealand* for their value to you (Circle VU for 'very useful', U for 'useful', NU for 'little or no use'):

| | | | |
|---|---|---|---|
| The *Travel facts* section on pages 14–25 | VU | U | NU |
| The *Driver's guide* section on pages 26–31 | VU | U | NU |
| The recommended driving routes throughout the book | VU | U | NU |
| Information on towns and cities, National Parks, etc | VU | U | NU |
| The maps of towns and cities, parks, etc | VU | U | NU |

Please use this space to tell us about any features that in your opinion could be changed, improved, or added in future editions of the book, or any other comments you would like to make concerning the book:

..................................................................................................................................

..................................................................................................................................

..................................................................................................................................

..................................................................................................................................

..................................................................................................................................

..................................................................................................................................

..................................................................................................................................

..................................................................................................................................

..................................................................................................................................

**Your age category:**    ❏ 21–30     ❏ 31–40     ❏ 41–50     ❏ over 50

Your name: Mr/Mrs/Miss/Ms ......................................................................................

(First name or initials) ...............................................................................................

(Last name) ................................................................................................................

Your full address: (Please include postal or zip code)

..................................................................................................................................

..................................................................................................................................

..................................................................................................................................

..................................................................................................................................

..................................................................................................................................

Your daytime telephone number:  .............................................................................

**Please detach this page and send it to: driving guides Series Editor,
Thomas Cook Publishing, PO Box 227, Coningsby Road, Peterborough PE3 8SB.**

**Alternatively, you can e-mail us at:** *books@thomascook.com*